# FORD MUSTANG

HOW TO BUILD & MODIFY

2011–2014

Wes Duenkel

S-A DESIGN

CarTech®

CarTech®

CarTech®, Inc.
6118 Main Street
North Branch, MN 55056
Phone: 651-277-1200 or 800-551-4754
Fax: 651-277-1203
www.cartechbooks.com



Edit by Bob Wilson
Layout by Monica Seiberlich

ISBN 978-1-61325-600-8
Item No. SA506

Library of Congress Cataloging-in-Publication Data Available

Written, edited, and designed in the U.S.A.
Printed in China
10 9 8 7 6 5 4 3 2 1



DISTRIBUTION BY:

*Europe*
PGUK
63 Hatton Garden
London EC1N 8LE, England
Phone: 020 7061 1980 • Fax: 020 7242 3725
www.pguk.co.uk

*Australia*
Renniks Publications Ltd.
3/37-39 Green Street
Banksmeadow, NSW 2109, Australia
Phone: 2 9695 7055 • Fax: 2 9695 7355
www.renniks.com

*Canada*
Login Canada
300 Saulteaux Crescent
Winnipeg, MB, R3J 3T2 Canada
Phone: 800 665 1148 • Fax: 800 665 0103
www.lb.ca

# CONTENTS

## ACKNOWLEDGMENTS

Similar to racing, book publishing is a team sport. As such, nothing between the covers of this book was possible without the steadfast support of aftermarket suppliers who invested their trust in this project.

Thanks to HP Motorsport's Mike Tederman and the late Paul Brown. You took a chance on a summer intern and inadvertently got me hooked on road-racing Mustangs.

Thanks to Dean Martin and Scott Whitehead with Rehagen Racing. Whether it was because I was a poor mechanic or a decent photographer, thanks for advising me to wrench less and take more photos.

Thanks to Evan Smith and Henry De Los Santos for their guidance through the minefield of enthusiast publications. Harry King offered unprecedented insight into the genesis of the Coyote engine. The book *Mustang: Anniversary Edition 1964–1994*, which was written by Nicky Wright, was an invaluable resource for the historical overview of the Mustang.

Finally, thanks to my family and patient wife, Kim, who tolerates my passion and doesn't complain (too loudly) about Mustangs in various stages of undress that occupy our garage.

## ABOUT THE AUTHOR

Wes Duenkel has wrenched on Mustangs since 1995. He didn't have a choice. His first car was a well-worn 1985 Mustang GT that needed lots of work.

After college and a stint working in the performance automotive aftermarket, Duenkel's passion for sports cars and creative photography skills led to a full-time career in motorsports photography and automotive writing. Since then, he has created hundreds of technical and feature articles for enthusiast publications.

Duenkel's motorsports photography career included covering the modern Ford GT sports car racing program in North America for Ford Motor Company. Duenkel continues to photograph racing and high-performance vehicles for corporate automotive clients.

A determined do-it-yourselfer, Duenkel has owned and/or modified dozens of 1965–present Mustangs. From carburetors to Coyotes and from road racing to rotating assemblies, he is well-versed in the engineering and mechanics of high-performance vehicles and enjoys using his words and photos to entertain, inform, and inspire his fellow automotive enthusiasts.

# PREFACE

Much like its grandfather did on April 17, 1964, the 2005 S197–chassis Mustang arrived in a market devoid of competition from traditional crosstown rivals General Motors and Chrysler. That soon changed, and mirroring the late 1960s, the competition pushed Ford Motor Company to infuse the Mustang with more power and performance.

The 5.0-liter Ti-VCT Coyote–powered 2011 Mustang GT was the result. The engine was borne of lessons learned from decades of Modular V-8 engine development. It catapulted the Mustang to the forefront of the category, and today the Mustang remains the sales and performance standard by which its competitors are measured.

However, performance enthusiasts aren't happy with the status quo. Every factory vehicle includes compromises to reduce noise, vibration, and harshness (NVH); to meet fuel-efficiency requirements; and (most commonly) to minimize cost. The aftermarket picks up where the factory left off. This book covers the aftermarket parts and procedures to increase performance on 2011–2014 Mustangs.

Ford produced several variations of the 2011–2014 Mustang, including those powered by the 3.7L V-6, the 5.0L Coyote V-8, the Boss 302 5.0L Roadrunner V-8, and the Shelby GT500 (both 5.4L Modular and 5.8L Trinity supercharged V-8s).

Regardless of what's under the hood, chassis modifications are common to most 2005–2014 Mustangs. The 2012–2014 Boss 302 is a close cousin to the 2011–2014 Mustang GT, as the Boss can be viewed as an enhanced Coyote-powered Mustang with specific engine and chassis improvements. Powertrain-wise, the Shelby GT500 is an entirely different animal; it has its own engine architecture, engine management, fuel system, and drivetrain.

The 2011–2014 GT models powered by the 5.0L Coyote V-8 are by far the most popular in both the total number produced and aftermarket support, so power upgrades for those models are the primary focus for this book.

*This photo was taken in June 1995, when I was about to give my mom her maiden voyage in my first car: a 1985 Mustang GT. I snagged it for $1,500, which was probably too much. I wasn't looking for a Mustang specifically, as I was looking for any car with a V-8 and a manual transmission. I saw this car for sale a few miles from my house, and the price was affordable. The wrench in my hand signaled not only this car's condition but also foreshadowed a future love of tinkering with Mustangs. (Photo Courtesy of Fuzzy Duenkel)*

*As with many car enthusiasts, I have my own Mustang memory: My first Mustang ride was in the back seat of my uncle's 1968 fastback that was purchased from a friend in 1989. I was 12 years old. I distinctly remember the noise that the 4-speed-backed 351 engine made on downshifts as we rumbled to a stop. (Photo Courtesy the Rehlinger family)*

# AN OVERVIEW

The Mustang has a special place in the heart of America's car culture. We all have a Mustang story, and it usually goes like this: "My [insert family member or friend] had a Mustang, and [insert fun memory]." The Mustang can accommodate a four-person family on an unforgettable trip across the country, or it can be used to merely run errands. What kid doesn't want to go to school in a Mustang?

## America's Blue-Collar Performance Car

Anecdotes are common because the Mustang's price is within reach for most American buyers. As a result, millions of Mustangs are in American driveways. Mustang ownership is accessible to both the blue-collar employee and the boss.

The Mustang's affordability makes it an unpretentious option for those who enjoy driving. From the moment the Mustang rolled into the 1964 World's Fair, Ford marketed the Mustang as a youthful alternative to contemporary ho-hum transportation. That included promoting the Mustang's sporty nature through aftermarket performance parts. From 1964 to today, Ford has offered performance upgrades so that owners can get the performance they desire along with the satisfaction of installing the parts themselves.

The 2011–2014 Mustang carries on this tradition as a competent, capable platform upon which enthusiasts can build the performance car of their dreams and make memories for themselves and their families.

## Bucking the Trend

In the decade following World War II, American manufacturing switched from churning out fighting machines to churning out consumer products. Meanwhile, returning soldiers' families churned out babies.

In 1960, an engineer-turned-marketing genius named Lee Iacocca

*The Mustang debuted at the World's Fair on April 17, 1964. It was a hit with the public. The Mustang was designed to please a broad demographic: young and old; male and female. Ford knew it had a hit when visitors lined the fence at the display, craning their necks for a look at the new Mustang. (Photo Courtesy Ford Motor Company)*

*From the beginning, Ford wanted to lure performance enthusiasts behind the wheel of Mustangs. Ford knew that customers who were enthusiastic about high performance were more likely to consider a Mustang if there were parts available to make them faster. Hot rodders often shopped for go-fast goodies even before taking delivery of their new Mustang. Advertisements such as this were printed in* Hot Rod *magazine just as brand-new Mustang owners were laying rubber out of dealership parking lots. (Photo Courtesy Ford Motor Company)*

*As this advertisement from 2011 shows, Ford Performance Parts continues to support horsepower lovers who want to enjoy their Mustangs on a racetrack, twisty back road, or from stoplight to stoplight. (Photo Courtesy Ford Motor Company)*

sniffed a coming opportunity: the surge of babies that clogged maternity wards in the late 1940s and 1950s were primed to make their mark on the world, rebel against their conservative parents, and buy a car. Iacocca, forever the salesman, wanted to pounce.

Small product glimmers, such as GM's Corvair, hinted that customers yearned for smaller high-performance cars, and Iacocca knew it. He wanted Ford to build a hip, sporty car that would capture the imagination of these new buyers—and loosen the grip on their wallets.

However, Iacocca had a problem: Robert McNamara. McNamara came to Ford as 1 of 10 financial Whiz Kids (veterans of the US Army Air Forces management science operation called Statistical Control) that Henry Ford II hired to run his grandfather's company in 1946.

It didn't take the Whiz Kids long to realize that statistical control didn't square with performance. That is, unless performance was of the financial kind. In wartime and in business, McNamara's specialty was minimizing risks. The development of an entirely new, youth-oriented product with a Zeppelin-sized marketing budget was the antithesis of McNamara's business philosophy.

Getting McNamara to accept Iacocca's plan would be impossible. That is, until a young man from Massachusetts named John F. Kennedy was elected president of the United States and asked McNamara to be his Secretary of Defense in 1961. With McNamara out as Ford's president, Iacocca was unleashed. Thirty-seven years old and full of ideas, Iacocca grabbed the controls of Ford Division and swung it into the 1960s. Once Henry Ford II (the Deuce) was on board, Ford Motor Company went from selling reliable appliances into the era of total performance. The linchpin of Ford's Total Performance program was Iacocca's new car: the Mustang.

The idea of the Mustang didn't arrive like a bolt of lightning in the night. Instead, it was like a building storm—a brainstorm of ideas from a group that Iacocca convened during a weekly dinner at Dearborn's Fairlane Inn. The Fairlane Committee commissioned a survey to determine what baby boomers wanted in a car. The committee learned that buyers overwhelmingly valued fun things (bucket seats and manual transmissions) over sensible things (expanded interior room and low operating costs).

The drafting rooms and prototype shops got busy. The two-seat Mustang I concept car was spawned, and it was subsequently scrapped because it didn't have the mass appeal that Iacocca envisioned. Market trends pointed toward young buyers who were single and young families looking to add a second car. This meant that interiors that prioritized comfort for rear-seat passengers weren't a priority. Then came the Mustang's 2+2 concept, which wasn't exactly a four-seater, but rather it was a two-seater with two smaller back seats.

Meanwhile, Iacocca knew that future customers were roaming high-school hallways and time was running out before these baby boomers began car shopping. Iacocca wanted them buying Mustangs. To accelerate development and lower cost, Ford engineers borrowed parts from the Fairlane and Falcon. A focus group of couples from varying tax brackets was chosen to gauge their reaction to the Mustang prototype. Everyone was impressed with the long-hood, short-deck design of the new pony car. The low retail price sealed the deal.

Such was the reaction of the general public when the Mustang officially debuted at the World's Fair in New York on April 17, 1964. A highly coordinated promotional campaign ensured the success of the Mustang. Thirty million people saw the Mustang unveiled the night before when Ford bought the 9 p.m. time slot on all three major TV networks.

Over the next two days, four million people flooded dealerships to see thousands of Mustangs that were already staged in dealerships across the country. Perhaps the campaign worked too well. According to legend, one dealership was forced to lock its doors to control the mobs of people that were hoping to see the new Mustang. In Garland, Texas, one eager buyer slept in his Mustang while his check cleared to ensure that no one bought the car out from under him—literally.

Iacocca and his team made sure that Ford marketed the Mustang to

***Those determining the size of the net that Ford's marketing team cast should look no further than these two advertisements. One targets older males "finding the fountain of youth," while the other has aspiring females in its sights. With a long list of options, it was easy to make the Mustang "the ideal car for me," as the second advertisement claims. (Photo Courtesy Ford Motor Company)***

*Even though Carroll Shelby, a Texas chicken farmer turned race car builder, dismissed the Mustang as "a secretary's car," Iacocca tasked Shelby with creating a high-performance niche model to bolster the Mustang's credentials among hard-core racing enthusiasts. By tossing the back seat, installing a fiberglass hood, and bolting a Holley 715-cfm carburetor and high-rise intake manifold to the Hi-Po 289 engine, Shelby created the GT350. (Photo Courtesy Ford Motor Company)*

*Big-block engine options were added in 1967 to compete with GM's new Camaro and Firebird. The combination of big-block engine and automatic transmission brought startling straight-line performance to the masses—and the missus. (Photo Courtesy Ford Motor Company)*

as many potential buyers as possible. Advertising from the period shows the wide net that Ford's advertising agency cast. Targeted advertising to both women and men of all tastes and budgets ensured that there was a Mustang for every buyer.

Prices for 1965 Mustangs ranged as widely as the options list: the figure nearly doubled from a hardtop's base price of $2,427 to $4,547 for a Shelby GT350 model. This ensured that there was a Mustang for every buyer—from the secretary with a trunk full of groceries to the corporate executive with a helmet and gloves ready for the weekend. Customization was the key to the Mustang's success, and a wide array of engine options, from the economical 170-ci 6-cylinder to the lumpy-idling 289 Hi-Po, ensured that the Mustang's power characteristics fit the person behind the wheel.

As buyer's tastes changed, so did the Mustang. The year 1967 brought market competition in the form of Chevrolet's Camaro and Pontiac's Firebird. The F-Body twins' big-block engine offerings gave the Mustang a run for its money, and the horsepower wars raged. Ford's FE-series 390- and 428-ci big-block engines were added to the Mustang's powertrain lineup.

By 1969, the trim, lightweight Mustang was restyled into a musclebound street brawler. The Sports Car Club of America's (SCCA) Trans-Am series spurred Detroit's Big Three (Ford, General Motors, and Chrysler) to offer special models with high-strung 5.0-liter engines to homologate their racing efforts. The Mustang Boss 302, Camaro Z28, Plymouth AAR 'Cuda, and Dodge Challenger T/A joined their big-block brethren in showrooms across the country.

The 1970s brought an even larger Mustang, one that felt the influence of former GM executive Semon "Bunkie" Knudsen, who joined Ford as president in 1968. As smog began filling urban areas, federal emissions standards crashed the horsepower party in Detroit. Sales began to slide and October, and 1973's oil crisis drove the nail in the coffin for the thirsty Mustang.

As buyers felt the horsepower party hangover, Iacocca knew that the Mustang needed to remain customer focused to survive. Unhappy with how long the Mustang had spent at the feed trough, Iacocca returned the Mustang to its small-car roots. Timing couldn't have been better, as the tidier, more economical 1974 Mustang II debuted in the fall of 1973, just as the oil crisis shocked American consumers out of their petroleum-drunk stupor.

With long lines at gas stations and manufacturers struggling to meet emissions standards, sticker and stripe decals atop hoods replaced the horsepower that once lurked underneath. However, buyers responded positively, as Ford sold well over a million copies of the Mustang II from 1974 through 1978.

As the 1970s drew to a close, the Mustang felt more market competition from Europe and Japan than from its neighbors in Detroit. Strait-laced and sensible, the Fox Body Mustang again reflected the taste of American buyers. The side scoops

***By the late 1960s, the Sports Car Club of America (SCCA) Trans-American Championship became the battleground for Detroit's Big Three automotive manufacturers to leverage their "Win on Sunday, Sell on Monday" philosophies. To both qualify for the series and capitalize on their involvement, Ford, Chevrolet, Pontiac, Dodge, and Plymouth created special models of their flagship pony cars to compete in the series. Ford captured the 1970 championship when drivers Parnelli Jones and George Follmer won 6 of the 11 races in their Mustang Boss 302s. (Photo Courtesy Ford Motor Company)***

and sideburns of the 1970s were replaced by sharply creased body panels and pleats on the C-pillars that matched those on buyers' trousers. Although the fresh styling and updated build quality enthused buyers, performance remained anemic.

However, the advent of electronic fuel injection and ceramic monolith catalytic converters allowed Ford to greatly improve performance while meeting the ever-stricter emissions standards. While it was a far cry from the horsepower heyday of the 1960s, the Mustang retained its conventional front-engine, rear-drive layout, and enthusiasts turned to the aftermarket to cure the boredom under the hood.

The Mustang remained popular with consumers through the early-to-mid 1980s, although buyers' eyes were clearly wandering elsewhere. Just as the Fox Body Mustang was hitting its stride, Ford product planners knew that the Mustang was one of the remaining rear-drive holdouts in dealership lots, where front-wheel-drive people-movers

***Iacocca was masterful at recognizing consumer trends, and in 1973, Iacocca's timing was impeccable. As long lines formed during the oil crisis in 1973, a smaller, more efficient Mustang II debuted. What the Mustang II lacked in performance, it gained in efficiency, and sales soared through the mid-1970s. (Photo Courtesy Ford Motor Company)***

***European cars caught the eyes of consumers and influenced Ford's designers when developing the next Mustang for 1979. The Fox-platform Mustang's sharp lines, modest proportions, and efficient drivetrains resonated with buyers. V-8 engines continued to be used, such as the 302 in this 1979 Mustang Cobra. However, with only 140 hp, this 302 was only a shadow if its former self. (Photo Courtesy Ford Motor Company)***

*In the mid-1980s, consumers gravitated toward the quality, efficiency, versatility, and all-weather traction of Japanese front-wheel-drive vehicles. Iacocca moved on to Chrysler and launched its wildly-poplar K-car platform, which arguably saved the company. For the Mustang to remain relevant to customers, Ford developed a new, front-wheel-drive Mustang with its partner Mazda. The plan was scrapped after Mustang enthusiasts (both inside and outside of Ford) protested loudly, but this styling study shows how close Ford was to completing the project. The vehicle later launched as the Ford Probe. (Photo Courtesy Ford Motor Company)*

*With the crisis of the front-wheel-drive Mustang averted, Ford gave the Fox-platform Mustang a facelift for 1987. The updated styling and improved power from sequential-port fuel injection made the Fox-chassis Mustang a sales success through its conclusion in 1993. (Photo Courtesy Ford Motor Company)*

*In the face of higher safety standards that required passenger-side airbags, Ford considered canceling the Mustang. A small skunkworks team within Ford burned the midnight oil to ensure that the Mustang continued. To keep development costs to a minimum, the SN-95 skeleton drew heavily from the previous Fox generation. The result was a Mustang that, while aesthetically new, was essentially a reskinned Fox Body Mustang. While previous Mustang generations broke new styling ground, the 1994 Mustang drew heavily from the Mustang's heritage. However, those styling aspects were smoothed over to satisfy contemporary "jellybean" automotive tastes. (Photo Courtesy Ford Motor Company)*

were torque-steering off lots at an alarming pace. Plans were underway to rebadge a Japanese-designed car as the next Mustang.

Throughout its history, the Mustang survived by being responsive to consumer trends, but moving to a Japanese-designed front-wheel-drive platform was a bridge too far for enthusiasts. Once the public got a whiff of Ford's plans, the mail room in Dearborn was flooded with angry letters from consumers.

Even though "M U S T A N G" text was already molded across the face of the imposter's prototype bumpers, an internal revolt within Ford forced the company to reverse course, and the Fox Body platform continued as the facelifted 1987 Mustang. It was a close shave for America's pony car. The almost-was Mustang debuted one year later as the Ford Probe.

In 1991, Congress passed the Surface Transportation Efficiency Act, which required all cars and light trucks sold in the United States to have airbags on the driver's side and passenger's side. Ford realized it would need to redesign the Mustang to meet this new requirement. Besides, the Fox platform had endured for 12 years. It was very long in the tooth.

The challenging financial landscape in the early 1990s meant that Ford considered canceling the Mustang instead of committing huge sums of money to develop a new platform. Many inside Ford resisted this idea, and a small group dedicated to the Mustang formed a skunkworks team to develop an alternate plan. Working after hours, the team hammered out a path forward that not only saved the Mustang but also saved a significant amount of money over the traditional development process. The

*The last hurrah of the Fox/SN-95 platform was the 2003–2004 Mustang SVT Cobra. A supercharged 4.6L, 32-valve V-8, channeled its underrated 390 hp through a 6-speed manual transmission to an independent rear suspension. It's mind-boggling that such performance could be squeezed out of a platform that was designed more than 25 years earlier. (Photo Courtesy Ford Motor Company)*

*It had been more than a quarter century since the Mustang received a completely new design when the 2005 Mustang debuted. The S197-chassis Mustang married retro styling with modern construction, handling, performance, and refinement. Roomier and more comfortable than its predecessor, the 2005 Mustang addressed longstanding ergonomic and performance complaints of earlier Mustangs. (Photo Courtesy Ford Motor Company)*

result was the FOX-4, or SN-95, chassis. The carryover of some major mechanical and body components classified it as a continuation of the Fox platform, but consumers saw it as a completely new car.

The SN-95 continued the Fox architecture for an astonishing 10 more years. During that time, the Mustang saw the departure of the original Ford small-block V-8, the introduction of Ford's overhead-camshaft Modular engine family, and the Mustang's first use of independent rear suspension (IRS). The latter's popularity (or lack thereof with drag racers) greatly influenced future Mustang development.

## Fifth-Generation Mustang: The S197 Platform

The dawn of a new millennium saw the demise of the Mustang's remaining crosstown nemesis, when the last Camaro rolled off its Canadian assembly line in 2002. By this time, Ford had learned its lesson and was committed to continuing the Mustang, but its chassis didn't meet contemporary consumer expectations or safety standards. An entirely new chassis was needed.

Ford knew that the retro styling cues of the 1994 Mustang were popular with buyers, so they were used on the new car.

Fresh from working on the Ford/Jaguar DEW98 rear-drive chassis platform came Chief Engineer Hau Thai-Tang, who set the goals for the car: 1) make it fun, fast, and affordable for the average person; 2) draw on the Mustang's popular past and mix it with good power, state-of-the-art safety, and modern levels of noise, vibration, and harshness (NVH); 3) create a shape that is unmistakably a Mustang.

The result equally drew in Mustang loyalists as well as casual observers who maybe hadn't considered a Mustang for a while. Maybe the retro styling rekindled a childhood memory or snatched a younger buyer's attention at a stoplight.

For the average buyer, the S197 chassis addressed many gripes about the previous generation. Chassis refinement, interior space, build quality, ergonomics, interior materials and styling, chassis dynamics, and structural-rigidity improvements all contributed to the success of the S197 chassis.

Racing enthusiasts lamented that the 2005–2014 Mustang was heavier

*Maintaining a basic level of chassis rigidity for convertibles was always a challenge with previous-generation Mustangs, as convertibles were essentially coupes with missing roofs and a few structural Band-Aids. However, Mustang convertibles were so popular that the S197 finally received its own chassis stampings to fortify convertibles from the ground up. (Photo Courtesy Ford Motor Company)*

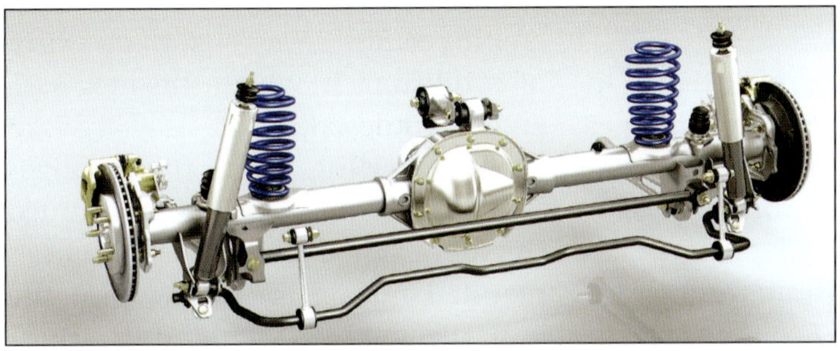

*If the S197 was "stuck" with a live rear axle, the choice of a three-link with a Panhard bar arrangement was leaps and bounds ahead of the Fox and SN-95's bind-prone converging four-link setup. (Photo Courtesy Ford Motor Company)*

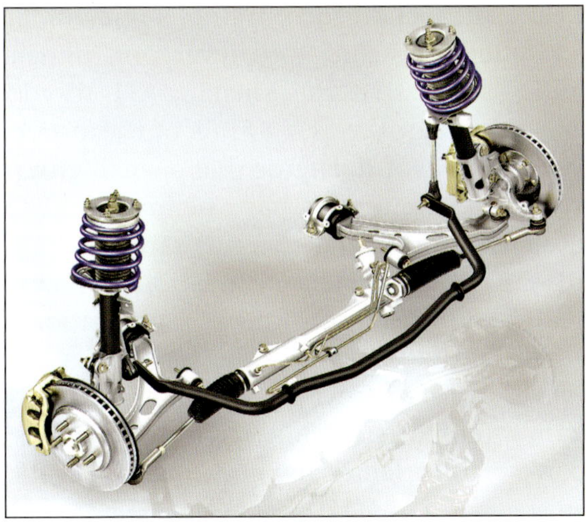

*Front suspension improvements also consisted of revised geometry and L-shaped control arms that direct cornering and braking loads through the front and rear bushings of dedicated stiffness, respectively. The front anti-roll bar links feature precision ball joints and direct sway-bar loads directly to the strut bodies rather than through the control arms. This reduces the loads on the lower ball joints to reduce friction and increase steering feedback. Combined with the three-link rear suspension, the S197 Mustang's suspension addressed many of the previous generations' shortcomings. (Photo Courtesy Ford Motor Company)*

than its predecessors but reasoned that the improvements in handling, NVH, and power were worth the extra heft.

Since the S197 chassis began life as an offshoot of Ford's DEW98 platform, the biggest head-scratcher for some was ditching the DEW98's IRS for a solid axle. Reasons for the decision vary and include cost, complexity, weight, durability, performance, and perception. Enthusiasts recall that the 1999–2004 Mustang Cobra's IRS wasn't a resounding success. The

*Extra headroom engineered into the front control-arm pocket and at the rear bushing mount are examples of how racing enthusiasts within Ford influenced the design of the S197 Mustang. Moving the control-arm pivot points higher corrects suspension geometry for lower ride heights. However, if the factory components don't have the necessary clearance and a racing series requires factory suspension components, options are limited. The previous-generation Mustang didn't have room above the factory location, which limited creative rule interpretations. Hence, savvy racers within Ford aggressively lobbied their cost-conscious counterparts to include this extra space.*

Mustang's first IRS was highly anticipated, but the results (particularly at the drag strip) were mixed. Perhaps that fed into Ford's decision to go back to a tried-and-true solid rear axle for the S197 Mustang.

## Coyote Engine: From Pipe Dream to Production

The new-for-2005 Mustang was a styling and sales home run. With the Chevrolet Camaro out of production since 2002, the Mustang had the American pony car segment all to itself. With solid sales figures, a broad market appeal, and no cross-town competition, the Mustang had become fat and happy. While the S197 chassis was superior to the outgoing SN-95 platform in countless

***First appearing in the 2011 Mustang GT, Ford's 5.0L Ti-VCT Coyote engine transformed the S197-chassis Mustang into a solid sports car contender. The first-generation Coyote produced 412 hp at a singing 6,500 rpm and a meaty 390 ft-lbs of torque. This was all from a modest 5 liters and affordable 87-octane gasoline. (Photo Courtesy Ford Motor Company)***

ways, it was also heavier. Combined with the Mustang GT's 300-hp, 4.6L V-8 engine, performance was . . . adequate. Things were stirring at GM and Chrysler that would spur Ford to not rest on its laurels.

Inside Ford Motor Company, the 4.6L 3-valve-per-cylinder engine wasn't universally loved, either. While most recognized that the new 3-valve architecture worked well for the 5.4L in the F-150, it would rapidly become outdated for sports car applications. When contemporary V-6 engines were producing comparable performance, the 4.6L 3-valve V-8 engine's 300 hp was a disappointment. Billed as offering "4-valve performance at a 2-valve cost," the 3-valve underachieved. It was as expensive to produce as a 4-valve engine but offered performance achievable from a 2-valve design.

With Chevrolet's reintroduced Camaro hitting dealerships two years later, Ford knew it had a horsepower problem. GM's 6.2L LS3 and Dodge's new 6.1L Hemi had a clear displacement advantage. The initial solution was to give the Mustang GT a new 6.2L that was under development for pickup applications. With packaging concerns aside, the 6.2L's 35-percent displacement increase would have yielded the horsepower figures for the Mustang GT to remain competitive, but the 6.2L engine never became a viable Mustang engine. The idea was shelved.

Besides new competition in Detroit, there were also changes coming from Washington, D.C. After remaining unchanged for more than two decades, the federal government increased corporate average fuel economy (CAFE) standards in 2011. With Ford's car sales volumes largely displaced by pickups, the once-less-significant Mustang GT now had a notable impact on the car side of Ford's CAFE calculations.

The bureaucracy of a 100-year-old, multinational company can discourage innovation, but the fundamentals of car-guy culture still thrived inside the cubicles at Ford. Frustrated with the company's conservative powertrain development, a small group of engineers sketched out new 5.0L engine options. However, due to its lack of official program support, origination from unconventional channels, and disinterest from mid-level management, the new 5.0 was relegated to after-hours virtual development by enthusiasts who longed for more muscle under a future Mustang's hood.

Then in 2006, Ford cut jobs and offered buyouts to tens of thousands of its employees as part of a massive restructuring plan. On the eve of the Great Recession, the move arguably saved Ford Motor Company from bankruptcy. The buyouts purged scores of Ford employees who were close to retirement—employees who had decades of institutional knowledge and in some cases decades of traditional thinking. The result was a generational change within Ford that cleared the way for questioning deeply entrenched design standards and practices.

The new market competition, CAFE standards, and generational employee shift was a perfect storm of conditions in which this new 5.0L engine could take root.

Still reeling from the changes within the company, Ford continued the development of the Mustang's planned update for 2011. With the 6.2L deemed too thirsty to meet upcoming CAFE standards, Ford needed a different engine. While watercooler conversations involved turbocharged inline 4-cylinder engines and V-6s, everyone understood that the Mustang GT should always have a V-8. Talk of the skunkworks 5.0L engine that a small group of engineers had penned spread within the engineering ranks at Ford.

Informal conversations quickly morphed into formal presentations, and a week later, the new 5.0L Coyote engine was in Ford's official Mustang cycle plan. As history shows, 5.0L engines also ended up under the hood of F-150 trucks.

Much of the team's effort went into the cylinder heads. A key factor was the size of the hydraulic lash adjuster. The Modular engine family's large lash adjuster limited the height of the intake runner. Use of such a tall lash adjuster was one of the traditional standards with which the Coyote engine crew disagreed.

The approval to use a shorter lash adjuster yielded a cascade of changes

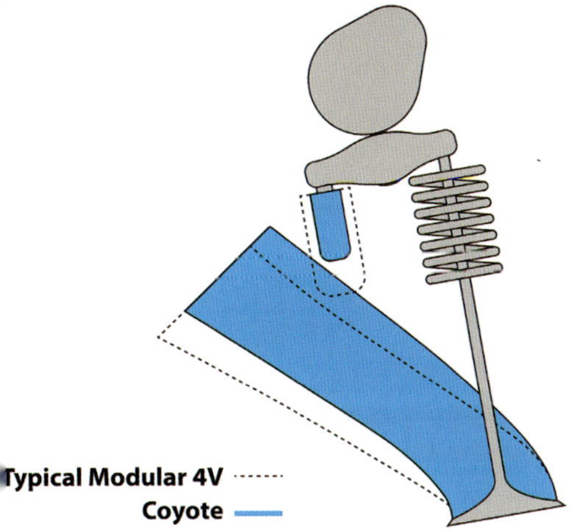


*The Modular 4V engine's large lash adjuster limited the height of the intake port and, ultimately, the flow around the valve. The performance potential of a smaller lash adjuster was proven on the lower-production 2000 Cobra R and Ford GT/GT500 cylinder heads, so the concept was employed on the Coyote cylinder head.*

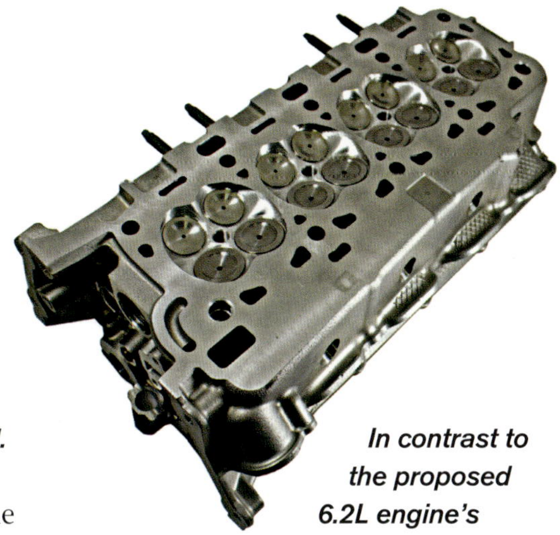

*In contrast to the proposed 6.2L engine's 2-valve cylinder heads, the centrally located spark plug of the Coyote's 4-valve heads offered a more complete burn and was less prone to detonation. The result was fewer emissions and an 11:1 compression ratio for more power and greater fuel efficiency—all while using 87-octane gasoline. (Photo Courtesy Ford Motor Company)*

that dramatically benefited engine performance. The shorter lash adjuster allowed the intake port to be raised, which gave the intake charge a straighter shot around the valve. The higher, 193-cc intake port spread the intake manifold runners wider across the vee, which increased the turn radius of the intake-manifold runners. The wider spread between the intake runners also increased the volume for the intake plenum. All of these seemingly minor changes dramatically increased the volumetric efficiency and power.

The engine also featured twin independent variable camshaft timing (dubbed Ti-VCT) on both the intake and exhaust cams. Not only did this innovation allow the 5.0L engine to maximize power, fuel economy, and minimize emissions but the system also harnessed torque from the camshafts for operation. Rather than use oil pressure to force the cams to advance or retard, the Ti-VCT system rerouted reserve oil from chambers at the precise time in a cam's rotation to allow the camshaft to advance or retard from the resulting forces acting on the cam from the valve actuation. Since the engine's oil pump wasn't doubling as a hydraulic pump to move the cams, the Coyote's oil pump used less power than the 4.6L 3-valve unit.

*Another key factor was moving the alternator out of the vee to make way for a front-feed intake manifold. Moving the throttle body to the front of the engine allowed the intake runners to be the tallest part of the intake manifold, enlarging their bend radius and improving cylinder breathing. (Photo Courtesy Ford Motor Company)*

There were a few reasons that engineers settled on 5 liters of displacement. To save on the manufacturing cost, the Coyote needed to utilize existing production equipment set to the Modular engine family's 100-mm bore spacing and 227-mm deck height. Engineers felt that the Coyote's 92.2-mm bore and 92.7-mm stroke were the practical limits within the Modular engine's architecture. The nearly square bore to stroke ratio yielded 4,951 cc, which rounded up is 5 liters. Besides, given the Mustang's heritage, "5.0" had a nice ring to it.

*A forged-steel crankshaft swung powdered-metal connecting rods and cast pistons inside a deep-skirt aluminum block with additional webbing for strength. The firing order reverted to that of Ford's flathead: 1-5-4-8-6-3-7-2. (Photo Courtesy Ford Motor Company)*

In the end, the Coyote engine was rated at 412 hp and 390 ft-lbs of torque from a relatively small 5 liters of displacement. The redesigned-for-2011 Mustang GT arrived in showrooms more than ready to take on the competition from Dodge and Chevrolet.

How did the "Coyote" code name come about? A V-8 engine planner won an informal engine-naming contest by referring back to Ford's first 32-valve V-8 from the early 1960s: the Coyote Indy V-8. It was attractive to draw upon Ford's rich racing heritage for this engine, and the name stuck.

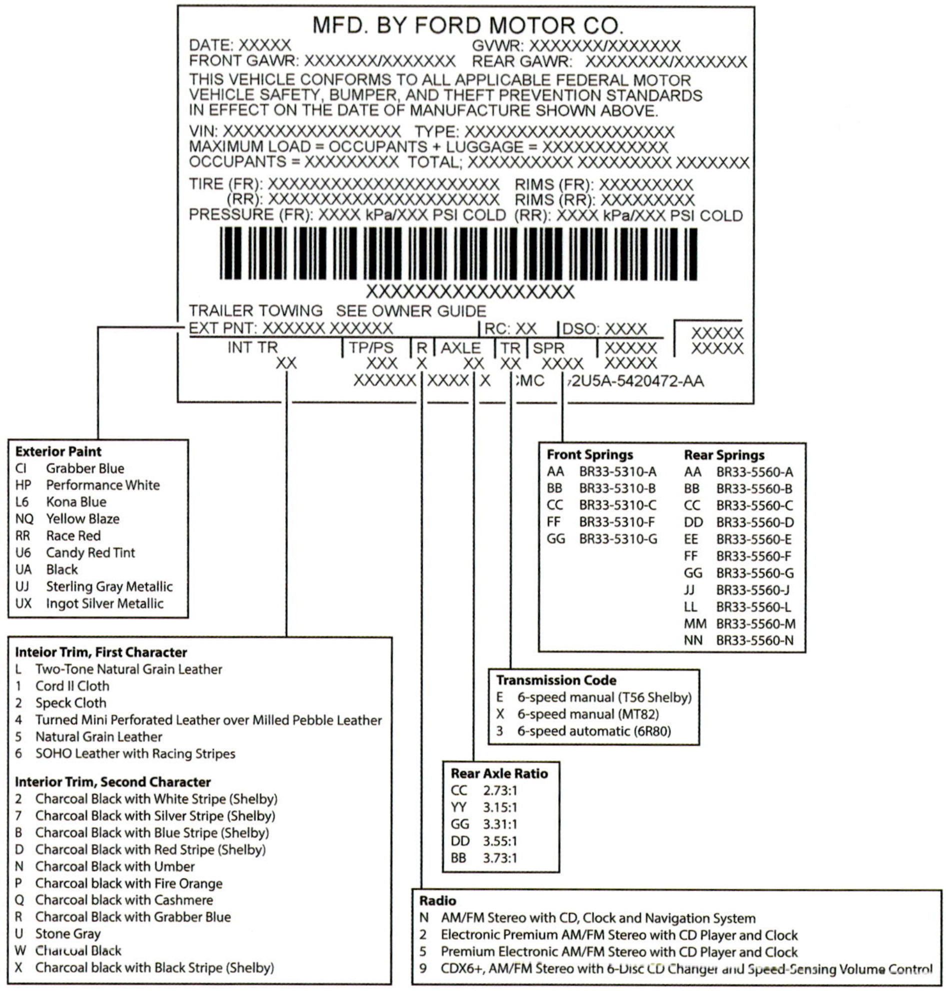


***The tag affixed to the rear edge of driver-side doorjamb contains useful information.***

## Buying and Modifying an S197 Coyote

A 2011 to 2014 Mustang (especially the GT) is an excellent platform for performance modifications, even if it's your first project car. It's relatively practical, economical, and powerful straight off the showroom floor. For performance enthusiasts, numerous factors work in the S197 Mustang's favor:

- 2011–2014 Mustangs are old enough to have depreciated considerably, but they are new enough that most collision repairs were reported and repaired while insured. This means that major body damage will show up on a vehicle history report. As vehicles age, bodywork is more commonly paid out of pocket and can only be found by in-person inspection.
- S197 Mustangs are plentiful, so it's not difficult to find unmolested examples in good condition. As cars exit their warranty period, many buyers move to newer vehicles, which leaves the last

***The 2011 to 2014 Mustang GTs are very rewarding project cars. They're plentiful, responsive to changes, and easy to work on.***

generation of Mustangs numerous and affordable for budget-minded enthusiasts to purchase.

- Durability is proven. Don't be afraid of cars with more than 100,000 miles. If maintained well, these cars have a lot of life left to enjoy.
- Ford used better materials and methods that resist corrosion and chassis fatigue than earlier generations. This makes 2011–2014 Mustangs a sound purchasing decision even in the rust belt.
- Modern fluid couplings and captured fasteners make disassembling and reassembling the S197 Mustang extremely straightforward. The larger chassis offers considerably more working room than previous (and later) generations, which greatly reduces frustration and busted knuckles. The chassis and component layouts are logical, conventional, and simple. Dare we say that working on a 2011–2014 Mustang is a pleasure.
- Modifying a Coyote-powered 5.0L car is especially rewarding because the powertrain responds well to modifications. The Mustang's popularity with enthusiasts means the aftermarket is awash with well-developed, proven components. There's no need to embark on your own research and development program; reputable companies already know what works and what doesn't. The paths to performance are well-beaten and clearly marked.

**2011 Mustang Engine Options**

| Type | 3.7L V-6 | 5.0L V-8 |
|---|---|---|
| Block | Aluminum, cast-iron liners, six-bolt main caps | Aluminum, pressed-in iron liners, six-bolt main caps |
| Displacement | 3,726 cc (227.4 ci) | 4,951 cc (302.1 ci) |
| Bore x Stroke | 95.5 mm (3.76 inches) x 86.7 mm (3.41 inches) | 92.2 mm (3.63 inches) x 92.7 mm (3.65 inches) |
| Bore Spacing | 100 mm | 100 mm |
| Crankshaft | Forged 4130 steel, cross-plane | Forged steel, cross-plane |
| Connecting Rods | Powdered forged steel | Powdered forged steel (150.7-mm length) |
| Pistons | Cast aluminum | Cast aluminum |
| Compression | 10.5:1 | 11.0:1 |
| Cylinder Heads | Aluminum, 4 valves per cylinder | Aluminum, 4 valves per cylinder |
| Valvetrain | Dual overhead cam (DOHC), twin independent variable camshaft timing (Ti-VCT), direct acting mechanical bucket (DAMB) lifters | Dual overhead cam (DOHC), twin independent variable camshaft timing (Ti-VCT), roller finger follower and hydraulic lash adjuster |
| Valve Diameter | Intake: 37.0 mm; Exhaust: 31.0 mm | Intake: 37.0 mm; Exhaust: 31.0 mm |
| Valve Lift | Intake: 10.0 mm; Exhaust: 97.0 mm | Intake: 12.0 mm; Exhaust 12.0 mm |
| Throttle Body Diameter | 68 mm | 80 mm |
| Fuel Delivery | Sequential multi-port fuel injection | Sequential multi-port fuel injection |
| Ignition | Coil on plug | Coil on plug |
| Firing Order | 1-4-2-5-3-6 | 1-5-4-8-6-3-7-2 |
| Horsepower | 305 hp (227 kW) at 6,500 rpm | 2011–2012: 412 hp (307 kW) at 6,500 rpm; 2013–2014: 420 hp (313 kW) at 6,500 rpm |
| Torque | 280 ft-lbs (380 N m) at 4,250 rpm | 390 ft-lbs (529 N m) at 4,250 rpm |
| Maximum RPM | 7,000 | 7,000 |
| Minimum Fuel Octane | 87 | 87 |
| Oil capacity | 6 quarts with filter | 8 quarts with filter |

# WHEELS AND TIRES

Upgrading rolling stock is vital to extracting the most performance out of a Mustang. After all, they're the only parts of a Mustang that should touch the ground.

## Wheels

The wheels are a vital connection between the tires and the suspension. The ideal wheel is perfectly rigid and lightweight. Accordingly, good wheel designs are a trade-off between stiffness and weight.

Design factors are a function of the material chosen and wheel construction. Most modern wheels are constructed of cast aluminum, cast and flow-formed aluminum, or forged aluminum (in order of increasing cost). Carbon-fiber wheels are slowly making their way into the market, but their high development, material and manufacturing costs result in use on high-end vehicles, such as the Ford GT, Shelby GT350R, and Shelby GT500.

Cast aluminum has a lower strength-to-weight ratio when compared to forged aluminum, so cast wheels must use more material to compensate for the material's reduced stiffness. Consequently, cast wheels are often much heavier than their forged counterparts. Cast wheels are formed by pouring liquid aluminum into a mold, where forged wheels are made from material squeezed between high-pressure dies or cut from a pre-forged block of aluminum.

A cast and flow-formed wheel is a bridge between a cast wheel and a forged wheel by using a cast blank and drawing the barrel of the wheel over a die. The process yields a wheel that has a higher stiffness-to-weight ratio than a cast wheel at a lower cost than a fully forged wheel.

| 2011–2014 S197 Mustang Factory Wheel and Tire Options | | | | | | | |
|---|---|---|---|---|---|---|---|
| Trim | Tire | Wheel Diameter (inches) | Wheel Width (inches) | Offset (mm) | Backspacing (inches) | Bolt Pattern (mm) | Center Bore (mm) |
| 3.7L | 215/65R17 | 17 | 7.0 | 40 | 5.6 | 5x114.3 | 70.6 |
| 3.7L | 225/60R17 | 17 | 7.0 | 40 | 5.6 | 5x114.3 | 70.6 |
| 3.7L | 235/50ZR18 | 18 | 8.0 | 44 | 6.2 | 5x114.3 | 70.6 |
| 3.7L | 255/40ZR19 | 19 | 8.5 | 40 | 6.3 | 5x114.3 | 70.6 |
| 5.0L | 235/50ZR18 | 18 | 8.0 | 41 | 6.1 | 5x114.3 | 70.6 |
| 5.0L | 235/50ZR18 | 18 | 8.0 | 44 | 6.2 | 5x114.3 | 70.6 |
| 5.0L | 245/45ZR19 | 19 | 8.5 | 50 | 6.7 | 5x114.3 | 70.6 |
| 5.0L (Brembo) | 255/40ZR19 | 19 | 9.0 | 42 | 6.7 | 5x114.3 | 70.6 |
| Note: The Brembo brake option includes a unique 19-inch wheel to clear the larger brake calipers. | | | | | | | |

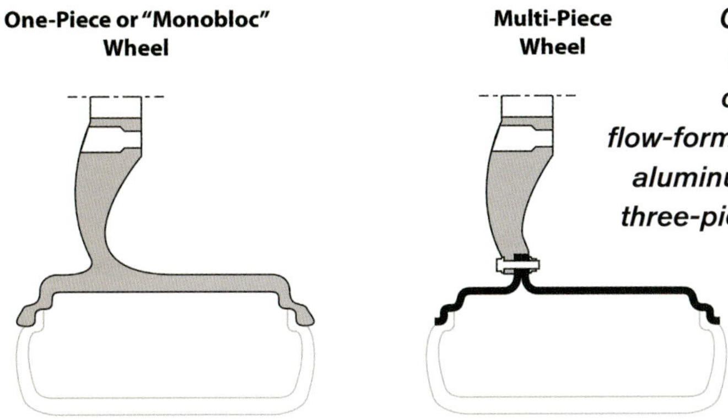


*One-piece, or monobloc, wheels (left) are usually cast aluminum, cast and flow-formed aluminum, or forged aluminum. Multipiece (two-and three-piece) wheels (right) offer flexibility in fitment and repair because wheel diameters, widths, and offsets can be tailored by replacing the center, inner, or outer rim halves.*

Most factory wheels are cast aluminum and are usually very conservatively designed to meet Ford's durability requirements. They're extremely durable but also very heavy. Forged wheels are often out of the budget for most enthusiasts, so a cast and flow-formed wheel is an excellent option for a wider-than-OEM wheel without the weight penalty of a casting or the price tag of a forged wheel.

Most factory-installed wheels are one-piece, or monobloc, wheels. Aftermarket wheels are available as one piece or multipiece. The latter allows fine-tuning of wheel fitment and component replacement.

Wheel choice often boils down to aesthetics. However, it's best to buy a name-brand wheel from a reputable retailer or Mustang specialist. A wheel is one of the most highly-stressed parts on a high-performance car, so beware: inexpensive and counterfeit wheels made from low-quality materials and questionable manufacturing processes are widespread and notorious for failing. At the very least, avoid inexpensive cast copies of forged and multipiece wheel designs, as cast aluminum is too weak for a design that has been optimized for stronger materials.

## Tires

Tires are more than just black rubber donuts; they're the link between the car and the pavement. Selecting a tire goes beyond the size that fits. Rubber compound and tire construction affect the traction, temperature range, handling, ride, noise, and wear characteristics of the tire. Compromises are made in each of these areas to deliver the performance that the customer expects.

The first factor when selecting a tire is to determine the driving conditions or season. An extreme-performance summer tire will have different characteristics than a winter tire or an all-season tire. The differences go beyond simply tread design, although that's an important variable.

Selecting the proper season of tire is dictated by the conditions in which the vehicle will be driven, and it is mostly a consumer preference. However, because of the compromises that are made to allow all-season tires to perform in a wide range of conditions, most tire experts agree that they should be avoided for a performance-minded application. If you plan to drive your Mustang regularly in snow or below-freezing temperatures, use specific summer and winter tires. Most Mustang enthusiasts focus on the summer tire category.

When selecting summer tires, consider this: as one moves up the ladder of dry traction, the risk of hydroplaning increases because when a tire rolls through a puddle, the water must evacuate through grooves in the tire. If all the water cannot escape from the contact patch, the tire will hydroplane.

Note that hydroplaning resistance is different than wet traction.

*The 255/40ZR19 Pirelli P Zero Nero all-season tire (left) and the 305/30ZR19 Michelin Pilot Sport Cup 2 tire (right) illustrate two tires for different applications. The Pirelli all-season tire's deeper grooves, channels, and sipes are designed for year-round use, including driving in light snow. Conversely, the Michelin Pilot Sport Cup 2 is a street-able track and competition tire that is optimized for dry-weather traction in warm climates. The Cup 2 tire features an asymmetric tread pattern with larger outside tread blocks and different rubber compounds across the tire to optimize durability and grip while cornering and accelerating.*

# Useful Tire Sidewall Information

The following information can be found on the sidewall of a tire.

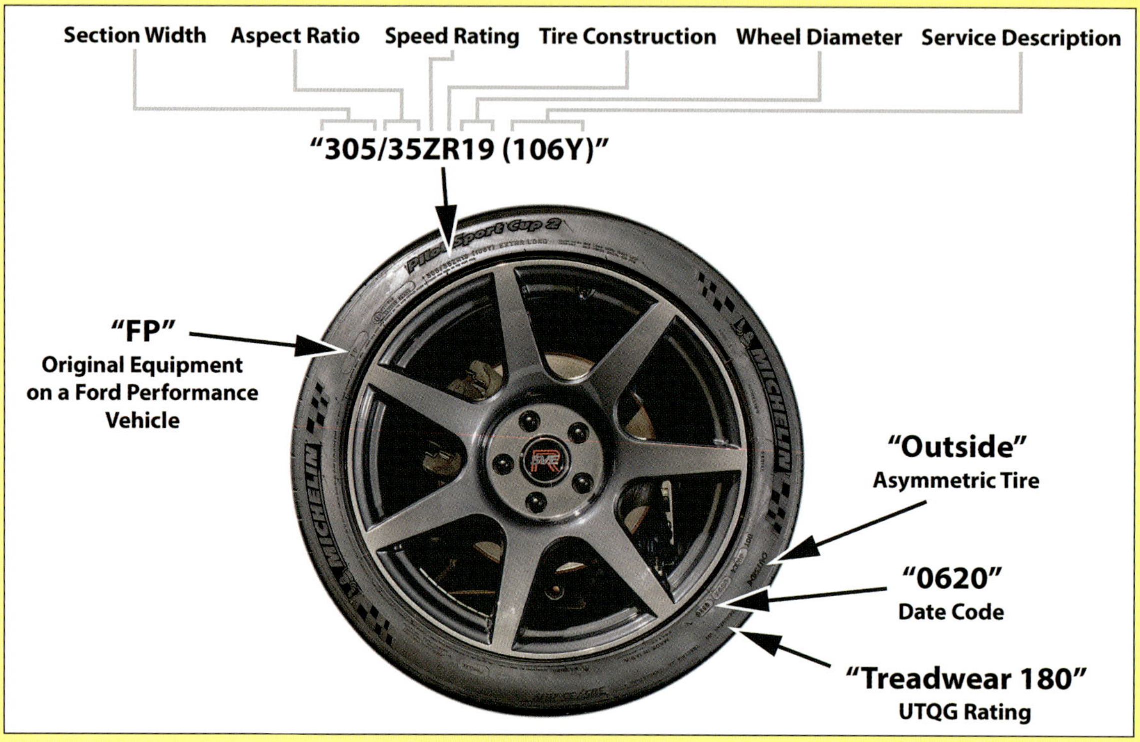


| Tire Size Specifications | | | | | | | | | |
|---|---|---|---|---|---|---|---|---|---|
| Tire | Size | Tread-wear, UTQG | Section Width (inches) | Measuring Rim Width (inches) | Diameter (inches) | Revolu-tions Per Mile | Weight (pounds) | Wheel width range, (inches) | Tread Depth |
| Pirelli P Zero Nero All Season | 255/40Z R19/XL (96W) | 400 | 10.2 | 9.0 | 27.0 | 746 | 29.0 | 8.5–10.0 | 7.2/32" |
| Michelin Pilot Sport Cup 2 | 255/35Z R19/XL (96Y) | 180 | 10.2 | 9.0 | 26.0 | 799 | 25.3 | 8.5–10.0 | 7.2/32" |
| Michelin Pilot Sport Cup 2 | 265/40Z R19/XL (102Y) | 180 | 10.7 | 9.5 | 27.4 | 760 | 26.3 | 9.0–10.5 | 7.2/32" |
| Michelin Pilot Sport Cup 2 | 275/35Z R19/XL (100Y) | 180 | 11.0 | 9.5 | 26.6 | 783 | 24.3 | 9.0–11.0 | 7.2/32" |
| Michelin Pilot Sport Cup 2 | 285/35Z R19/XL (103Y) | 180 | 11.4 | 10.0 | 26.9 | 774 | 27.4 | 9.5–11.0 | 7.2/32" |
| Michelin Pilot Sport Cup 2 | 295/35Z R19/XL (104Y) | 180 | 11.8 | 10.5 | 27.1 | 767 | 28.2 | 10.0–11.5 | 5.5/32" |
| Michelin Pilot Sport Cup 2 | 305/35Z R19/XL (106Y) | 180 | 12.3 | 11.0 | 27.4 | 758 | 29.7 | 10.0–12.0 | 6.0/32" |
| Michelin Pilot Sport Cup 2 | 325/30Z R19/XL (105Y) | 180 | 13.0 | 11.5 | 26.7 | 778 | 30.5 | 11.0–12.0 | 7.2/32" |

### Size

The basic size of a tire is shown, including nominal section width, aspect ratio, speed rating, and wheel diameter.

### UTQG Treadwear Rating

The uniform tire quality grade (UTQG) refers to how much a tire wears when driven on a test loop when compared to a known control tire. Since manufacturers conduct their own tests and there are countless variables that affect real-world tire wear, the UTQG may not accurately predict one tire's performance over another. So, a tire with a UTQG treadwear of 200 from one manufacturer may last longer and have less grip than a 280-treadwear tire from another manufacturer. Consequently, take UTQG treadwear rating with a large grain of salt. Some motorsports classes require tires with a 200 UTQG treadwear rating, making this class of tire very competitive.

### Section Width

The section width (in millimeters) is the nominal width of tire. The actual width of a tire varies with sidewall design, construction, and the presence of any rim-protection features.

### Aspect Ratio

The ratio of the sidewall height to section width x 100 is the aspect ratio. All else being equal, higher-aspect-ratio tires have taller sidewalls and are larger in diameter.

### Tire Construction

The letter "R" indicates a radial tire, which is rather moot today, as all road and most racing tires are radials.

### Wheel Diameter

The diameter of a wheel (in inches) for which a tire is designed is shown after the "R" for radials. A larger-diameter wheel will require a tire with a smaller aspect ratio to maintain the OEM tire circumference (and speedometer accuracy).

### Measuring Rim Width

This is the wheel width on which a tire's section is measured. A tire's effective section width will change depending upon the wheel's width.

### Tire Diameter

The tire diameter is the diameter of a tire at the center if its tread without any load on the tire. This is helpful in matching front and rear tires of different section widths.

### Revolutions Per Mile

The number of times a tire rotates over the course of a mile based upon calculations or actual measurements by the manufacturer is shown. This is helpful for recalculating a speedometer after different size tires are fitted.

### Tire Weight

Equally as important (if not more) as wheel weight is the tire weight because the wheel and tire together are unsprung and affect ride and handling.

### Wheel Width Range

The manufacturer-approved wheel width range for a specific tire is often specified. Mounting tires on wheels within the approved width range keeps a tire's internal stresses within its design parameters.

According to Michelin, "For the best performance (both cornering and straight line), it is advantageous to select the maximum recommended rim width for a given tire size. A wider rim increases the lateral stiffness of the tire, which increases steering response and high-speed stability. Even drag racers running in radial tire classes have found benefits by choosing wider rims to help control the contact patch. A wider wheel is better in all cases."

### Tread Depth

Tread depth, usually measured in 1/32 of an inch, is measured in the deepest groove of a tire.

### Service Description

A tire's load index and speed rating comprise a tire's service description. "106" corresponds to a load index of 950 kg (2,094 pounds), and "Y" indicates a tire rated for 300 kilometers per hour (186 mph). Since the service description is enclosed in parentheses, the rating exceeds the 300 kilometers per hour.

### Date Code

Tires have a shelf and service life besides only wear. The date code indicates the two-digit week and year of manufacture. "0620" means that a tire was manufactured the sixth week of 2020.

### Other Sidewall Markings

Asymmetric tires often have special tread patterns and/or tire compounds that are designed for the conditions seen by the outside edges of the tire. "Outside" indicates an asymmetric tire, and this side of the tire should be mounted to face the outside of the vehicle.

Tires with a tread pattern designed to evacuate water best when rolled in a particular direction will have also have directional arrows on the sidewall.

If a tire is designed specifically for an O.E.M. application, such as Porsche or Ford, there is an indication on the sidewall. "FP" means that a tire is original equipment for a Ford Performance vehicle. ■

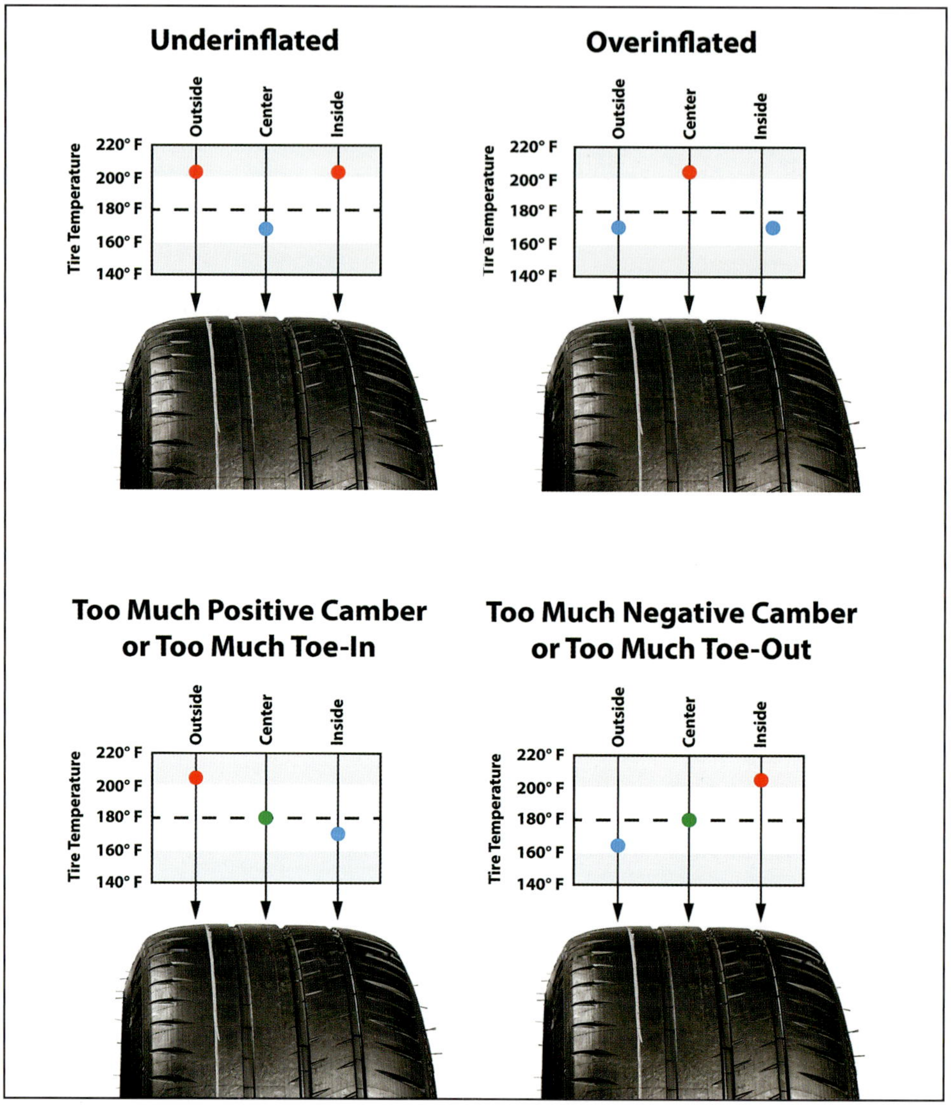


*Using a quality tire pyrometer and tire-pressure gauge can tell you a lot about how your tires are reacting to the car's setup. Alignment, tire pressure, and driving style all affect tire temperatures. Use your tire manufacturer's recommended target tire temperature as a guide in tuning. Race tires have a higher target temperature than street tires. Michelin's target for the Pilot Sport Cup 2 tire is 180°F.*

A tire with a shallow tread depth can also have excellent grip on wet surfaces, just not through puddles. So, an aggressive summer tire optimized for dry traction can be driven on a wet track, but standing-water conditions should be approached with caution.

A tire specification chart includes vital information that will help with final tire selection. This chart covers the specifications for an OEM–replacement Pirelli P Zero Nero all-season tire and specifications for a streetable track and competition tire, the Michelin Pilot Sport Cup 2.

## Maximum Tire Performance at the Track

Tire manufacturers, including Michelin, cater to enthusiasts and often publish recommended tire-temperature targets, tire-pressure ranges, and maximum camber specifications for track use. Regarding Michelin Pilot Sport Cup 2 tires, Michelin offers the following guidelines:

- While not necessary, there is a small benefit to a heat cycle before sustained track use. A heat cycle is defined as running enough laps to bring the tires to more than 160°F and then letting them cool and rest for 24 hours or more before running an extended track session.
- Maximize the negative camber setting allowed by the factory specifications, but do not exceed 4 degrees of negative camber (1.5 to 3 degrees of negative camber is optimal).
- The Cup 2's target tread temperature is around 180°F for average for maximum grip. At 220°F, the grip will begin to degrade, and the tire will feel greasy. Temperatures higher than 260°F can permanently damage the tire.
- Avoid burnouts with street tires. Burnouts may help competition tires that are designed to run at higher temperatures, but high-performance street tires can be overheated by an extended burnout. Anything more than a short burnout should be avoided.
- The optimum hot tire pressure is between 34 and 38 psi for the best combination of grip and wear.
- Do not run cold pressures below 28 psi and avoid hitting curbs until the pressure increases to the running pressure. Also, don't

forget to reset the pressures to the auto-manufacturer-recommended setting before driving home.

## How-To Project: Wheel and Tire Upgrade

Fitting a wider set of wheels that are wrapped in grippy rubber is one of the best ways to increase the performance of your Mustang. Maximizing the rubber under the fenders of an S197 Mustang requires research and attention to detail. Fortunately, several suppliers cater to S197 Mustangs, including Late Model Restoration (LMR). LMR's in-house SVE brand offers the R350 wheel in 19x10 and 19x11 to fit some of the widest rubber possible under the fenders of a S197 Mustang while saving weight.

We chose to wrap the SVE R350 wheels with Michelin's Pilot Sport Cup 2 tires sized 285/35 and 305/35 front and rear, respectively. Ford and Michelin collaborated on the development of the latest-generation Ford GT road- and Le Mans-winning race cars and worked together early in the process.

Since 2016, all Ford Performance vehicles come with Michelin tires as original equipment. Given Michelin's prominent position and reputation in motorsports, we chose the company's Pilot Sport Cup 2 tire to get the most out of our current and future suspension improvements.

Here's a rundown of our shopping list:

- Late Model Restoration Supply SVE R350 Wheel Kit (part number WK-177913A)
- Late Model Restoration Supply Tire Pressure Monitoring Sensor (TPMS) Kit with Training Tool (part number LRS-20315B)
- Michelin Pilot Sport Cup 2 tires, 285/35-19, 305/35-19

***Late Model Restoration Supply SVE R350 Wheel Kit (part number WK-177913A) includes a pair of 19x10-inch front and 19x11-inch rear wheels that are finished in Liquid Graphite. They're cast and flow-formed wheels that are designed exclusively for 2005-and-newer Mustangs. The included spline-drive lug-nut set eases installation. (Photo Courtesy Late Model Restoration Supply)***

***Michelin's Pilot Sport Cup 2 tire is a track-focused tire that can be driven on the street. Every aspect of the tire is designed to maximize dry-weather grip but to still be road-friendly on trips to and from the track. We chose 285/35ZR19 and 305/35ZR19 tires to match our 10- and 11-inch-wide wheels, respectively. (Photo Courtesy Michelin)***

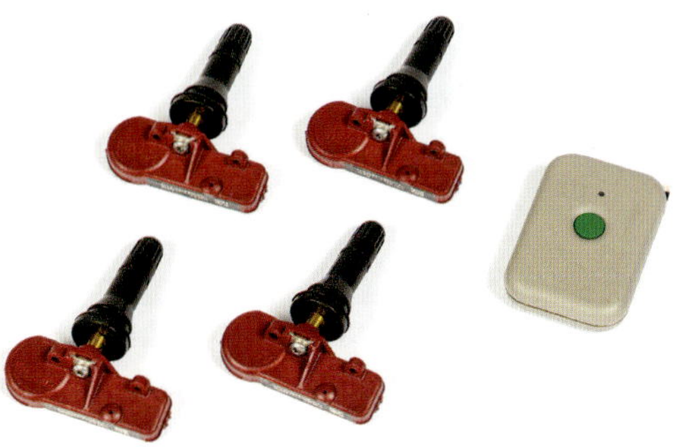

***So that we could easily swap to our OEM wheels and tires for daily and winter use, we fitted our SVE R350 wheels with a new tire pressure monitoring system (TPMS) kit from Late Model Restoration Supply. It includes a training tool that pairs the new TPMS sensors to the Mustang to retain convenience and safety.***

***Besides weight savings, one of the major reasons to fit a new set of wider wheels is to accommodate wider tires. Fortunately, the fender lips on S197 Mustangs are very thin and don't require rolling in most cases. To get a basic idea of how much room we had on the outside, we measured the existing fender gap at ride height front and rear.***

*There are a few areas of concern that limit wheel and tire width on the inside. Up front, clearance between the strut and the wheel/tire limits width. We like at least 1/4-inch clearance. In our experience, the rest of the front wheel housing and suspension usually won't interfere at full steering lock in either direction if clearance exists at the strut.*

*In the rear, a limiting factor is clearance between the wheel/tire and the shock.*

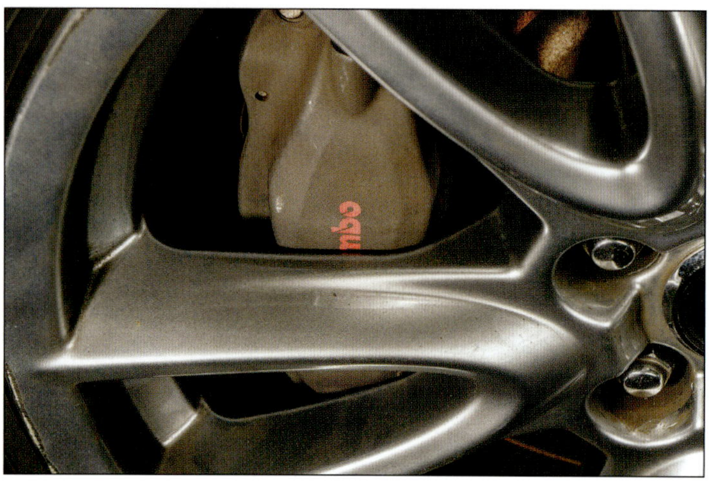

*Brake clearance must also be considered when selecting aftermarket wheels. Note how the factory Brembo package wheels tightly hug the brake calipers. Most aftermarket brake kit manufacturers offer templates to assist in checking brake-component clearance when fitting aftermarket wheels and brakes.*

*We trial-fit the SVE R350 wheels front and rear to double-check the clearance.*

*Everything looked good up front. However, at the rear, the fender liner was bowed out to where it could drag on the wheel and tire. We used a heat gun to reform the fender-liner tab.*

*Reforming the fender liner with the heat gun provided the clearance that we needed.*

*Wide wheel and tire options can also interfere with the bump-stop bracket that's spot welded to the frame rail. The R350 wheels cleared this troublesome area with ease because the Street Performance Coilover kit from H&R Special Springs limits droop travel before the wheel can interfere with the bump-stop bracket. The clearance is shown between the arrows.*

*When mounting wheels and tires, it's helpful to find an installer that specializes in performance wheel and tire setups. TNT Wheel in Goodlettsville, Tennessee, is our go-to shop for mounting tires. TNT Wheel used a valve-stem puller tool to seat the sensors in the wheels.*

*Then, TNT Wheel used special no-contact tools to mount the Michelin Pilot Sport Cup 2 tires on the SVE R350 wheels.*

*TNT Wheel used its precision dynamic balancer to balance the combination with adhesive weights.*

*It's not uncommon for adhesive weights to come loose when exposed to high brake heat. We used aluminum tape (commonly available at hardware stores) to reflect heat away from the weights.*

*With the tires mounted, we installed the new wheels on this 2012 Mustang GT and verified clearance.*

*Because the lug nut holes in the SVE R350 wheels are smaller than the OEM wheels, SVE includes spline-drive lug nuts.*

*With the Mustang back on its feet, we used the TPMS training tool to pair the new TPMS sensors to the Mustang's monitoring system.*

**OEM (with Brembo) and SVE R350 Wheel Comparison**

| |  |  | |
|---|---|---|---|
| **Wheel** | **OEM 5.0L with Brembo (Front)** | **SVE R350 (Front)** | **SVE R350 (Rear)** |
| Wheel Diameter (inches) | 19 | 19 | 19 |
| Wheel Width (inches) | 9 | 10 | 11 |
| Offset (mm) | 42 | 35 | 50 |
| Backspacing (inches) | 6.7 | 6.9 | 8.0 |
| Wheel Weight (pounds) | 32.0 | 24.2 | 25.0 |
| Tire | Pirelli P Zero Nero All Season | Michelin Pilot Sport Cup 2 | |
| Size | 255/40ZR19 | 285/35ZR19 | 305/35ZR19 |
| Tire Weight (pounds) | 29.0 | 27.4 | 29.7 |
| Total Weight (pounds) | 61.0 | 51.6 | 54.7 |
| Weight versus OEM (pounds) | – | -9.4 | -6.3 |

Although the SVE R350 wheels from LMR and Michelin Pilot Sport Cup 2 tires are significantly wider than the factory Brembo package wheel setup, the wider SVE and Michelin wheel/tire combination shaves 9.4 and 6.3 pounds from each front and rear wheel, respectively. That's a significant savings in both rotational and unsprung mass.

*Compared to the OEM wheel setup, the SVR R350 wheels and Michelin Pilot Sport Cup 2 tires give this 2012 Mustang GT an all-business look to match its performance.*

*The staggered width fitment on the same aspect ratio means that the rear tires are slightly taller than the front tires, which enhances this Mustang's slight front rake.*

*The SVE R350 wheel from Late Model Restoration is a handsome wheel for S197 Mustangs that fits extremely well, clears all but the biggest racing brake packages, and mounts much-needed wider tires, all while cutting weight.*

*The wider footprint from the 285- and 305-mm-wide Michelin Pilot Sport Cup 2 tires gives this Mustang world-class levels of grip.*

# Chassis and Suspension

The chassis and suspension are critical to not only 2011–2014 Mustangs but any vehicle. These systems and the components within them are explained in this chapter.

*Jacking rails provide a convenient place to jack up the side of the car and position jack stands. They make jacking up and supporting Mustangs much easier and safer.*

## Chassis

With few exceptions, the stiffer a car's chassis is, the better it is. A rigid chassis allows the suspension to work better, allows less harshness to be transmitted to occupants, and suffers fewer creaks, shudders, and rattles. Use of high-strength materials, contemporary manufacturing techniques, and computer-aided design tools took chassis rigidity to new levels with the S197 Mustang.

In addition, convertibles received different stampings to comprise their structure, rather than resorting to only bolt-on supports to combat convertible chassis flex. Ford described the body structure as 31-percent stiffer in torsion than the previous model. It's so stiff that it takes 15,500 ft-lbs to deform the body 1 degree.

Since the S197 Mustang's unibody structure is so much stiffer than previous models, there isn't as much low-hanging fruit for the aftermarket to pluck. Most aftermarket chassis modifications are designed to add strength, convenience, and safety, or to reduce weight.

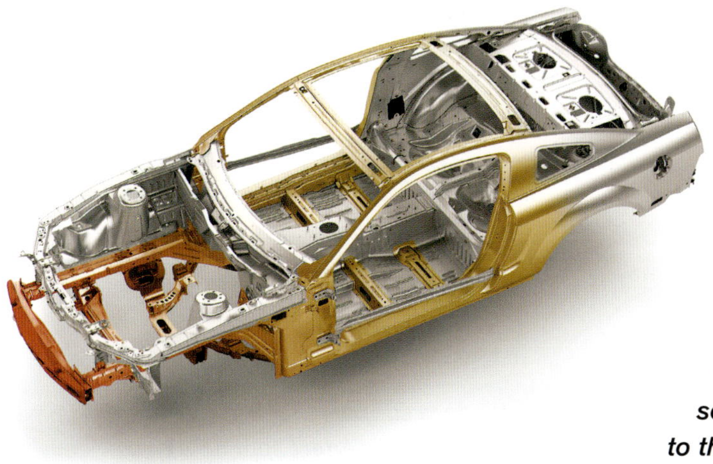

*In addition to adding more suspension travel, the 2005–2014 Mustang's taller transmission tunnel adds a stiffer backbone to the floor pan. The S197's taller and thicker door sills and rocker panels have generous radii to add stiffness. Note that the section from the A-pillar to the taillight panel is one sheet-metal stamping, which further enhances chassis rigidity. (Photo Courtesy Ford)*

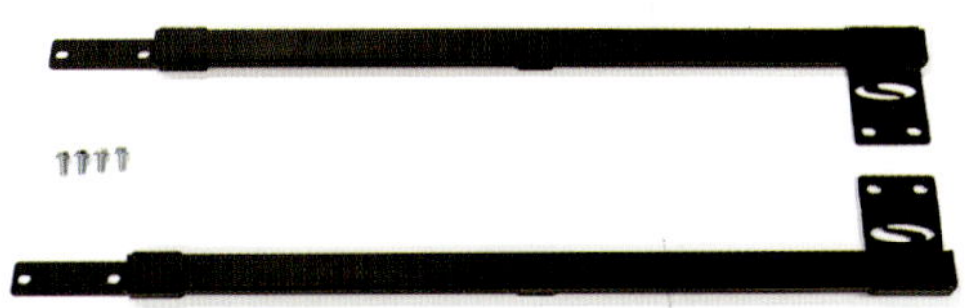

*Steeda's jacking rails are unique in that they don't require welding to install and bolt to existing chassis fastener locations.*

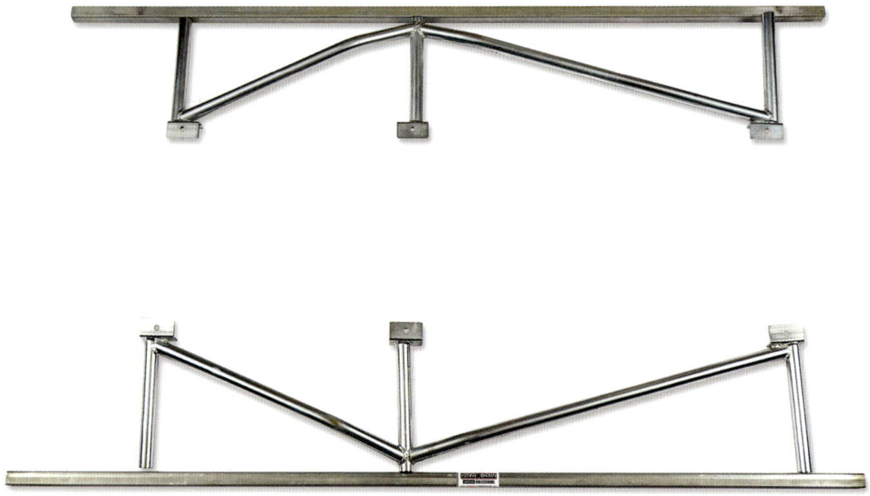

*A variation on jacking rails is the Extreme Matrix system from Kenny Brown. It includes a jacking rail that welds to the rocker-panel pinch weld and ties that rail to the unibody's frame rail with a web matrix. Not only does the arrangement add rigidity to the floor but it also arguably adds some side-impact protection.*

*The Stifflers FIT system expands on the jacking rails and matrix brace idea by tying into the chassis end rear lower control-arm mounts. (Photo Courtesy Stifflers)*

*Steeda's frame rail and torque box braces support the flexible lower control-arm mount and distribute its loads directly to the rocker and the subframe to make this area of the chassis stiffer. (Photo Courtesy Steeda)*

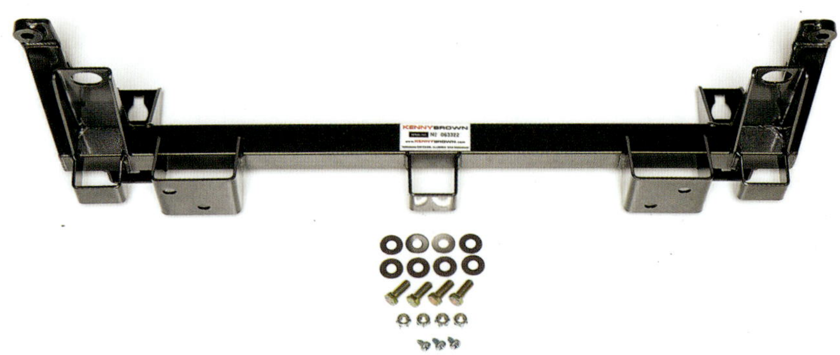

*Replacing the stamped-steel radiator core support with a lighter-weight unit like this from Kenny Brown cuts weight from a perfect spot on a nose-heavy Mustang: ahead of the front wheels. The result is improved weight distribution and sharper handling. (Photo Courtesy Kenny Brown Performance)*

The strut towers are on a major load-bearing area on the S197 Mustang chassis, so tying them adds a measure of rigidity. A strut tower brace was factory-installed on convertible and performance-package-equipped Mustangs. Note that some intake manifolds and superchargers interfere with various strut tower braces. While the factory GT strut tower brace is much lower, the Boss 302 strut tower brace clears most aftermarket intake manifolds, including the Ford Performance Parts Cobra Jet.

On the limited-edition Boss 302 Laguna Seca, Ford removed the rear seat and installed an X-brace in its place. To provide a similar structural benefit, Steeda offers its rear chassis X-brace (part number 555-5093), which ties the rear shock towers to the chassis without requiring rear seat removal. (Photo Courtesy Steeda)

If your Mustang will see significant track use and you don't mind losing the back seat, a roll bar (such as this bolt-in unit from Watson Racing) adds chassis rigidity, rollover protection, and a convenient place to mount safety harnesses. (Photo Courtesy Late Model Restoration)

## Suspension

A Mustang's suspension not only isolates the driver from bumps in the road but also affects how a Mustang handles, which is how well it accelerates, stops, and goes around corners. At the risk of oversimplification, we'll cover the basics of vehicle dynamics and how they apply to 2011–2014 Mustangs.

### Why Tires Matter

Before getting into chassis and suspension, we must discuss tires. The cliché "where the rubber meets the road" is a perfect way to think about how tire behavior affects a Mustang's handling. Understanding the basic physics of rubber tires is critical to understanding handling balance.

First, tires are made of rubber, which has different properties than other materials. For a given tire, two major factors determine grip: vertical load and slip angle.

### How Vertical Load Affects Grip

The more force (weight) that is on a tire, the more grip is available from that tire. If you remember what was taught in high school physics class, static friction (or grip) is a function of pressure and a material's coefficient of friction. Push down on something with twice the force, and the effort that is needed to move it doubles. More significantly, the amount of force that is needed to move something is independent of surface area. If the load doesn't change, a smaller surface area takes the same force to move as the larger surface area. This is assuming that the coefficient of friction between the surfaces is constant and the grip related to load is linear.

This diminishing of returns with regard to load and grip has two important takeaways: 1) A tire has more grip if the load is more evenly distributed across the tire. This is why wider tires have more grip than skinny tires and why wheel camber affects grip. 2) A pair of tires has more grip if the load is more evenly distributed between them. This is why spring rates, dampers, anti-roll bars, wheel alignment, and suspension geometry affect handling balance.

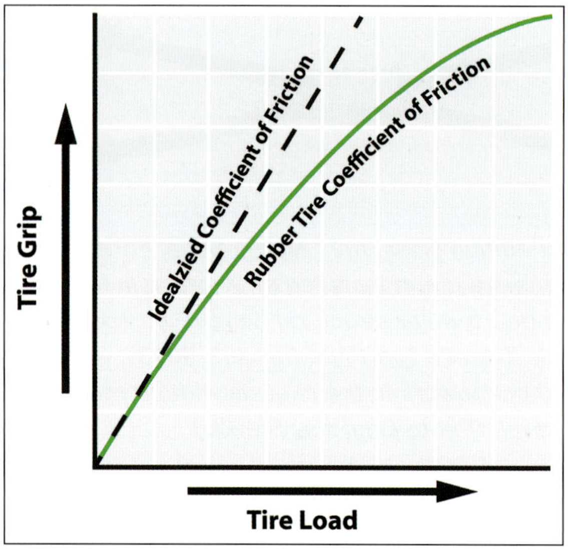


*Here's where behavior of rubber tires diverges from what was taught in high school physics class: a rubber tire's coefficient of friction decreases with load. That's not to say that a more heavily loaded tire doesn't generate more grip (it does), but the relationship between load and grip is not linear. In other words, a tire with double the load does not have double the grip.*

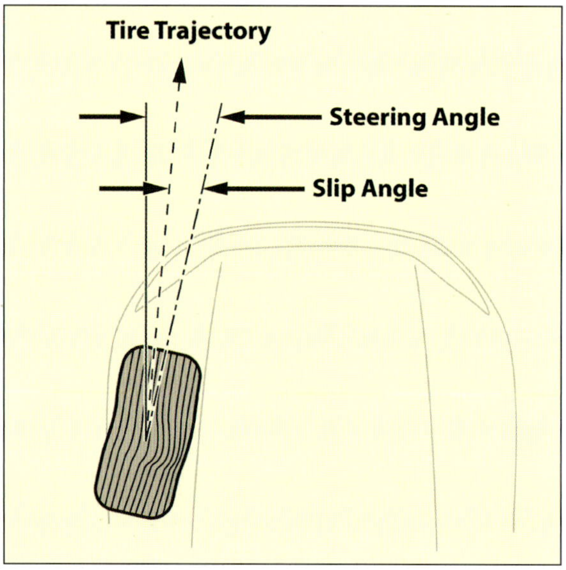


*In tire physics, there's a big difference between slip and slide. When the steering wheel is turned, the tires don't follow the exact path where they're pointing. Rather, rubber tires "crab walk" a certain amount. The difference between the direction in which the tires are pointed and the direction in which they're traveling is called the slip angle.*

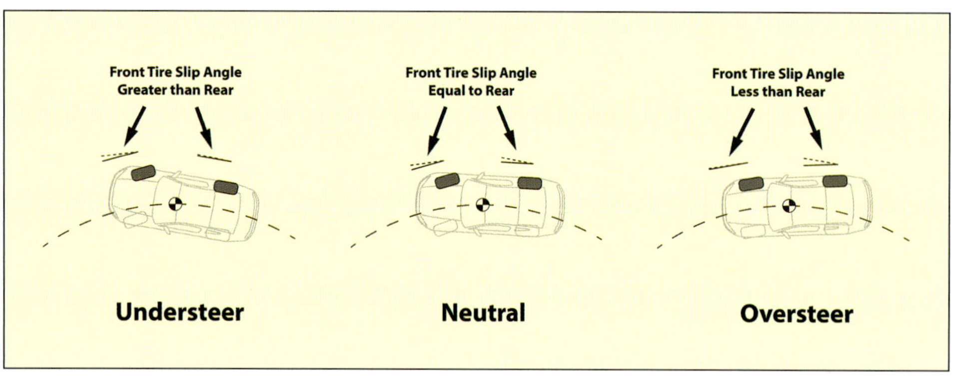


*Handling balance is often described as understeer, neutral, or oversteer. If the slip angle of the front tires is greater than the slip angle of the rear tires, the car is understeering. Conversely, if the slip angle of the front tires is less than the slip angle of the rear tires, the car is oversteering. Neutral describes equal front and rear tire slip angles.*

Turning the steering wheel farther commands a greater slip angle, which generates additional lateral grip. However, beyond a certain point, the slip angle exceeds the tire's ability to generate additional grip, and the tires begin to slide. We're all familiar with how sliding tires leave black marks on the pavement.

### *Handling Balance*

Keep in mind that when turning a corner, both the front and rear tires have a slip angle. A relative comparison between the slip angles of the front and rear tires is described as handling balance.

A car that understeers underperforms its steering angle and thus requires more steering angle to generate lateral force at higher cornering speeds. Conversely, a car that oversteers requires progressively less steering angle as cornering speeds increase. A neutral-handling car doesn't require steering angle changes as speeds increase.

To help illustrate the concept, here's a thought experiment: You're driving 20 mph in an empty parking lot. With the wheel turned a half turn to the left, the Mustang will drive in a circle of a certain radius. If you increase the speed to 40 mph and the radius of the circle gets wider, that's understeer (the Mustang needs more steering angle to follow the same path). If the circle gets smaller, that's oversteer (the Mustang needs less steering angle to follow the same path). If the steering angle doesn't change to follow the same path regardless of speed, the car is said to be neutral.

Understeer is also described as "push" or "plow." Conversely, a car that oversteers is described as "loose" or "tail happy." All Mustangs (as most modern production cars) are engineered to understeer to some extent. This behavior makes a car's handling more predictable, and therefore, safer. When improving cornering grip, the car is only as fast as its weakest end. If the front grip goes away long before rear grip, the overall cornering capability of the car is compromised. The goal is to maximize grip through the entire corner to increase corner exit speed.

Tuning the handling balance is all relative. The various adjustment knobs (alignment, springs, dampers, anti-roll bars, and suspension geometry) dictate the car's response to driver input and change balance relative to the other end of the car.

### Static Alignment

One of the first and most consequential adjustments to a Mustang is the static alignment. The rear is pretty much fixed, so we'll discuss the front.

Static camber angle is the angle of the tire relative to the ground when viewed from the front. Negative camber is when the top of the tire points toward the center of the car. Static negative camber generates a lateral force that increases cornering

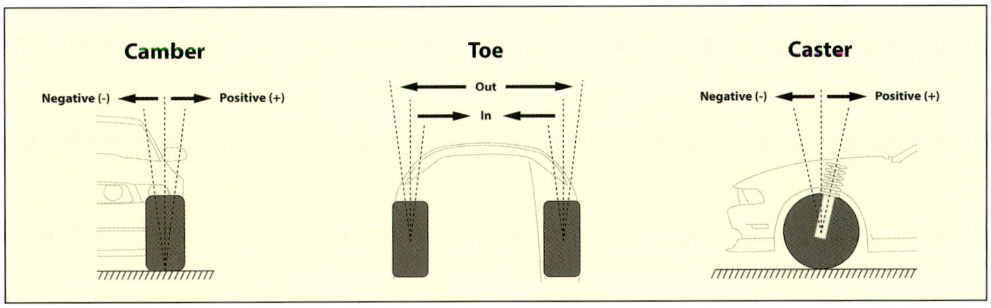


*Basic tire alignment terms are camber, toe, and caster.*

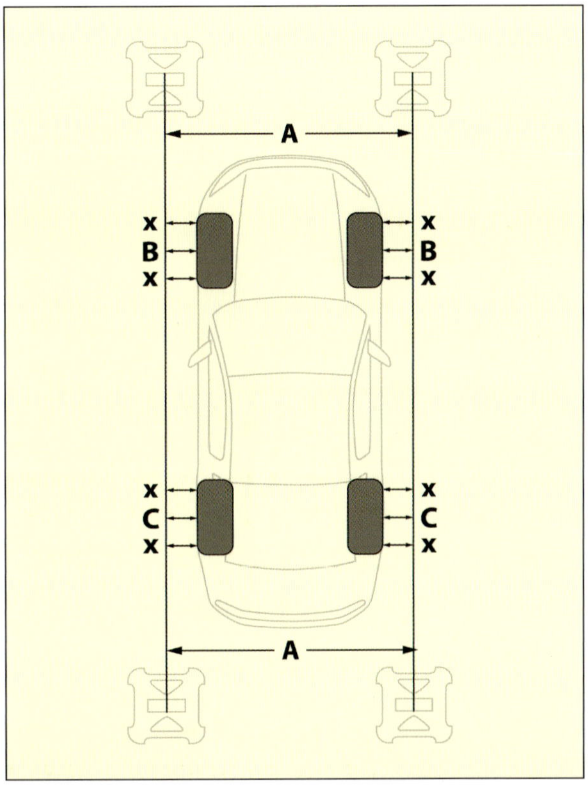


*You can perform four-wheel alignment in your garage using strings and jack stands. Loop the strings on jack stands and extend them until the string is as high as the center of the wheels. Arrange the jack stands so that the distances (A) are equal and that the strings are square to the car by equalizing distances B and C. With the steering wheel pointed straight ahead, compare measurements at the front and rear edges of the wheels to measure toe. Where toe plates only measure front toe, a string setup can verify if the rear axle is centered and straight (thrust angle is zero).*

*A quick way to check front toe is to use a pair of tape measures and straightedges. Have a helper hold one side while you check the relative distances on the other.*

*With the car parked on a level surface, a square and a digital level can be used to measure wheel camber.*

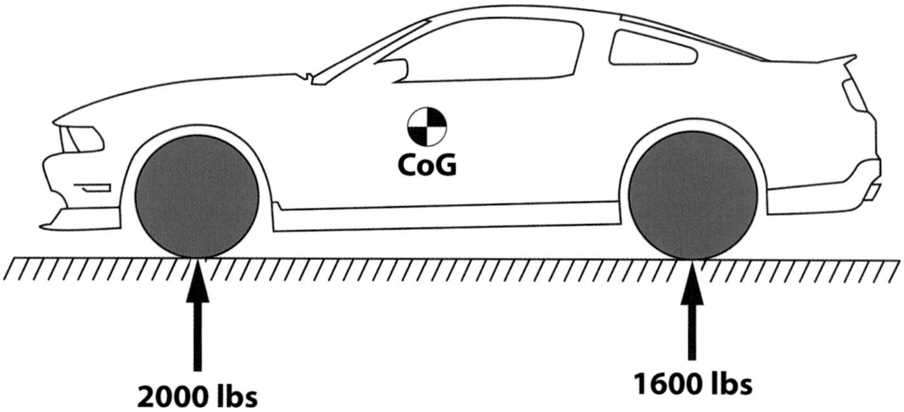


***Weight transfer occurs when a Mustang accelerates, brakes, or turns. At rest, a typical 3,600-pound Mustang with a 55-percent front/45-percent rear weight distribution has about 2,000 pounds on the front tires and 1,600 pounds on the rear tires. CoG refers to the center of gravity.***

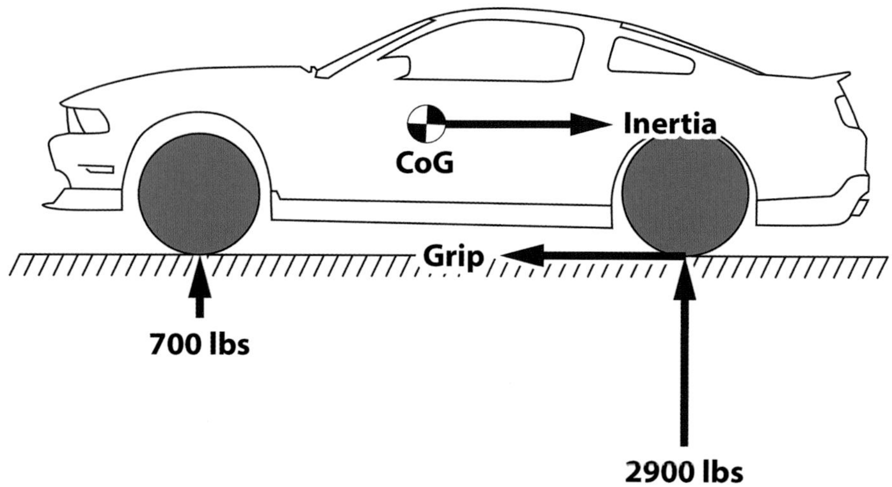


***When accelerating, the load (weight) transfers to the rear tires. Note that regardless of how hard the car accelerates or brakes, the sum of the load on all tires equals 3,600 pounds.***

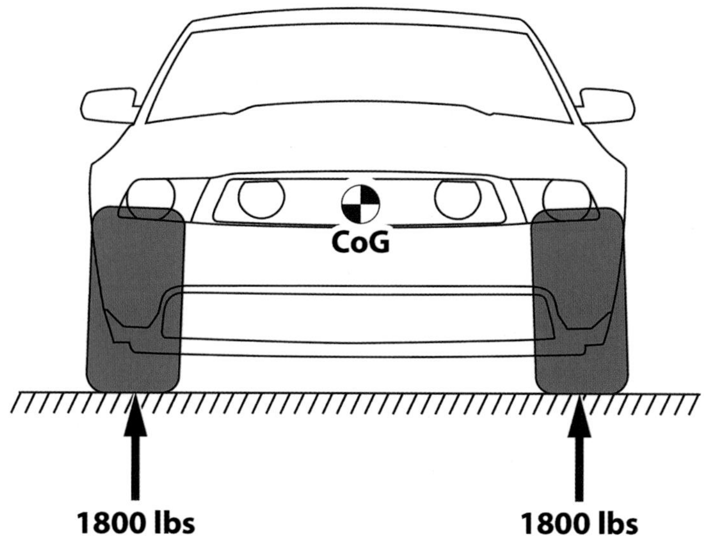


***Similar to accelerating and braking, provided that the left/right weight distribution is equal, the static weight distribution on each side of the car is 1,800 pounds (half of the Mustang's 3,600-pound total weight).***

performance and also counteracts camber gain during body roll through a corner. However, because the tire's contact patch is uneven, camber angle compromises longitudinal grip (accelerating and braking).

Caster is the angle of the steering axis from vertical as viewed from the side. Besides increasing the self-centering feel of the steering, positive caster adds negative camber to the outside tire and positive camber to the inside tire as the wheels are steered left or right.

Toe angle is the alignment of the tires relative to each other when viewed from the top. Toe-in is when the leading edges of the tires are closer together than the trailing edges; toe-out is the opposite. Toe angle affects the straight-line stability and turn-in behavior of a Mustang.

### *Weight Transfer*

Acceleration (which includes braking and cornering) results in weight transfer. For example, as a Mustang accelerates forward, weight is transferred from the front tires to the rear tires. Similarly, when a Mustang turns a corner, weight is transferred from the inside tires to the outside tires. The amount of total weight transferred depends upon the amount of acceleration, the Mustang's weight, and how high the center of gravity is from the ground. The amount of acceleration determines how much weight is transferred in each direction,

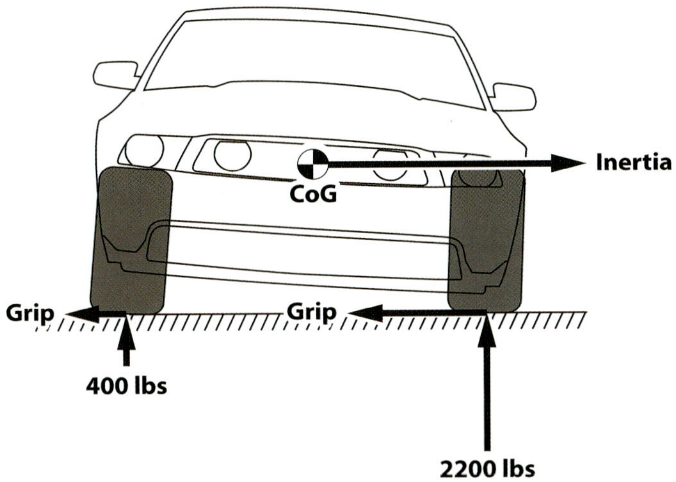


*When cornering, weight transfers from the inside tires to the outside tires, yet the sum load remains constant.*

*A set of lowering springs is a great way to give a Mustang a more aggressive stance, lower the center of gravity, and improve handling response. The Road & Track springs from Maximum Motorsports for 2005–2014 Mustang coupes feature progressive-rate front springs that begin at 320 in-lbs at ride height and increase to 360 in-lbs at 2 inches of bump travel. The rears begin at 260 in-lbs and ramp up to a lofty 380 in-lbs over the same compression range. (Photo Courtesy Maximum Motorsports)*

and the suspension springs, dampers, and geometry determine the rate at which the weight is transferred and the distribution of the weight among the four tires.

### *Springs*

The basic function of a suspension spring is to absorb road imperfections while keeping the car off the ground, but they also play an important role in vehicle dynamics. Stiffer springs transfer weight faster than softer springs. A stiffly sprung Mustang will have quicker reactions to driver inputs, but a Mustang that is too stiffly sprung is less compliant and can overwhelm the tires. Springs work in concert with dampers to absorb bumps, damp chassis movements, and tune handling balance. Stiffer springs on one end of the car increase the side-to-side weight transfer differential, which shifts the handling balance to the other end. Be mindful that when a Mustang is lowered, the suspension geometry is altered. We'll cover this in more detail later in this chapter when discussing roll centers and anti-squat.

*The H&R Special Springs Street Performance coilover kit for 2011–2014 Mustangs (part number 51656-2) takes the guesswork out of selecting a spring/strut/shock package for spirited street and moderate track use. H&R's ride-height adjustable system includes gas-charged monotube shocks and inverted monotube struts that are matched to higher-rate H&R springs. The strut bodies are threaded to set the ride height 1.0 to 2.5 inches lower than stock. To maximize tire clearance, the rear springs mount in the factory location but use an adjustable threaded lower spring perch to set the ride height 1.0 to 2.0 inches lower than stock.*

*Maximum Motorsports also offers shorter bump stops that are compatible with lowering springs and increase bump travel. (Photo Courtesy Maximum Motorsports)*

| Common S197 Mustang Spring Options | | | | | |
|---|---|---|---|---|---|
| | | Rate (in-lb) | | Ride Height Change (inches) | |
| **Description** | **Part Number** | **Front** | **Rear** | **Front** | **Rear** |
| OEM Boss 302 | N/A | 150 | 180 | N/A | N/A |
| OEM Boss 302 Laguna Seca | N/A | 145 | 190 | N/A | N/A |
| OEM GT Performance Pack/ Brembo | N/A | 130 | 170 | N/A | N/A |
| OEM GT Standard | N/A | 125 | 155 | N/A | N/A |
| OEM GT500 Coupe | N/A | 223 | 180 | N/A | N/A |
| OEM GT500 Convertible | N/A | 175 | 13 | N/A | N/A |
| FPP Street Lowering | M-5300-KA | 150–200 | 120–150 | -1.5 | -1.5 |
| FPP Track Lowering | M-5300-PA | 150–200 | 120–150 | -1.0 | -1.0 |
| FPP Boss 302 Lowering | M-5300-T | N/A | N/A | -0.6 | -1.4 |
| FPP GT500 | M-5300-L | N/A | N/A | -0.8 | -1.0 |
| Steeda Ultra-Lite 555-8206 | 555-8206 | 195 | 175 | -1.3 | -1.5 |
| Steeda Sport 555-8215 | 555-8215 | 200 | 175 | -1.0 | -1.3 |
| Steeda Competition | 555-8241 | 225 | 185 | -1.0 | -1.3 |
| Eibach Pro Kit | 35125.14 | 160–275 | 126–279 | -1.0 | -1.5 |
| Eibach Sportline | 4.12535 | 180 | 100–220 | -1.3 | -2.0 |
| Maximum Motorsports Road & Track | 435H0 | 320–360 | 260–380 | -1.9 | -2.0 |
| H&R Sport | 51690 | 200 | 245 | -1.0 | -1.6 |
| H&R Super Sport | 51690-77 | 250 | 200 | -1.7 | -2.4 |
| H&R Race | 51690-88 | 300 | 275 | -1.5 | -1.4 |
| BMR Lowering | SP0009 | 165 | 160 | -1.5 | -1.5 |
| BMR Handling | SP065 | 240 | 200 | -1.5 | -1.5 |
| BMR Handling | SP072 | 260 | 220 | -1.5 | -1.5 |
| Vogtland Sport | 953084 | 180–240 | 180–220 | 1.2 | 1.2 |
| H&R Street Performance Coilover | 51656-2 | 400 | 290 | Adjustable | Adjustable |
| H&R RSS Coilover | RSS29170-2 | 630 | 515 | Adjustable | Adjustable |
| H&R Optional RSS Coilover Springs | 29170CS3 | 715 | 600 | Adjustable | Adjustable |
| Note: Many spring rates are progressive, and determining actual spring rate can be difficult. As such, the above data should only be used as a rough guide. | | | | | |

***Dampers (Struts and Shocks)***

Suspension dampers (on Mustangs, these consist of struts and shock absorbers) are fluid-filled devices that absorb the energy sent through the suspension by bumps and chassis movement. The dampers dissipate this energy as heat. Dampers control the unsprung mass spring while going over bumps (compression) and control the chassis during rebound (extension).

If the dampers are too weak in compression, hitting a bump launches the tire over bumps, and the tires lose grip. Stiffer springs, heavy wheels, and massive brakes require more compression damping to control the unsprung mass.

Rebound damping is a powerful tuning tool for adjusting transitional weight transfer. Adding rebound damping at the front or rear reduces weight transfer to the opposite end during transitions, such as launching, hitting the brakes, and entering or exiting a corner.

Some dampers are adjustable for rebound and/or compression damping and can feature additional adjustments for high- and low-speed damping to tailor the damping characteristics to tune the handling during various suspension and chassis motions. Specifically, high-speed compression damping (blow-off) can reduce the tendency of a chassis to be upset by hitting a hard bump or curb mid-corner.

### *Anti-Roll Bars*

An anti-roll bar, or sway bar, is a simple torsion spring that connects the wheels on either side of the car. It increases roll resistance by using the chassis to apply load to the outside tire and subtract load from the inside tire. The result is less body roll but more load differential between the outside and inside tires.

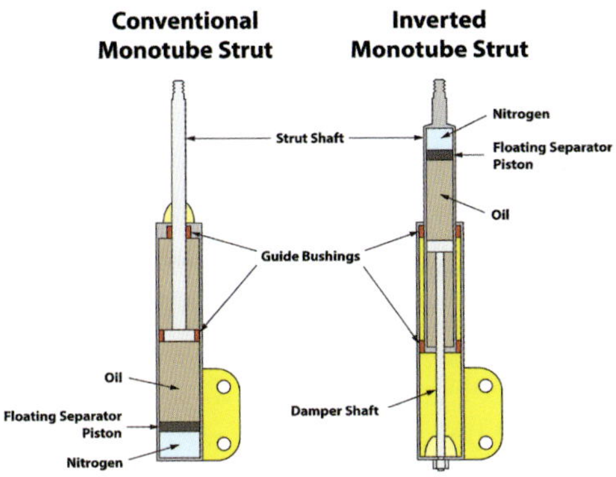


*Suspension loads on a McPherson strut suspension are carried by the strut shaft. On a conventional strut, the strut shaft doubles as the damper shaft. An inverted strut separates the suspension loads from the damper by using the damper housing as the strut shaft. The large-diameter damper housing is less prone to flex and uses larger bushings that better handle heavy suspension loads.*

*Koni Sport struts and shocks feature a rebound adjustment to tune the transitional characteristics of the chassis. Adjustments are made via a knob at the top of the strut and shock shafts. (Photo Courtesy Maximum Motorsports)*

*Maximum Motorsports offers Bilstein HD-series struts and shocks for 2005–2014 Mustangs. These Bilstein struts feature an inverted design where the damper shaft is connected to the bottom of the strut housing, and the shaft and guide bushings are much larger than a conventional strut. The HD valving controls higher spring rates than the OEM dampers. (Photo Courtesy Maximum Motorsports)*

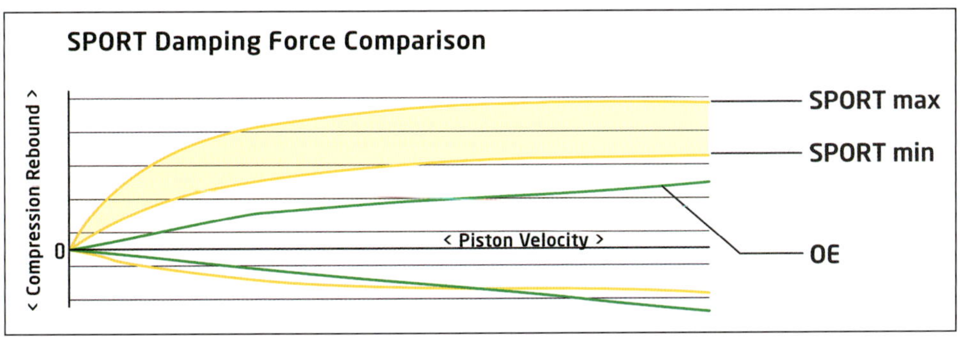


*This chart shows Koni's Sport damper curves compared to a typical factory damper. Note how the rebound force adjustment range exceeds the OEM damper and also how the compression damping is higher at slower piston speeds but blows off at high piston speeds (e.g., hitting a sharp bump). (Illustration Courtesy Koni North America)*

*Track-focused cars with high spring rates benefit from high-end adjustable dampers. These JRZ Motorsport 11 Series dampers from Kenny Brown feature independent adjustments for compression and rebound. Remote-reservoir canisters ease rebound adjustments and increase damper capacity for less heat soak. A digressive blow-off valve allows stiff compression valving while maintaining compliance over curbs. Both the front strut and rear shocks use standard-size coilover springs to simplify spring rate changes. (Photo Courtesy Kenny Brown Performance)*

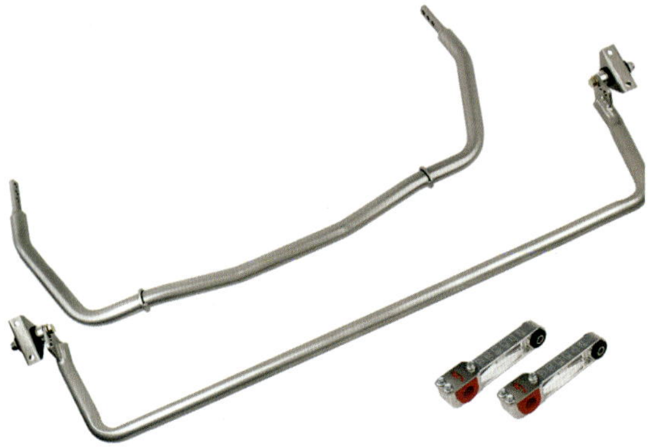

*Adjustable front and rear sway bars, such as this kit from Steeda (part number 555-1080), sharpen a Mustang's response to steering input. In addition, moving the links to different mount holes changes the chassis' leverage on the sway bar, which adjusts the bar's spring rate, and, as a consequence, the Mustang's handling balance between understeer and oversteer. (Photo Courtesy Steeda)*

Anti-roll bars differ from suspension springs in that their effect is confined to cornering—they merely pivot in their mounts under acceleration and braking. Thus, anti-roll bars are a convenient way to adjust cornering balance without affecting weight transfer during straight-line braking and acceleration. The drawback of anti-roll bars is that they reduce some of the independence of the suspension, as bumps that affect one tire

**Common S197 Mustang Front Sway Bar Options**

| | Part Number | Diameter (mm) | Adjustments |
|---|---|---|---|
| OEM V-6 2010 | N/A | 28.6 | N/A |
| OEM V-6 2011–2014 | N/A | 33.2 | N/A |
| OEM GT 2005–2010 | N/A | 34.0 | N/A |
| OEM GT 2011–2014 | N/A | 34.6 | N/A |
| OEM Boss 302 | N/A | 34.6 | N/A |
| OEM Boss 302 Laguna Seca | N/A | 34.6 | N/A |
| FRPP GT Coupe Sway Bar Kit | M-5490-A | 35.0 | 3 |
| FRPP GT500 Sway Bar Kit | M-5490-B | 35.0 | 3 |
| Eibach | 35125 0.310 | 36.0 | 3 |
| H&R | 70655-2 | 36.0 | 2 |
| BMR | SB022 | 35.0 | 3 |
| BMR | SB041 | 38.0 | 5 |
| Whiteline | BFF55Z | 33.0 | 4 |
| Addco | K2-260-0U-406 | 35.0 | N/A |
| Steeda | 555-1070 | 35.0 | 3 |
| Steeda Competition | 555-1067 | 35.0 | 3 |
| Pedders | 428025-35 | 35.0 | 3 |

Note: You can't always compare the outside diameter of bars to determine the spring rate because some bars are hollow or have different lever arms. As such, using sway-bar for rate should be taken with a large grain of salt.

**Common S197 Mustang Rear Sway Bar Options**

| | Part Number | Diameter (mm) | Adjustments |
|---|---|---|---|
| Boss 302S | N/A | 13.0 | N/A |
| OEM Convertible | N/A | 18.0 | N/A |
| OEM V-6 2011–2014 | N/A | 22.0 | N/A |
| OEM GT 2005–2010 | N/A | 20.0 | N/A |
| OEM GT 2011–2014 | N/A | 24.0 | N/A |
| OEM Boss 302 | N/A | 25.0 | N/A |
| OEM Boss 302 Laguna Seca | N/A | 26.0 | N/A |
| FRPP GT Coupe Sway Bar Kit | M-5490-A | 22.0 | N/A |
| FRPP GT500 Sway Bar Kit | M-5490-B | 24.0 | N/A |
| Eibach | 35129 0.312 | 25.0 | 3 |
| H&R | 71655 | 26.0 | N/A |
| BMR | SB023 | 22.0 | N/A |
| BMR | SB042 | 25.0 | 4 |
| Whiteline | BFR65Z | 27.0 | 4 |
| Addco | K2-253-0U-407 | 22.2 | N/A |
| Steeda | 555-1071 | 22.2 | N/A |
| Steeda GT500 | 555-1071-GT500 | 25.4 | N/A |
| Steeda Competition | 555-1073 | 31.8 | 3 |
| Pedders | 429025-24 | 24.0 | N/A |

also unload the tire on the other side.

Changing the anti-roll bar spring rate is one of the easiest and most effective ways to adjust handling balance. In fact, race cars have cockpit-adjustable anti-roll bars (where allowed) so that drivers can adjust the handing balance during the course of a race.

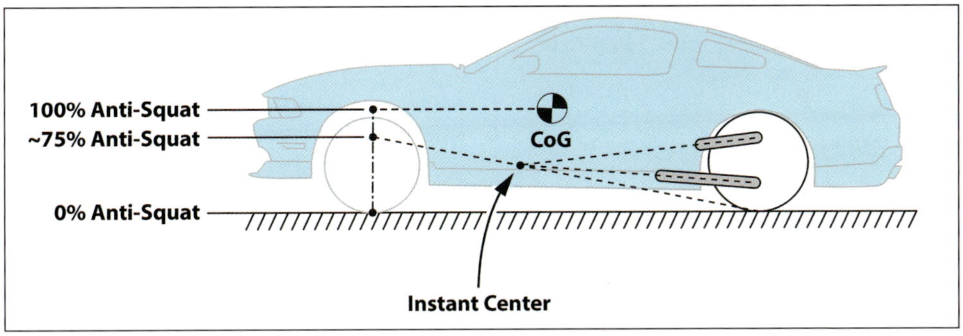


*Under acceleration, a Mustang's rear tires begin rotating and the vehicle's weight shifts to the rear tires. The usual result is that the rear suspension compresses and the front end lifts. This is called squat. For a given amount of mass and torque, the amount of squat is the result of the rear suspension geometry, specifically, the "instant center" and its relationship to the center of gravity's height. The point where lines that are drawn through the upper and lower suspension links converge is the instant center. The relationship between the distance from a line drawn from the tire's contact patch through the instant center, to the front wheelbase, and to the center of gravity's height describes the percentage of anti-squat. More anti-squat transfers weight to the rear tires faster, while less anti-squat softens the hit to the rear tires when launching. Note that lowering the rear ride height on a 2011–2014 Mustang changes the rear suspension geometry and reduces anti-squat.*

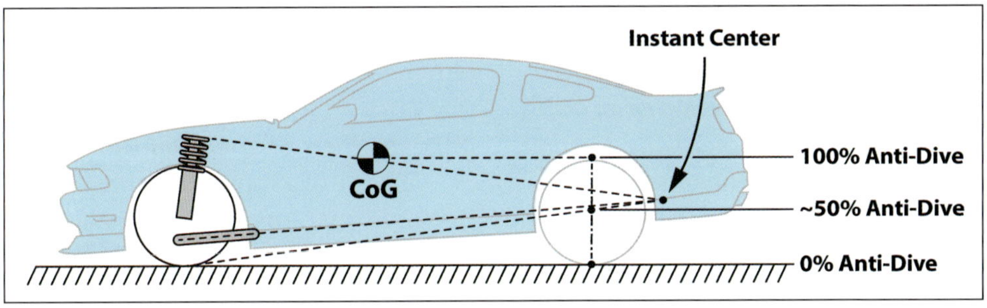


*In a similar manner to anti-squat, anti-dive refers to the relationship of the front suspension links to the wheelbase and the center of gravity. More anti-dive reduces how much the nose dives under braking and increases the rate of weight transfer to the front wheels. However, because anti-dive opposes the suspension's natural tendency to compress under braking, too much anti-dive can cause the front suspension to lock when braking. Additionally, since road bumps naturally want to push the tires rearward, anti-dive can make the front suspension less compliant over bumps, especially when braking.*

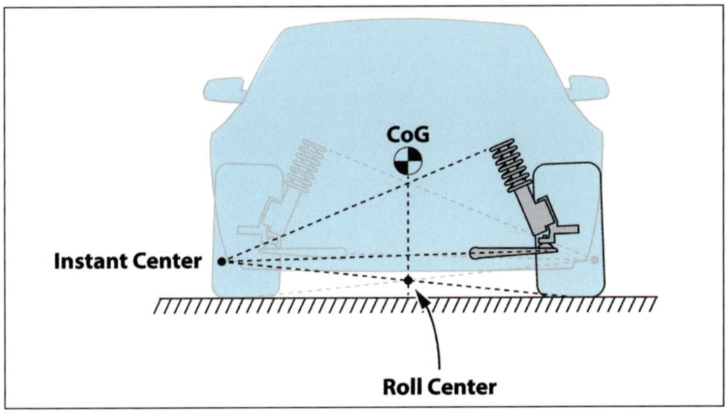


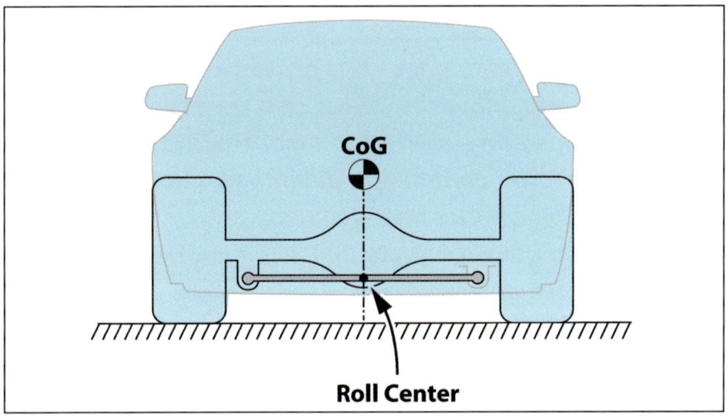


*When turning, the point around which each end of the car rotates is the roll center. The roll center's relationship to the center of gravity describes how the tires are loaded. A higher roll center transfers weight to outside tires more quickly. However, the higher the roll center is above the ground, the greater the jacking effect is on the suspension. Jacking is the tendency of the outside tire's suspension to "fold under" the chassis, which raises the ride height, and overloads the tire. Simultaneously on solid-axle rear suspension, jacking unloads the inside rear tire, further reducing grip.*

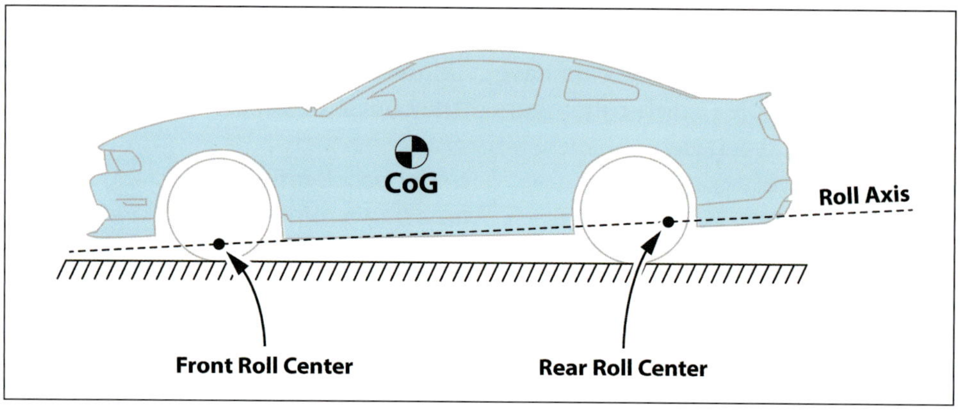


*While roll centers are important, their relationship to each other affects the cornering balance of the chassis. A line drawn through front and rear roll centers is the roll axis. During steady-state cornering, the end of the car with a lower roll center will have more grip. Consequently, a roll axis that inclines toward the rear favors oversteer, while a roll axis that inclines toward the front tends toward understeer. However, the effects are reversed on the initial turn-in, as the end of car with a lower roll center is lazier to respond than the other.*

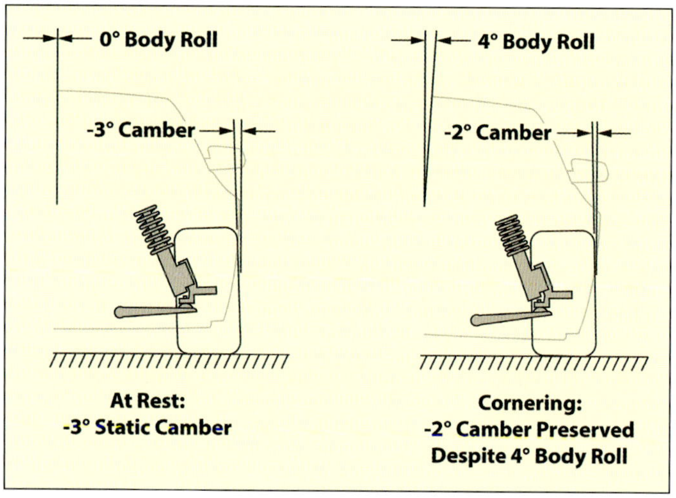


*Negative camber generates a lateral force that enhances cornering grip, but, as mentioned earlier, camber compromises longitudinal (accelerating and braking) grip. Suspension geometry that tips the top of the tire toward the center of the car when it compresses has "negative camber gain." This preserves longitudinal grip under acceleration and braking and enhances lateral grip via negative camber gain during cornering. With a Mustang's strut front suspension, the relationship between angles of the strut and lower control arm determine camber gain. As the body rolls over in a turn, negative camber gain geometry preserves camber to counteract camber change due to body roll. Note that when lowering a Mustang, not only does the roll center move downward but also the angle of the lower control arms diminishes negative camber gain geometry.*

### *Suspension Geometry*

In addition to tires, alignment, springs, and dampers, suspension geometry plays a critical role in how these components work together in reaction to driver inputs.

### *Mustang Front Suspension Geometry*

Although it still utilizes struts, the 2011–2014 Mustang's front suspension geometry is a large improvement over the previous generation. The front uses a true McPherson strut where the spring is coaxial (over) the strut, which relieves the control arms and bushings from most of the spring's forces. Additionally, the control arms are L-shaped to bias the front and rear control-arm bushings toward different purposes: cornering forces primarily go through the front bushing, and braking forces are handled mostly by the rear bushing. This arrangement means that a stiff front bushing can be used to benefit cornering performance, and a soft rear bushing reduces harshness under braking.

Lowering a Mustang's ride height lowers the center of gravity, which benefits handling. However, the front roll center drops precipitously, which reduces the front suspension's roll resistance and slows weight transfer when cornering. So, methods to raise the front suspension's roll center are beneficial on a lowered Mustang.

### *Mustang Rear Suspension Geometry*

The use of a robust, tried-and-true, live-axle rear suspension makes the S197 Mustang a favorite of the aftermarket. While the S197's three-link suspension with Panhard bar arrangement is leaps and bounds ahead of the previous Mustang's four-link rear suspension design, there's still room for improvement, especially when the Mustang is lowered.

The K-link provides the best of both worlds: the axle moves in a straight line like a Watts link, and the roll center can be low like a Panhard bar. Since the roll center is defined by the theoretical intersection of the radius rods, the roll-center height can be anywhere along the centerline of the linkage—or even underground.

### *How Mustangs Do (and Don't) Follow the Rules*

Remember that every component (e.g., wheels, tires, springs,

*Steeda's X11 ball joints (part number 555-8136) raise the front roll center by lowering the outer-ball-joint pivot. (Photo Courtesy Steeda)*

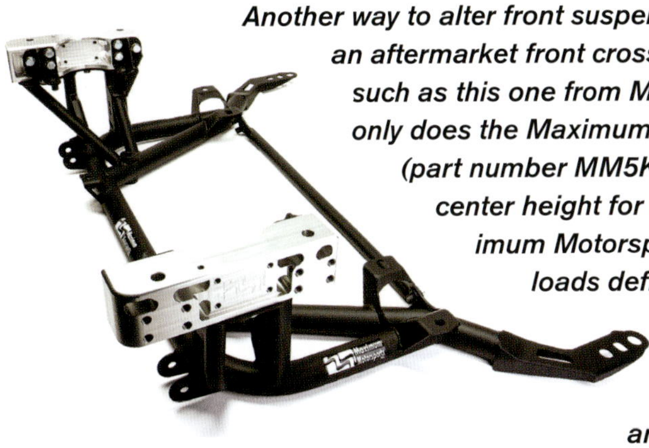

*Another way to alter front suspension geometry is to install an aftermarket front crossmember, or K-member, such as this one from Maximum Motorsports. Not only does the Maximum Motorsports K-member (part number MM5KM-7) optimize the front roll center height for lowered Mustangs but Maximum Motorsports also claims cornering loads deflect its K-member 30 percent less than the factory crossmember. It works with the factory control arms and engine mounts to maintain stock levels of noise, vibration, and harshness. (Photo Courtesy Maximum Motorsports)*

*To correct bump steer geometry when using extended ball joints, tie-rod ends that similarly lower the outer steering pivot are also required. This bump steer kit from Steeda (part number 555-8106) includes spacers of varying thicknesses to fine-tune the bump steer curve. (Photo Courtesy Steeda)*

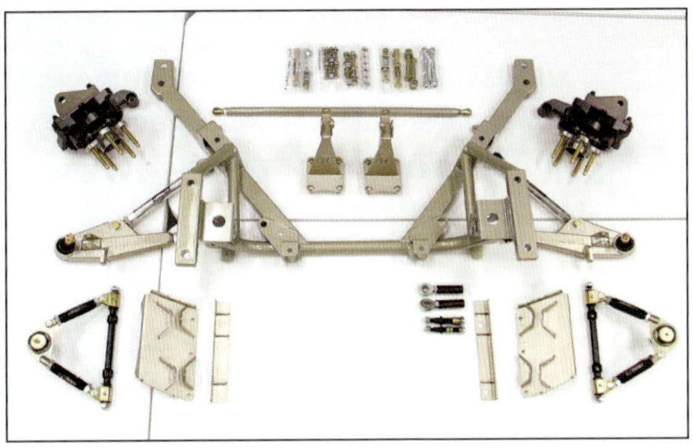

*Another option is to scrap the Mustang's McPherson strut suspension altogether in favor of a short-long-arm (SLA) or double wishbone setup. Even the best McPherson strut suspension has geometry compromises that are addressed with an SLA suspension. One of the greatest benefits stems from an SLA's improved camber curve. SLA geometry can gain more negative camber in bump than a strut, so less static camber is required. The result is a larger contact patch at ride height for better braking performance and more negative camber in bump for greater cornering grip. CorteX Racing's Xtreme-Grip SLA suspension is a clean-sheet suspension design for S197 Mustangs. CorteX Racing claims superior camber gain, roll center stability, and additional tire clearance over a strut design. It accommodates a wide range of shock designs and radial-mount brake systems. (Photo Courtesy CorteX Racing)*

*Unlike previous Mustangs, the S197 Mustang's factory upper strut mounts are not adjustable. Maximum Motorsports' caster/camber plates allow users to adjust camber and caster individually. Caster can be maximized while camber can be changed to suit street or track driving to maximize grip and minimize tire wear.*

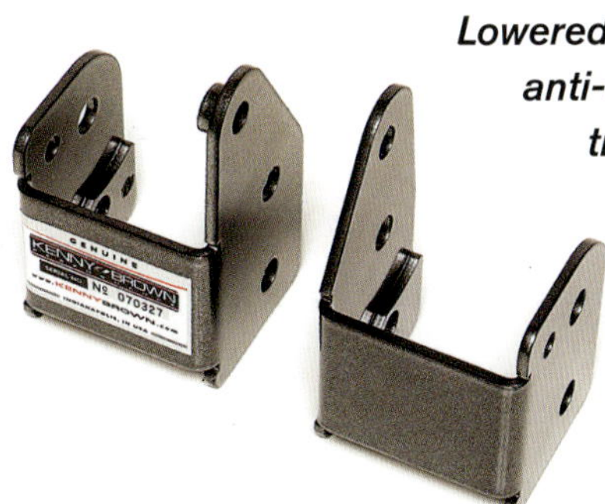

*Lowered Mustangs greatly benefit from increased anti-squat geometry. Kenny Brown's anti-squat traction brackets lower the rear lower control-arm pivot point to raise the side view instant center and restore anti-squat and anti-lift geometry to lowered S197 Mustangs. The result is less squat and greater rear tire bite under acceleration and less rear suspension lift while braking. (Photo Courtesy Kenny Brown Performance)*

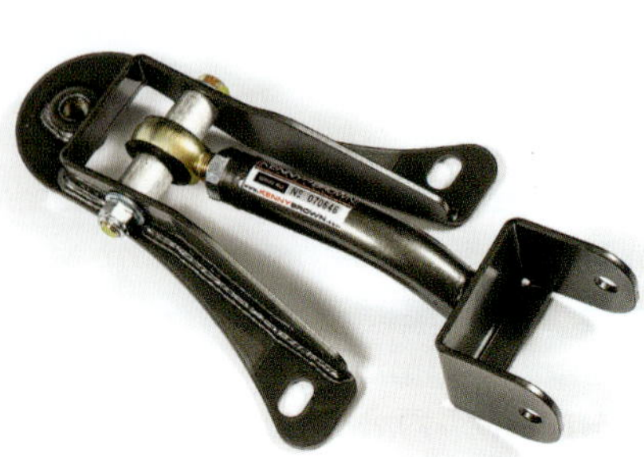

Kenny Brown Performance's U-link upper control-arm module further improves rear suspension geometry by incorporating a longer upper control arm, or third link, and a raised front pickup point. The arm is shaped to maintain bump travel and uses a race-quality rod end with dust seals on the chassis end. (Photo Courtesy Kenny Brown Performance)

The factory control arms are splayed (wider at the front than the back) so Kenny Brown's double-adjustable aluminum rear lower control arms include spacers that bring the rear lower control arms closer to parallel. The OEM arm's soft rubber bushings are replaced with race-quality lined rod ends that are left-hand threaded on one end to allow for adjustment when installed. The Kenny Brown arms are more than eight pounds lighter than the factory parts. (Photo Courtesy Kenny Brown Performance)

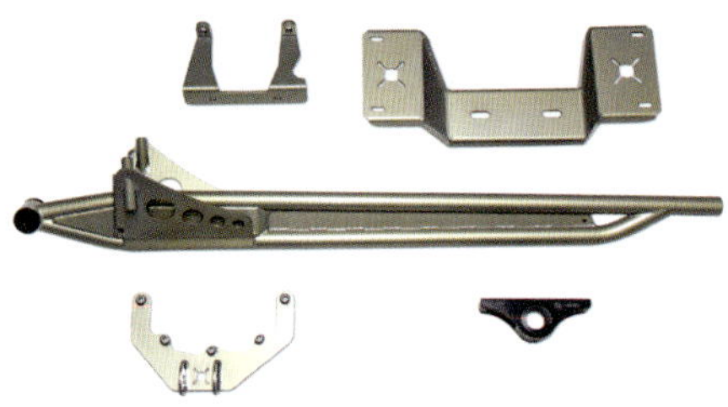

CorteX Racing's Xtreme-Grip torque arm replaces the rear suspension's third link with a torque arm mounted rigidly to the bottom of the axle. Because the front pivot attaches to the floor pan near the Mustang's center of gravity, acceleration and braking forces affect the attitude of the chassis less than the OEM arrangement, thereby increasing anti-squat and anti-lift effects. Because the side view swing arm geometry is dictated by the torque arm pivot rather than derived by control-arm angles, rear axle roll steer is minimized for stable, predictable handling. (Photo Courtesy CorteX Racing)

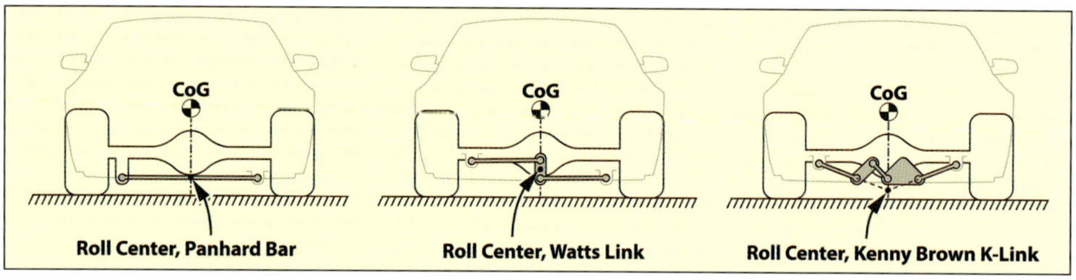


When it comes to the rear axle lateral location, there are three main options: a Panhard bar, Watts link, or Kenny Brown K-link. The factory setup is a Panhard bar, although a few aftermarket companies have opted to convert S197 Mustangs to a Watts link. There are pros and cons to both. A Panhard bar is simpler, and the roll center can be set lower than that of a Watts link. However, the axle moves up and down in an arc dictated by the length of the Panhard bar (but the length of the S197 Mustang's Panhard bar minimizes this effect). The axle housing located with a Watts link moves up and down in essentially a straight line, but the linkage is more complex, and (when the bell crank is mounted vertically to the chassis or rear axle) the roll center is at bell crank pivot. The roll center relocation is limited by ground clearance under the linkage.

Kenny Brown Performance's roll center relocation kit includes brackets that move the Panhard bar mounts several inches lower than stock to lower the roll center to improve rear grip and chassis balance when cornering. The aluminum Panhard bar includes left-hand threads on one end to allow precise axle location within the chassis at varying ride heights. The bar itself is half the weight of the OEM Panhard bar, and spherical rod ends replace the factory bar's rubber bushings. (Photo Courtesy Kenny Brown Performance)

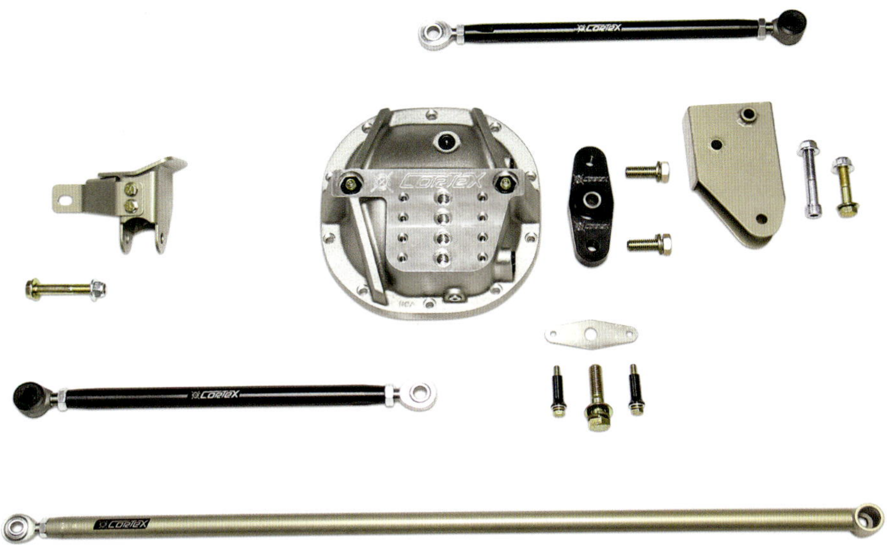

*CorteX Racing replaces the factory Panhard bar arrangement in favor of a Watts link. Its Xtreme-Grip Watts link kit includes an aluminum differential cover with four different bell crank pivot locations so that users can adjust the roll center and tune handling balance. By nature, the Watts link locates the axle vertically regardless of bump, droop, or ride height. Spherical bearings are used throughout for precise location and immediate reactions to driver inputs. (Photo Courtesy CorteX Racing)*

dampers, and weight distribution) is part of a complex system that works together. Racing-specification shocks and springs are worthless if a set of all-season hockey-puck tires can't put enough load into the chassis. Conversely, a set of sticky slicks will overload a stock Mustang suspension, and the car will be a scary, wallowing mess.

All of the theory is moot if your Mustang doesn't react to a change in the way that you expect. A Mustang is a complex and less-than-precise collection of parts, most of which are built by the lowest-bidding supplier, where low cost is valued over ultimate performance. That's not a knock against Ford, as this philosophy makes Mustangs plentiful and affordable.

Here's the point: tuning a Mustang involves lots of variables, many of which are unknown and uncontrollable. Extracting the most performance from a Mustang involves some trial and error. Have patience, take good notes, and (most importantly) have fun.

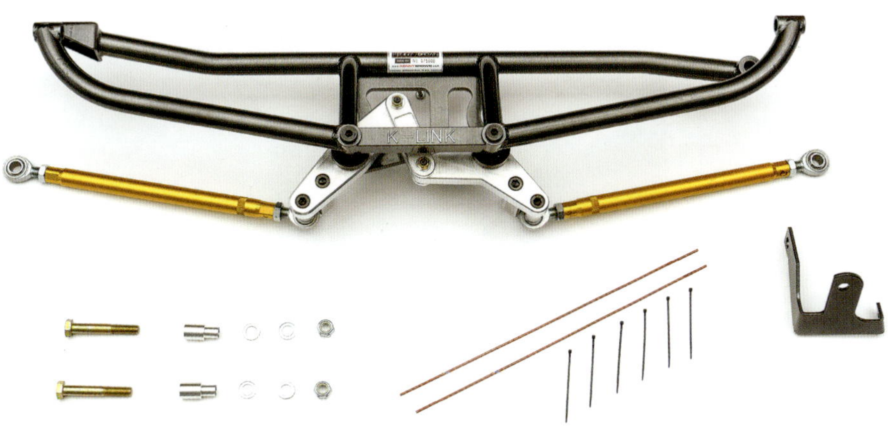


*Part of Kenny Brown Performance's Rear Grip Kit 2 is the K-link. It's a complete bolt-in lateral axle locating device for S197 Mustangs; no drilling or welding is required. The unique system boasts quick installation and easily adjustable roll center height. The linkage features billet aluminum components, lined rod ends, and heavy-duty bushings for long life and quiet operation. (Photo Courtesy Kenny Brown Performance)*

## How-To Project: Coilover Spring and Shock Package

The Street Performance coilover kit for 2011–2014 Mustangs (part number 51656-2) from H&R Special Springs goes beyond traditional lowering springs by including struts and shocks that are matched to higher-rate front and rear springs. The ride height is adjustable via the threaded front strut bodies and adjustable rear spring perches. While offering the adjustability that is often reserved with high-end spring and damper packages, the H&R Street Performance coilover kit allows users to fine-tune the ride height and corner weights without sacrificing street manners.

We installed this H&R coilover kit on a 2012 Mustang GT with an otherwise-stock suspension. The quality of the H&R kit was excellent, and the ride was slightly firmer yet more controlled than the factory springs, struts, and shocks. Everything fit perfectly, and installation went smoothly.

*The H&R Special Springs Street and Performance coilover kit for 2011–2014 Mustangs is a complete spring and damper package for serious street and moderate track use. The monotube struts and shocks are matched to higher, progressive-rate springs for enhanced control while maintaining a comfortable ride. Adjustable spring perches front and rear allow the ride height and corner weights to be fine-tuned for maximum performance.*

Besides a standard tool kit, you'll need the following items to complete the job:

- H&R Special Springs Street Performance coilover kit (part number 51656-2)
- Maximum Motorsports strut to spindle mounting hardware kit (part number MMF-3)
- Basic tool kit
- Floor jack and jack stands
- Strut spring compressor (available to borrow from most auto parts stores)
- Torque wrench that exceeds 166 ft-lbs
- Impact wrench

*Besides addressing its high-rider stance, this 2012 Mustang GT could benefit from a lower center of gravity, higher-rate springs, and firmer dampers.*

## Front Installation

**1** *Note the ride height by measuring the distance between the fender lips and the ground before beginning installation.*

**2** *With the car on jack stands, remove the wheels and tires and slide them under the car for safety.*

**3** *Using a wrench to hold the sway-bar link joint from spinning, remove the sway-bar end link nut from the strut.*

**4** *Next, remove the bolt that secures the brake hose to the strut.*

**5** *Free the wheel speed sensor wire from the strut ear.*

**6** *With a floor jack supporting the lower ball joint, remove the strut-to-spindle bolts.*

**7** *Remove the four nuts securing the upper strut mount to the strut tower.*

**8** *Use nylon cable ties between the spindle and the sway bar to support the spindle while removing the strut.*

**9** *With everything disconnected, remove the front strut assembly.*

**10** *Using a strut spring compressor that you can borrow from a local auto parts store, compress the spring and zip off the strut mount nut with an impact wrench.*

**11** *Comparing the factory strut assembly (left) with the H&R setup (right), it's clear how the factory spring is much longer and wider than the H&R coilover spring. In addition, the H&R strut assembly weighed 4.5 pounds less than the factory setup.*

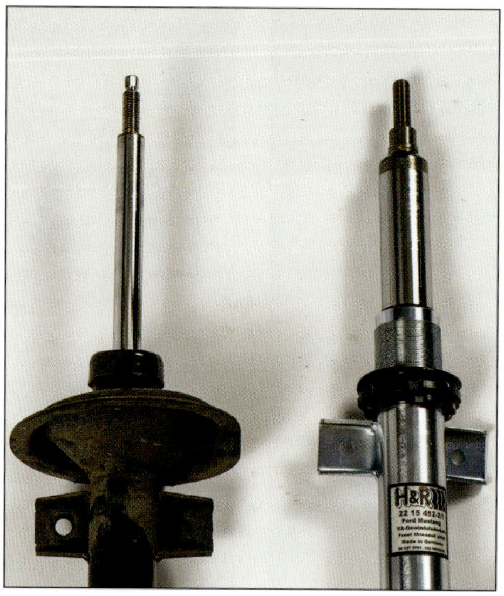

**12** *The OEM strut (left) has a conventional design, whereas the H&R strut (right) is an inverted monotube design that is shared with high-end racing struts. The massively larger strut shaft on the H&R inverted monotube makes the strut assembly significantly more rigid, which minimizes strut shaft flex, increases assembly durability, and reduces friction.*

**13** *Slip the OEM strut mount over the H&R strut shaft and index the spring end accordingly in the mount. Tighten the strut nut using an impact wrench incrementally, being mindful not to overdo it.*

**14** *With the H&R spring and strut assembled, feed it up into the strut tower.*

**15** *Tighten the four strut mount nuts to 26 ft-lbs.*

**16** *Ford says the strut-to-spindle bolts cannot be reused. New bolts and nuts are available from Maximum Motorsports as part number MMF-3. After removing the nylon cable ties restraining the spindle, slip the strut ears over the spindle and tighten the fresh strut-to-spindle bolts to 166 ft-lbs.*

**17** *Next, reattach the brake hose and speed sensor to the H&R strut.*

**18** *Finally, torque the end-link nut to 85 ft-lbs.*

## Rear Installation

**1** *Moving to the rear, support the rear axle with a floor jack and disconnect the rear sway-bar end links from the chassis.*

**2** *To allow the rear axle to droop enough to remove the springs, remove the rear brake hose retaining-bracket screw from the chassis.*

**3** *Peel back the trunk wall trim lining and remove the upper shock isolator.*

**4** *To remove the shock, unscrew the lower shock bolt.*

**5** *After confirming that the axle is supported by the floor jack, pull the factory shocks from the car.*

**6** *Lower the floor jack until you can remove the factory rear springs.*

**7** *To make room for the H&R lower spring perch, remove the factory rubber spring isolator.*

**8** *A side-by-side comparison of the factory shock and spring (left) and the H&R shock and spring (right) reveals how the shorter H&R spring combines with the adjustable perch to allow for ride-height adjustments. Note how the H&R spring is progressive, in that the rate increases as the spring is compressed. The H&R spring, shock, and perch combination was 1 pound heavier than the stock pieces.*

**9** *Place the H&R spring-and-perch package into position between the axle and the upper spring perch.*

**10** *We used a hex wrench to seat the perch set screws into the factory spring perch so that it doesn't turn when making ride-height adjustments.*

**11** *Before installing the H&R monotube shock, transfer the OEM rubber isolator from the factory shock to the H&R damper.*

**12** *Then, put the inserted H&R shock shaft through the hole in the trunk and jack up the rear axle until the lower mount hole aligns with the shock bushing.*

**13** *With the H&R shock in position, torque the lower shock mount bolts to 85 ft-lbs.*

**14** *Use a hex socket to hold the shock shaft while tightening the isolator nut to 30 ft-lbs.*

**15** *Next, reattach the brake line bracket to the chassis.*

**16** *Reinstall the rear sway-bar end links and torque the bolts to 85 ft-lbs.*

**17** *To document your ride-height settings, spin the front spring perch jam nut all the way down and measure the distance between it and the spring perch.*

**18** *At the rear, measure the distance between the axle pad and the spring perch to note the ride-height settings.*

**19** *Use the same method as before (fender lip-to-ground distance) to measure the ride-height changes.*

**20** *Once satisfied, lock the front ride-height setting with the jam nut and the included spanner wrenches.*

**Ride Height**

| Front Coilover Distance "A" | Front Ride Height "X" | Departure from Stock | Rear Spring Perch Distance "B" | Rear Ride Height "Y" | Departure from Stock |
|---|---|---|---|---|---|
| Stock Suspension | 28.750 inches | – | Stock Suspension | 29.750 inches | – |
| 0.000 inch | 26.500 inches | -2.250 inches | 0.350 inch | 27.500 inches | -2.250 inches |
| 0.500 inch | 27.000 inches | -1.750 inches | 0.600 inch | 27.750 inches | -2.000 inches |
| 1.000 inch | 27.500 inches | -1.250 inches | 0.850 inch | 28.000 inches | -1.750 inches |

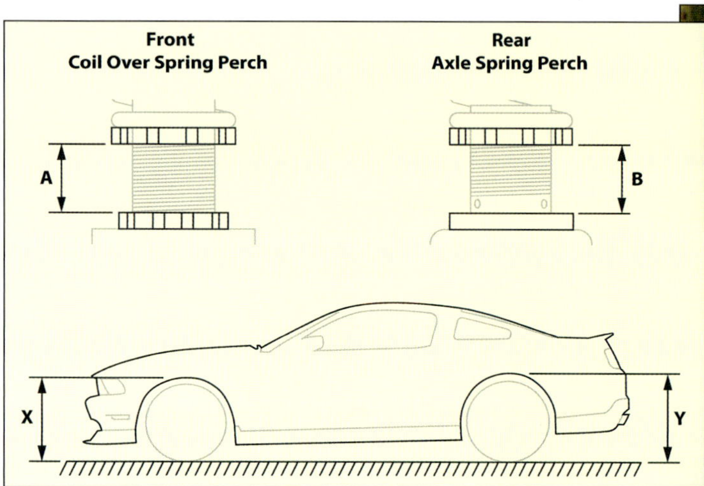


*We recorded our ride heights at different perch positions for future reference.*

*Ah, that's more like it. Besides adding a more aggressive stance, the H&R Street Performance coilover kit allowed us to lower the center of gravity and sharpen the chassis responses of this 2012 Mustang GT.*

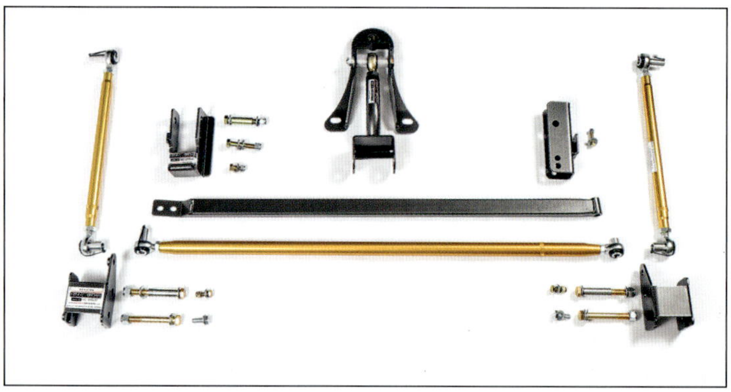

*The rear grip kit for S197 Mustangs from Kenny Brown Performance is a complete bolt-on system that revises the rear suspension geometry to add straight-line and cornering grip.*

## Rear Suspension Geometry Upgrade

The S197 Mustang's three-link with Panhard bar rear suspension is leaps and bounds ahead of any previous Mustang's live-axle rear suspension. However, there's room for improvement, especially when a Mustang is lowered.

As part of Kenny Brown's AGS 4.0 philosophy, the Kenny Brown Performance rear grip kit revises the Mustang's rear suspension geometry by lowering the rear roll center for enhanced cornering grip, increases anti-squat geometry to add forward bite, and reduces body pitch under braking.

Although the geometry alterations are comprehensive, the installation process only requires basic hand tools. This is what we used:

- Kenny Brown S197 rear grip kit (part number 2153.300)
- Basic tool kit
- Blue threadlocker
- Floor jack and jack stands
- Torque wrench
- Drill with 5/16- and 7/16-inch drill bits

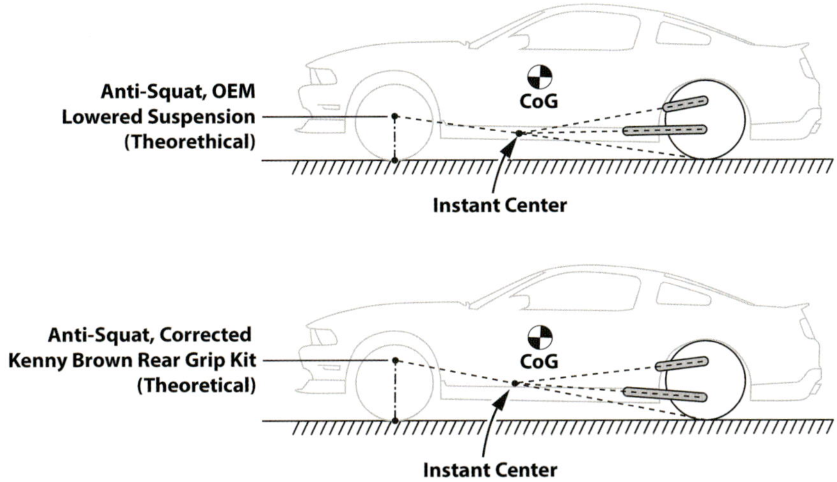


*The Kenny Brown Performance rear grip kit adjusts the side view swing-arm geometry of the rear suspension by lowering the rear lower control-arm pickup point on the axle and raising the chassis end of the upper control arm.*

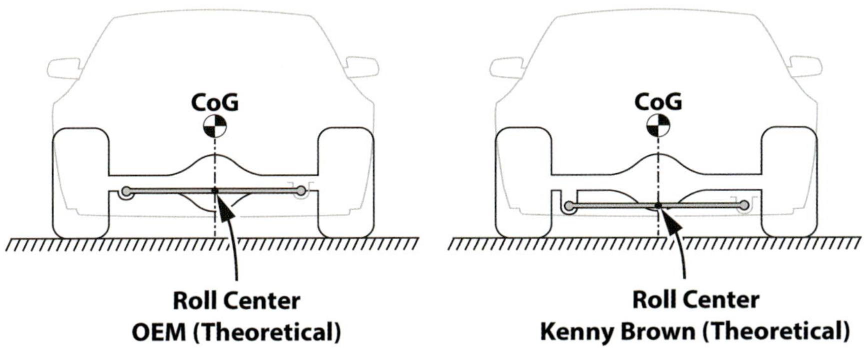


*The Kenny Brown Performance rear grip kit lowers the rear roll center to increase rear grip around corners.*

*The Kenny Brown U-link upper control-arm module features a longer arm with revised geometry to reduce instant center migration as the rear suspension moves around.*

*The front joint on the Kenny Brown U-link upper control-arm module features a race-grade spherical bearing with rubber seals to further protect the bearing from dirt and debris.*

*All of the Kenny Brown Performance parts are serialized for quality control and production tracking.*

*Kenny Brown uses lined rod ends with anti-rattle O-rings for precision, noise-free operation and long life. The control arms and Panhard bar utilize a left-hand-thread rod end to allow length adjustment without removal.*

## Performance Rear Grip Kit Installation

**1** *The weather was great, so we installed the Kenny Brown S197 rear grip kit on this 2012 Mustang GT in a driveway on jack stands. Remove the wheels and place them under the car for added safety.*

**2** *Use a floor jack and a block of wood to support the rear axle assembly under the differential.*

**3** *Depress the clips on either side of the back seat and remove the lower cushion.*

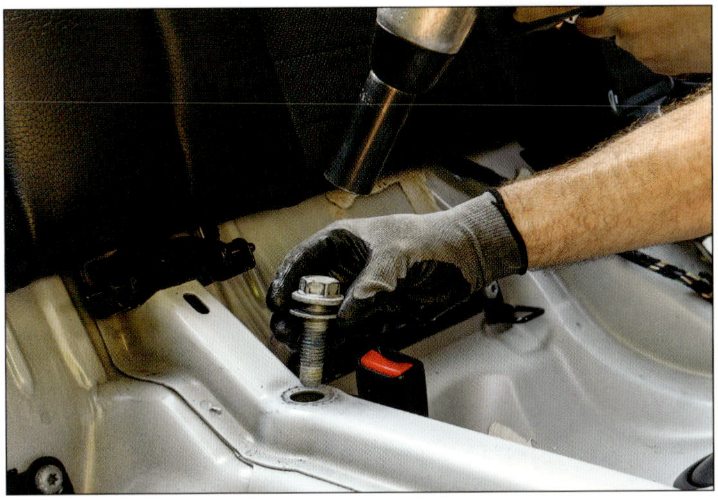

**4** *With the back seat cushion removed, unscrew the upper control-arm mount bolt with a 24-mm socket. The factory uses blue threadlocker on this bolt, so an impact gun makes the job easier.*

**5** *Next, remove the remaining two upper control-arm link mount bolts with an 18-mm socket.*

**6** *Use a 21-mm socket to remove the axle-end control-arm pivot nut, and pull the bolt from the bushing.*

**7** *With all the fasteners removed, route the factory upper control-arm link around the right side of the axle housing.*

**8** *Compare factory upper control-arm module (left) to the Kenny Brown U-link upper control-arm module (right). Besides replacing the forward control-arm bushing with a large rod end, the Kenny Brown U-link module features revised geometry to improve anti-squat, anti-lift geometry, and reduce instant-center migration.*

**9** *Feed the Kenny Brown U-link upper control-arm module into position over the axle bushing and against the floor pan.*

**10** *Clean the factory bolts and apply a few drops of blue threadlocker to the three bolts, securing the U-link bracket to the chassis.*

**11** *Torque the factory rear mount bolts to 85 ft-lbs and the factory differential bushing bolt to 129 ft-lbs.*

**12** *The factory forward front mount is torqued to 129 ft-lbs.*

**13** *With the Kenny Brown U-link module installed, move on to the control arm installation. First, use a pair of locking pliers to remove the parking-brake cables from the caliper levers.*

**14** *Then, remove the clips retaining the cables to the calipers.*

**15** *Work one side at a time so that the axle housing is sufficiently restrained, and remove the right-side lower control-arm bolts.*

**16** *With the bolts removed, pull the factory control arms.*

**17** *The factory control arm (top) features large rubber bushings and weighs 4.2 pounds more than the Kenny Brown lower control arm (bottom).*

**18** *Install the Kenny Brown lower control arm. Torque the forward bolt to 110 ft-lbs and loosely install the rear bolt.*

**19** *Use nylon cable ties to secure the parking brake cable to the lower control arm and repeat the lower control arm installation process for the other side of the axle.*

**20** *Next, begin the Kenny Brown anti-squat traction bracket installation by first removing the factory axle weights from the inside of the axle brackets.*

**21** *Then, slide the Kenny Brown anti-squat traction brackets over the factory axle brackets and slide the supplied hardware into place where the factory control arm mounted.*

**22** *Next, loosely install the supplied 12-mm bolt where the factory axle weight was attached.*

**23** *With all the hardware installed, torque the 12-mm bolt to 59 ft-lbs and the 9/16-inch bolts to 95 ft-lbs.*

**24** *Make sure that the jam nuts on both ends of the control arms are tight.*

**25** *Note how the rear lower control-arm mount on the Kenny Brown anti-squat traction bracket is significantly lower than the factory pivot. This is instrumental in revising the geometry and improving traction and braking performance on Mustangs, especially lowered ones.*

**26** *Remove the rear sway bar. Kenny Brown recommends leaving it off entirely to balance the handling with the rear grip kit. As such, we shaved the factory sway bar's 19 pounds from the rear.*

**27** *Remove the factory Panhard bar by removing the bolts and prying the bar from the chassis mount.*

**28** *Next, remove the left-side factory Panhard brace bolts.*

**29** *With the Panhard bar out of the way, remove the factory Panhard bar brace from the chassis.*

**30** *The factory Panhard bar (top) includes rubber bushings and is filled with loose shot for vibration damping. At 3.8 pounds, the Kenny Brown Panhard bar is less than half of the OEM bar's 7.8-pound weight and features race-grade lined spherical rod ends.*

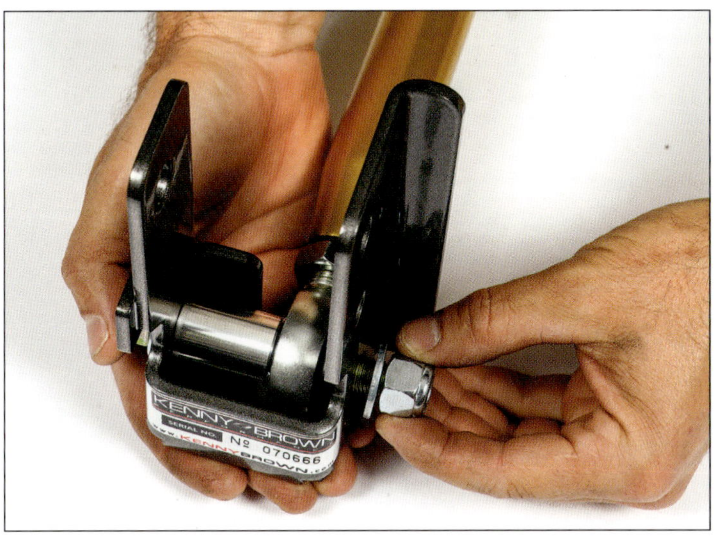


**31** *The left side of the Panhard bar is captured inside the Kenny Brown axle end bracket. Slide it into the axle end bracket and loosely install the supplied hardware.*

**32** *Hang the Kenny Brown Panhard cross-brace from the left side of the chassis using the factory bolts.*

**33** *With the right end of the Kenny Brown Panhard cross-brace inside the chassis side bracket, slide both up inside the factory Panhard bar mount until the holes align with the factory Panhard-bar bolt hole.*

**34** *Use the factory Panhard-bar bolt to secure the assembly, and torque it to 129 ft-lbs. Torque the bolts on the left side to 46 ft-lbs.*

**35** *Use a 5/16-inch bit to drill a hole through the factory Panhard bar chassis bracket.*

**36** *After drilling the hole, install the supplied hardware and torque it to 14 ft-lbs (168 in-lbs).*

**37** *Slide the Kenny Brown axle side bracket over the factory bracket and install the supplied spacer and factory hardware.*

**38** *After positioning the factory flag nut up inside the axle bracket, torque the factory bolt to 95 ft-lbs.*

**39** *Using a series of drill bits, make a 7/16-inch hole in the factory axle bracket.*

**40** *Install the supplied hardware and torque it to 41 ft-lbs.*

**41** *After positioning the Panhard bar between the brackets, install the supplied bolt and torque it to 95 ft-lbs.*

**42** *On our lowered Mustang, we used the upper chassis bracket hole so that the Panhard bar would be relatively level when at ride height.*

**43** *Use a large straightedge and adjust the Panhard bar until the axle is centered in the chassis.*

**44** ***With the axle centered in the chassis, tighten the Panhard bar jam nuts.***

***Here's the finished installation. Besides the added grip from the Kenny Brown S197 rear grip kit, we were extremely impressed with the ease of installation.***

***Front Suspension Geometry Upgrade***

Kenny Brown Performance's front grip kit for 2011–2014 Mustangs benefits Mustangs in three major ways: it raises the front roll center on lowered Mustangs, it adds anti-dive geometry for less front nose droop during braking, and it cuts 22 pounds from an already nose-heavy Mustang.

Installation is simpler than one would expect, and it only requires a few specialized tools:

- Kenny Brown GT4 tubular front K-member (part number 2153.202)
- Kenny Brown GT4 front control-arm module (part number 2151.201)
- Kenny Brown forged bump-steer tie-rod ends (part number 2151.203)
- Maximum Motorsports 2005–2014 engine support beam (part number MMT-11)
- Pair of 2-inch ratchet straps (600 pounds minimum load capacity)
- Basic tool kit
- Floor jack and jack stands
- Torque wrench
- Tie-rod end puller

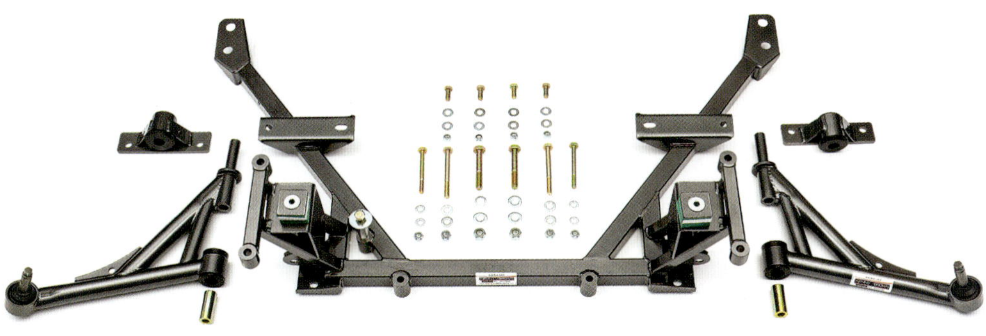

***Kenny Brown Performance's front grip kit for 2011–2014 Mustangs includes the company's GT4 tubular front K-member (part number 2153.202), Kenny Brown gt4 front control-arm module (part number 2151.201), and Kenny Brown forged bump-steer tie-rod ends (not shown, part number 2151.203). Build quality and fitment are excellent.***

## Performance Front Grip Kit Installation

**1** *We prepped for the installation process by supporting this 2012 Mustang GT securely on jack stands and placed all four wheels under the car to protect in the event of a jack stand failure.*

**2** *The Maximum Motorsports engine support beam is a handy, simple device that bolts in place of the factory strut tower brace and uses two 2-inch tow straps to lift and hold the engine during a K-member swap.*

**3** *Remove the front engine mount nut on either side.*

**4** *Hook a 2-inch tow strap under the engine-mount brackets on both sides. (We shot this photo after removing the K-member.)*

**5** *Hang the ratchets from the beam and shorten the straps until they fully support the engine's weight.*

**6** *Next, turn your attention to the suspension. Use a tie-rod-end puller to free the tie-rod ends from the steering knuckle.*

**7** *Remove the clevis pinch bolts from the lower ball joints.*

**8** *Remove the underbody panels and Z-brace that ties the K-member to the radiator support.*

**9** *The 2011–2014 Mustang's steering is electrically-assisted; so, rather than disconnecting hydraulic lines, simply unplug the steering rack's electrical connectors.*

**10** *Remove the bolt securing the steering shaft to the rack.*

**11** *After removing the eight nuts and bolts that fasten the factory K-member to the chassis, use a board and a floor jack to carefully lower the factory K-member from the chassis.*

**12** *With the factory K-member on the ground, remove the three bolts that fasten the steering rack to the K-member.*

**13** *Also remove the factory hardware from the control arm's rear pivot to reuse with the Kenny Brown control-arm module.*

**14** *Lubricate the included polyurethane control-arm bushings with the supplied specialized grease.*

**15** *Fasten the Kenny Brown control arms to the Kenny Brown K-member and torque the fasteners to 110 ft-lbs.*

**16** *Next, attach the steering rack to the Kenny Brown K-member using the supplied hardware. The bolt with the sleeve is used at the rear mount.*

**17** *Using a wide board for support, lift the new assembly into place and loosely install the factory nuts and bolts.*

**18** *Loosely install the Kenny Brown engine mounts and bolts.*

**19** *Once everything is lined up, torque the K-member's front nuts and rear bolts to 90 ft-lbs and 65 ft-lbs, respectively.*

**20** *With the K-member's fasteners torqued, release the tension on the ratchet straps and rest the engine on the mounts.*

**21** *Torque the engine-mount bolts to 33 ft-lbs.*

**22** *While using a wrench to align the notch with the hold in the spindle, attach the ball joints to the spindle and torque the pinch bolts to 76 ft-lbs.*

**23** *We replaced the factory tie-rod ends with the Kenny Brown forged bump-steer tie-rod ends that alter the bump-steer curve to match the Kenny Brown front grip kit's revised suspension geometry.*

**24** *Attach the tie-rod ends to the spindle and torque the nut to 35 ft-lbs.*

**25** *For good measure, pump a little grease into the fittings on the ball joints and tie-rod ends.*

**26** *Next, rejoin the steering shaft to the rack joint.*

**27** *Reconnect the steering-rack electrical plugs.*

**28** *Reinstall the factory Z-brace using the supplied hardware.*

**29** *Lastly, reinstall the underbody panels.*

**30** *With the car back on the ground, we used a string setup to adjust the toe to zero for street driving.*

**31** *We used a digital level and a square to measure camber.*

**32** *Once we were satisfied with the settings, we tightened the strut-mount hardware.*

# Brakes

Brakes use friction to turn kinetic energy into heat. A track car presents different braking system design challenges than a grocery getter. Slowing 3,800 pounds from 160 mph is no easy task. While road car brakes are primarily designed to stop a car safely, a track car's brakes must deliver repeated performance under grueling conditions, lap after lap.

Mustangs with a lowered center of gravity and stickier tires have more braking performance available before the wheels approach lockup. This means that more braking pressure can be applied before the anti-lock braking system (ABS) intervenes, which shortens braking distances. However, while just about any braking system may be able to survive one of these shorter panic stops, it will undoubtedly be overwhelmed with heat on repeated attempts. This is where high-performance braking systems come into play.

Improving braking performance involves increasing three factors: friction, capacity, and cooling. Increasing friction slows a Mustang quicker, different components absorb and tolerate the heat better, and enhanced cooling sheds the heat faster before the next stop.

*The physics of braking is on full display with this Grand-Am Mustang Boss 302 slowing for Turn 1 at Kansas Speedway. Hot brake discs often visibly glow as they heat up under heavy braking. The needs of a track-oriented braking system are vastly different than an ordinary road car. Components must be designed to operate at high temperatures for repeated and long duty cycles.*

## Brake Pads

Selecting brake pads that have a higher coefficient of friction is one way to increase braking performance. Different brake-pad materials not only have different friction characteristics but they also have different temperature ranges where they perform best. A street-oriented pad will thrive at lower temperatures but will quickly overheat and wear quickly when driven on a road course. Conversely, track-oriented pads can be noisy and abrasive when cold but perform more consistently and last longer at high temperatures while on track.

Unfortunately, there isn't a magic brake pad that does it all. Choosing a brake pad involves a compromise between noise, wear, operating temperature, and desired friction. If you have a dual-purpose car and are serious about on-track performance, it's best to have dedicated sets of street and track pads and swap them at the track.

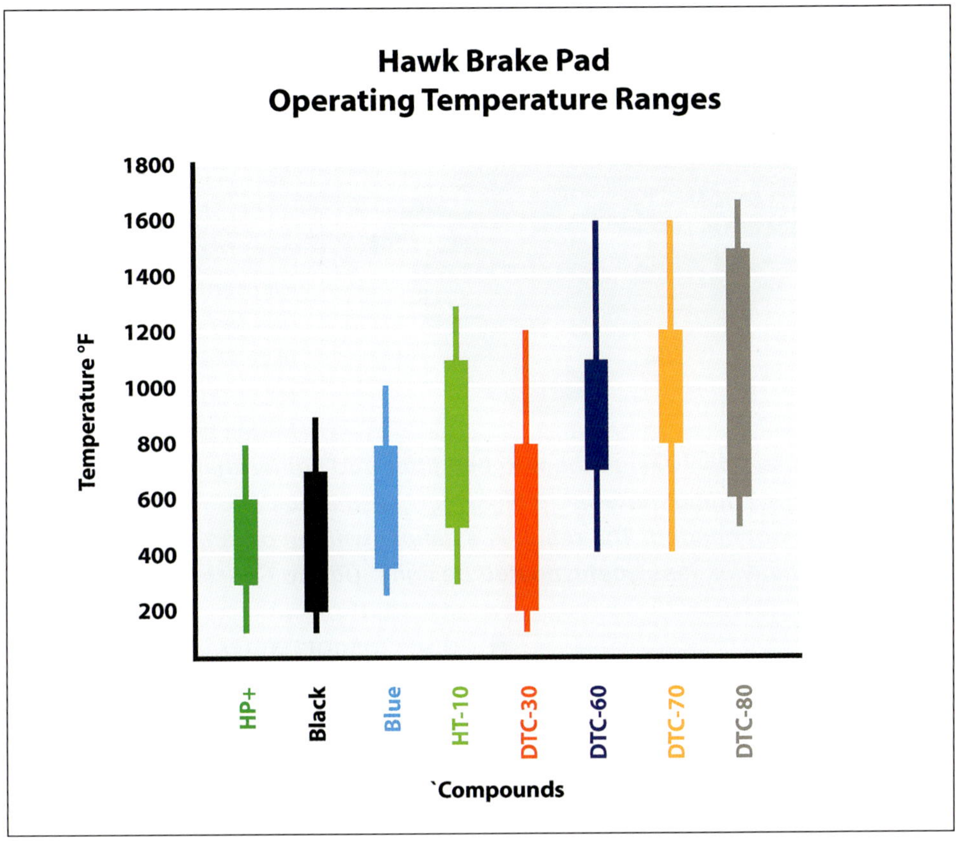


*This chart compares the minimum/maximum (thin line) and optimal (thick line) operating temperature ranges for several Hawk Performance brake-pad compounds. Note that there isn't one pad that does it all. There are trade-offs in friction, wear, and temperature range for each pad compound.*

## Brake Calipers

Friction is also affected by mechanical factors, such as clamping force, swept area, and leverage. A Mustang's brakes are operated via hydraulics, and braking force depends upon the ratio of the master cylinder and the combined brake piston sizes. If the brake-caliper pistons have more surface area than the factory brakes, the pistons will squeeze the pads and discs harder for the same pedal effort.

The same holds true for installing larger discs that place the pad's swept area farther from the center of the brake disc. If the brake pads have more leverage on the wheels, less pedal effort results in more braking torque.

However, it's important to keep both the hydraulic and levered mechanical advantages in mind when changing brake components, as these directly affect the balance of the front and rear braking systems (commonly called brake bias).

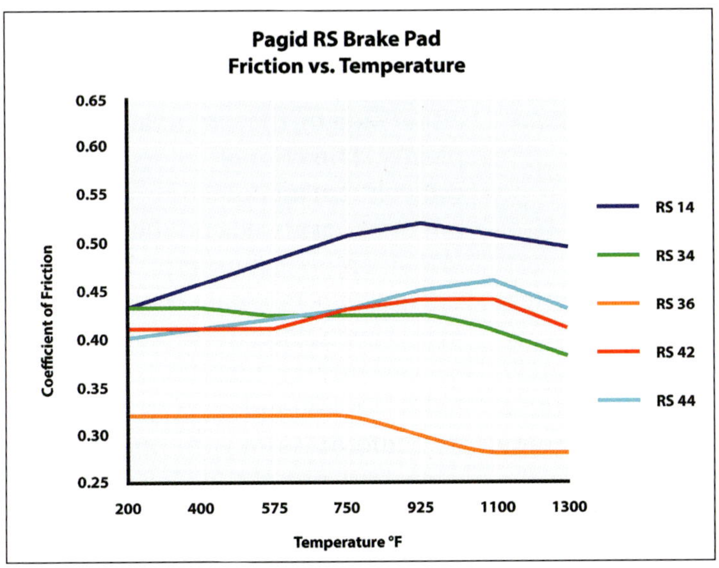


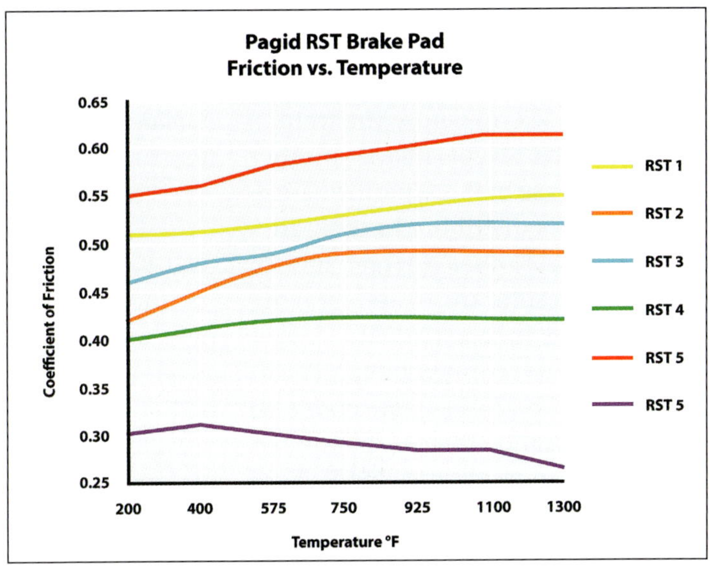


*These charts show the various friction characteristics for some Pagid Racing brake-pad compounds and illustrate how each compound's coefficient of friction varies with temperature. As the brakes are applied, the friction surface temperature increases. The coefficient of friction of some compounds increases with temperature (described as progressive), while the coefficient of friction of other compounds decreases as the pads heat up (digressive). Besides the average coefficient of friction, progressive or digressive pads can be used to tailor braking behavior.*

*This AP Racing CP9668 Radi-CAL Pro5000R caliper has six pistons that distribute the hydraulic force over the surface of the pad. Note that the pistons get larger from the leading to the trailing edges of the pad to reduce pad taper and increase pad life. These pistons are stainless steel and notched to reduce heat transfer to the brake fluid and aid in piston cooling. (Photo Courtesy Essex Parts Services)*

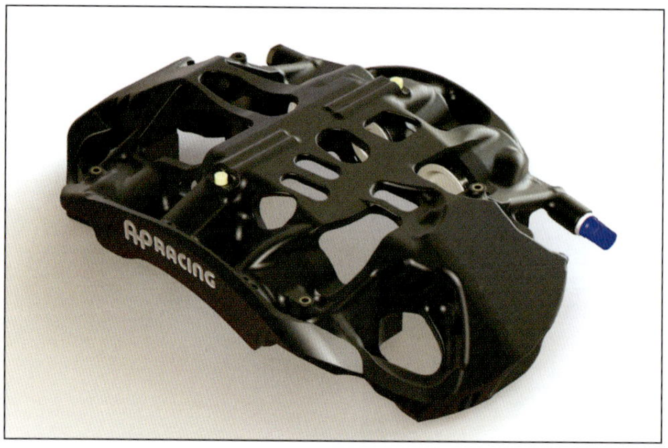

*While larger calipers with more pistons increase swept area, they also can increase weight (the least-desirable, unsprung kind). Over the past few decades, Finite Element Analysis (FEA) has led to new advances in brake caliper design. By understanding the forces acting on a brake caliper, engineers can design them to be stiffer and lighter than their traditional counterparts by adding material to highly stressed areas and removing material where it's not needed. The result is a caliper with an organic shape that outperforms heavier, less sophisticated designs. (Photo Courtesy AP Racing)*

Increasing front disc size, piston surface area, or pad friction will shift the brake bias toward the front, which will increase the share of the braking force that the front contributes. Conversely, increasing rear mechanical advantage shifts brake bias to the rear. If ABS fails, a car can spin if there is too much rear brake bias and the rear brakes lock up before the front.

Increasing swept area is another way to increase braking performance, as larger pads distribute braking friction (and heat) over a larger surface area. This results in greater braking capacity and longer pad life. Larger brake pads are clamped by larger calipers with a higher piston count so that the hydraulic force is distributed across the pad to wear the pads more evenly. Multi-piston calipers often stagger the piston diameters to further reduce pad taper.

Reputable big brake kit manufacturers size their caliper pistons accordingly to maintain a balanced brake bias.

*This is a cutaway of an AP Racing J Hook disc. Note the directional vanes that use the centrifugal force of the spinning disc to draw air from the center of the disc and expel it to the outside to cool the disc. (Photo Courtesy Essex Parts Services)*

## Brake Discs

Increasing disc diameter, thickness, and design affects brake torque, swept area, heat absorption capacity, and cooling. Disc, or rotor, material is usually iron. While carbon-ceramic braking systems show up inside the wheels of contemporary supercars, the bulk of the OEM and performance aftermarket still relies on traditional ferrous discs.

While increasing unsprung weight, more massive discs can absorb more heat, which reduces disc temperatures and improves brake system endurance. Most modern discs are vented, meaning that air flows through the inner and outer friction surfaces to cool the disc. Thicker discs often have larger cooling passages through the disc, which increases cooling efficiency.

Vented discs can be nondirectional or directional. The terms refer to the cooling features inside the disc. Nondirectional rotors are easier to manufacture and can be installed on either side of the car, reducing complexity. Directional rotors are more difficult to manufacture and stock but offer improved cooling over their nondirectional counterparts.

Besides internal cooling, discs may have different features on the friction surface. Manufacturers create holes, slots, dimples, or other features in the disc surface to increase the pad's bite and aid in pad degassing. Do not drill your own rotors. Holes drilled in a disc not designed for them can result in disc cracking and failure!

When discs get hot, they expand. The center of the disc is sandwiched between the wheel and hub. This interface is a large heat sink that keeps the center of the disc cool. The temperature differential between the hot outer disc surface and the cool wheel interface distorts the brake disc, and in extreme cases, the disc forms a cone shape. Two-piece "floating" discs were developed to address this problem.

Two-piece floating discs are comprised of an aluminum center section, or hat, and the outer iron disc. Various fastening methods are employed to retain the iron disc to the aluminum hat while still allowing the disc to expand when hot.

## Brake Fluid

Brake fluid is a simple yet critical part of any brake system. The brake fluid acts as the hydraulic connection between the master cylinder and the brake calipers. Hydraulic systems rely on the incompressibility of a liquid. However, every liquid has a boiling point. Since the brake fluid flows through the brake calipers and contacts the caliper pistons, it needs to do its job without boiling. If bubbles form in the fluid, they make the pedal spongy at best and render the brake system useless at worst. This phenomenon is called brake fade.

Brake fluids compatible with a Mustang's brake system are glycol-ether based, which is also hygroscopic (it absorbs water). As the brake fluid absorbs water over time, its boiling point is reduced. As a result, most brake fluids will list both a dry and a wet boiling point. The former represents fresh fluid, and the latter represents fluid that has absorbed water.

As a precaution, brake fluid should be flushed on a regular basis (annually on Mustangs that see heavy track use) with a glycol-ether based fluid that has the highest dry and wet boiling points you can afford.

## Brake Hoses

Compression and expansion are enemies of brake feel. Any flex in the braking system can result in a spongy pedal feel. One of the biggest contributors to brake-system flex are the hydraulic brake hoses that connect between the chassis and the calipers. Aftermarket brake "stainless-steel" brake hoses are usually comprised of a polytetrafluoroethylene (PTFE) hose that is covered by a stainless-steel braid. The result is a hose that expands less under pressure than OEM-style hoses.

## Cooling

Increased friction creates heat, and that heat needs to be removed before it overwhelms the brakes. As mentioned before, vented brake discs pump air through the disc using centrifugal force. Supplying a steady stream of cool air to the center of the disc can lower operating temperatures, which prolongs pad and disc life and avoids boiling of the brake fluid. The most common solution is brake ducting that routes air from a high-pressure area to the center of the brake discs.

While brake duct kits are available, AP Racing warns that a poorly designed or undersized brake duct is worse than none at all. The best way to check brake duct efficiency is to monitor brake component temperatures using an infrared thermometer, temperature paint, or temperature strips.

*Prospeed RS683 brake fluid is one of the best on the market. It exceeds DOT 3 and DOT 4 specifications, so it's compatible with road car braking systems. It features a 583°F dry boiling point (fresh from the bottle) and boils at 394°F when it has absorbed water. Prospeed claims it uses a patented manufacturing process that reduces the amount of dissolved air in the fluid to make it less compressible than other fluids, which leads to a firmer, more responsive brake feel.*

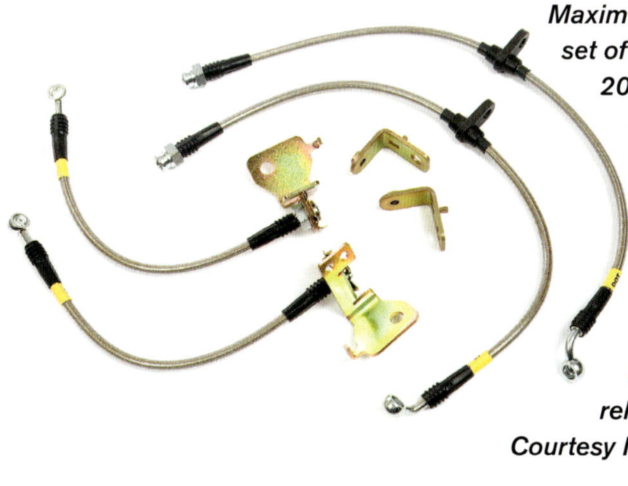

*Maximum Motorsports offers a set of brake hoses for 2005–2014 Mustangs (part number MM5BK1F and MM5BK1R) that includes fittings and brackets to secure them like the OEM hoses. Poorly designed and installed brake hoses can fail near the fittings if they don't have the strain relief and support. (Photo Courtesy Maximum Motorsports)*

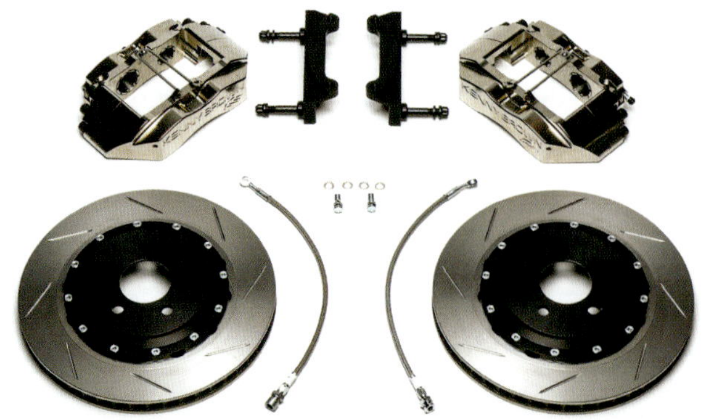

Kenny Brown's Pro 4 race brake package is unique in that it uses a large, 4-piston caliper that is designed exclusively for Kenny Brown based upon lessons learned from World Challenge GTS competition. It's a lighter and less expensive alternative to larger 6-piston kits. It uses 25-mm brake pads for endurance applications. (Photo Courtesy Kenny Brown Performance)

Kenny Brown offers a brake duct kit for S197 Mustangs that includes spindle-mounts, a 3-inch high-temperature brake duct hose, and bumper-mount brake duct inlets. The spindle mounts feature an oval-shaped nozzle to channel fresh air completely inside the disc and avoid disc distortion from uneven cooling. (Photo Courtesy Kenny Brown Performance)

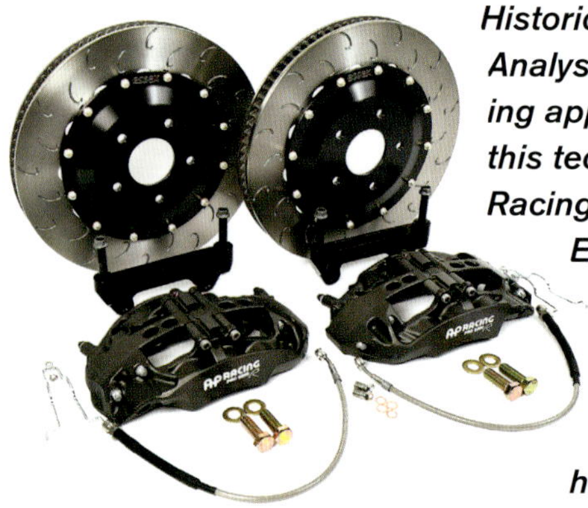

Historically, calipers designed using Finite Element Analysis have been limited to bespoke, high-end racing applications. However, Essex Parts Services offers this technology for lowly Mustangs by incorporating AP Racing's Radi-CAL Pro5000R 6-piston calipers into the Essex-designed competition brake kits for 2005–2014 Mustangs. Configured as a bolt-on replacement for Mustangs equipped with the factory Brembo brake option, the Essex kits include 372-mm discs and braided stainless brake hoses. They're also designed to work with the factory rear brakes. (Photo Courtesy Essex Parts Services)

While carbon-ceramic braking systems in the aftermarket are rare, Wilwood Engineering offers its AERO6 WCCB brake kits that feature carbon-ceramic technology. Carbon-ceramic brakes deliver performance that turns conventional brake-system thinking on its head. Carbon-ceramic materials offer higher thermal performance that exceeds traditional iron or titanium rotors and resists distortion, warping, cracking, and wear. Systems include 6-piston calipers and 14.00-inch WCCB discs front and rear but are bolt-on replacements for the factory brakes. Even the parking-brake function is retained, as the rear kit includes an integral drum parking brake mechanism. (Photo Courtesy Wilwood Engineering)

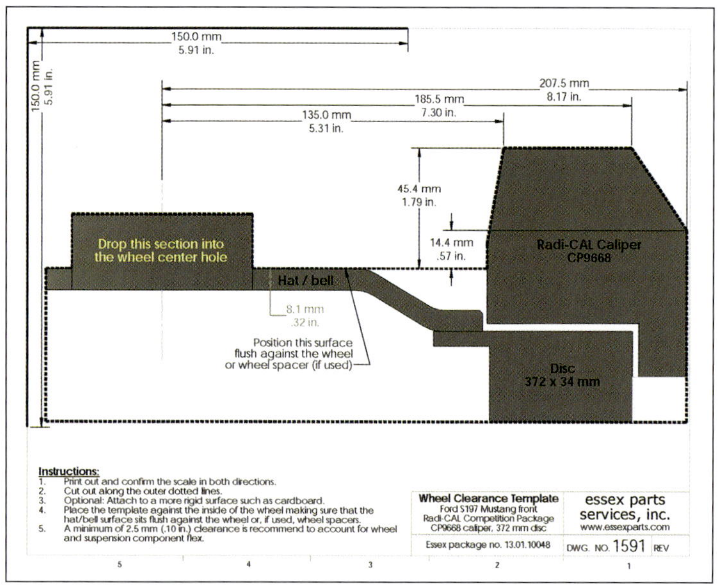


Larger brake calipers can interfere with some wheels. Most brake kit manufacturers publish dimensions or a template that, when printed at full scale, can be cut out and used to evaluate wheel clearance. (Photo Courtesy Essex Parts Services)

## How-To Project: Complete Brake Upgrade

While the standard brakes that Ford fitted on 2011–2014 Mustangs are adequate for mild performance expectations, the optional Brembo Brake Package on 2011–2014 Mustangs upped the ante considerably. However, a more capable brake package is necessary for S197 Mustangs that will see aggressive track duty, especially if more horsepower is under the hood.

*The Ford Performance Parts 6-piston 15-inch brake upgrade kit (part number M-2300-T) is a complete, OEM-quality brake upgrade package for 2011–2014 Mustangs. Not only does it offer a massive braking performance increase over the factory options but it's also one of the few kits that upgrades the rear brakes.*

*The 6-piston Brembo calipers were developed for the 200-mph 2013–2014 Shelby GT500, so we know they're up to just about any task. They come loaded with pads and bolt to the front spindles without any modifications.*

*The M-2300-T kit also upgrades the rear rotors to 13.8 inches to round out the package. The rear calipers remain a single-piston sliding arrangement with an integrated parking brake.*

The basic recipe for better braking includes some combination of increasing mass, swept area, and cooling. The Ford Performance Parts 6-piston 15-inch brake upgrade kit (part number M-2300-T) and the Kenny Brown brake duct kit (part number 2151.503) offer all three ingredients in spades.

Since the rear differential cover is removed for the rear brake installation, we replaced the cover with the Ford Performance Parts finned aluminum axle cover (part number M-4033-KA).

The M-2300-T kit is essentially the brake package developed for the extremely capable 2013–2014 Shelby GT500. As such, it includes 15-inch front rotors (up from 13.2 inches for a standard Mustang or 14 inches with the Brembo package) and 13.8-inch rear rotors (up 2 inches from 11.8 inches). The Brembo 6-piston front calipers offer significantly more clamping capability over the factory 2-piston sliding calipers or the optional factory 4-piston Brembos.

Besides what's shown on a specification sheet, M-2300-T offers additional benefits over other big brake kits on the market:

- It's a complete brake package that upgrades the front and rear brakes to maintain proper front/rear brake bias.
- The parts are 100-percent OEM quality and come directly from the proven 2013–2014 Shelby GT500.
- Aftermarket pad, rotor, and hose options are widely available as direct replacements for GT500 components.
- The front calipers fit behind factory 19-inch Brembo package wheels, so new wheels aren't necessary if upgrading a factory Brembo-equipped Mustang.

Although the rear brake setup adds complexity to the installation, the results are well worth the effort. Despite being super-car capable, the GT500 brakes offer a factory feel and modulation. Combined with the Kenny Brown cooling ducts, these brakes are ready to shrug off the next track day!

Here are the details of what we used for this installation:

- Ford Performance Parts 6-piston 15-inch brake upgrade kit (part number M-2300-T)
- Ford Performance Parts finned aluminum axle cover (part number M-4033-KA)
- Kenny Brown front brake cooling duct kit (part number 2151.503)
- 500 mL bottles (3) of Prospeed RS683 brake fluid
- Pressure brake bleeder
- Brake bleeding bottles (at least two)
- 2½-inch hole saw
- 13-mm flare-nut wrench
- 85W-140 gear oil (2 quarts) with friction modifier
- Permatex gear oil gasket maker (part number 81182)
- Basic tool kit
- Floor jack and jack stands
- Torque wrench

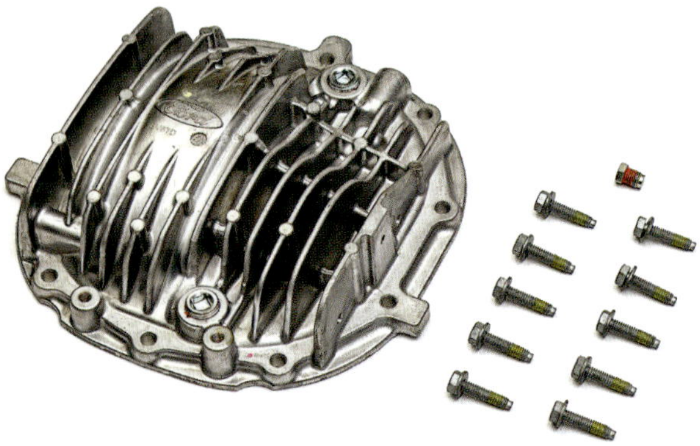

*The rear brake installation requires pulling the axle shafts, so while the differential cover was off, we replaced it with the Ford Performance Parts finned aluminum axle cover (part number M-4033-KA). The die-cast aluminum cover is finned inside and out to cool the differential fluid while on track. Ports for a differential cooler and temperature sensor are also incorporated into the cover's design.*

## Complete Brake Upgrade

**1** *Begin the installation process by disconnecting the front brake hoses from the hard lines. Use a 13-mm flare-nut wrench to ensure that you don't damage the flare nuts.*

**2** *To minimize fluid loss during installation, seal off the hard lines with rubber vacuum caps.*

**3** *Next, remove the front brake calipers and hoses.*

**4** *Then, remove the brake splash shields.*

**5** *Compared to the factory 14-inch rotor and 4-piston Brembo package (left), the GT500 6-piston and 15-inch rotor setup (right) clearly offers more swept and clamping area. The OEM front rotors weigh 22.2 pounds, while the 15-inch GT500 pieces weigh 31.8 pounds. While that's a big difference in unsprung weight, the additional mass also increases the thermal capacity of the braking system. The 6-piston Brembo calipers were only 1.8 pounds heavier than the 4-piston factory calipers.*

**6** *The Kenny Brown brake duct adapters bolt in place of the factory splash shields. Note that the oval nozzle directs air into the center of the rotor where the air can be drawn through the internal rotor vanes.*

**7** *Slide the 15-inch rotors onto the hub and install the 6-piston Brembo brake calipers by torquing the bolts to 85 ft-lbs.*

**8** *Connect the supplied brake hose to the brake caliper and torque the flow bolt to 41 ft-lbs.*

**9** *The included GT500 brake hoses are direct replacements for the factory brake hoses.*

**10** *Moving to the rear, use a screwdriver to free the parking-brake cables from the calipers.*

**11** *Then, remove the two caliber-bracket bolts from the backing plates.*

**12** *Securely hang the calipers off to the side using a cable tie.*

13 *Next, remove the rear rotors.*

14 *Remove the splash shields.*

15 *Remove the ABS sensor to avoid damaging it during axle removal and installation.*

16 *Next, drain the rear axle fluid and remove the differential cover.*

**17** *Rotate the differential to remove the lock bolt and pinion shaft.*

**18** *With the pinion shaft out of the way, push the axle shafts toward the center of the axle housing and pull the C-clips with a magnet.*

**19** *Pull the axle shafts from the housing and set them aside.*

**20** *Remove the factory brake-caliper support bracket.*

**21** *Next, remove the anti-moan bracket from the axle. The GT500 rear brakes' harmonics don't require the additional bracket for stabilization.*

**22** *The new brake-caliper support bracket bolted to the axle housing the same way as the factory bracket. Torque the bolts to 50 ft-lbs.*

**23** *Being careful not to damage the axle seals, slide the axle shaft back into the housing.*

**24** *Now, it's time to reinstall the ABS sensor.*

**25** *Permatex's gear oil sealant is specially formulated to resist gear oil better than other sealants. We've had good luck with this product, so we used it on the Ford Performance axle cover.*

**26** *Differential covers are notorious for leaking because of improper sealant use, so it's extremely important to follow Permatex's instructions to the letter. Loosely install the cover and wait an hour before torquing the bolts to 24 ft-lbs.*

**27** *Per the sealant's instructions, the sealant was allowed to cure 24 hours before filling the axle with 85W-140 gear oil. You can use a drill pump to hasten the process of filling the differential. Pump the fluid through the top port in the cover. Two quarts yield the right fluid level (5 mm below the fill hole at the front of the axle housing).*

**28** *Next, loosely install the brake calipers, disconnect the fluid hoses, remove the copper crush washers and flow bolt, and plug the banjo fittings with a rubber vacuum cap to minimize brake-fluid loss.*

**29** *The GT500 rear brake rotors (right) are a full 2 inches larger in diameter than the factory rotors (left).*

**30** *Hang the new rotors on the rear axle flanges.*

**31** *Then, bolt on the new rear calipers and torque the bolts to 76 ft-lbs.*

**32** *Bolt the brake hose to the new calipers using the original flow bolt and new copper crush washers that were supplied with the Ford Performance Parts kit.*

**33** *Brake-system flushing and bleeding can be tedious. Not only does a pressurized brake bleeder speed up the process but it also eliminates the need for an assistant, and the results are often as good or better than having someone pump the pedal.*

**34** *The six-piston Brembo brake calipers have an inner and outer bleeder. Bleed both sides of the caliper simultaneously using two bleeder bottles.*

**35** *When installing new rear brake calipers, Ford recommends bleeding them with the pistons fully extended. To do so, remove the outer brake pad and replace it with a rag. Then, remount the caliper and slowly press the brake pedal until the rear pistons are fully extended.*

**36** *With the calipers pistons fully extended, bleed the rear calipers while using a rear brake-piston retraction tool to screw the pistons back into the calipers.*

**37** *To provide an air inlet for the Kenny Brown brake cooling duct kit, make a 2½-inch hole in the front lower grille opening using a hole saw. (Another option is a 2012–2014 Boss 302 lower grille that already has brake duct inlet provisions.)*

**38** *To adapt the 2½-inch holes to the 3-inch hose included with the Kenny Brown brake cooling kit, we used a section of 2½-inch stainless exhaust tubing with a 1/4-inch strip of rubberized matt riveted around one end. We painted it flat black for appearance.*

**39** *The inlet adapters fit snugly into the lower grille openings to provide fresh air to the front rotors.*

**40** Route the brake duct hoses from the front grille openings, along the sway bar, and over to the spindle adapter. It's important to make sure that the ducts don't bind or interfere with the wheels or other suspension parts throughout the suspension motion and steering range.

It was close, but there was about 0.060 inch of clearance between the factory 19-inch Brembo Package wheels and the Brembo 6-piston brake calipers. This was a very welcome surprise, as new wheels were not required for a separate street or cold-weather wheel/tire package.

The Brembo 6-piston calipers and 15-inch brake rotors really fill the front wheels. This is one serious front brake setup.

The rear brakes now have a bigger-diameter rotor (13.8 inches) than the standard GT front brake rotors (13.2 inches).

# Drivetrain

The drivetrain's job is to get the power from the engine to the wheels. It seems simple, but it's not—especially if the engine is producing significantly more torque than stock. A smooth clutch and easy-shifting transmission can make driving your car a joy, whereas an ornery clutch and balky shifter can make driving a chore. A good rule of thumb is to upgrade drivetrain components as necessary but don't go overboard. Racing components often involve compromises that can impact street manners. Choose wisely.

## Clutches

The main reason to upgrade a clutch is to increase holding power in response to higher engine torque. As with most aftermarket parts, there's no free lunch. Clutch choice is a compromise between torque capacity, drivability, and pedal effort. That's because holding power is a direct result of friction surface area, friction material, and clamping load.

Surface area is usually limited to the diameter of the flywheel and is likely maximized from the factory. Because the starter is a fixed distance from the crankshaft center line, it's

*Centerforce's dual-friction clutch kit for 2011–2014 Mustangs with the MT82 transmission is a great upgrade from the factory clutch. The pressure plate features centrifugal weights that increase holding capacity while maintaining low pedal effort. The clutch disc includes a full organic facing on one side and a segmented face on the other for smooth engagement. Centerforce claims a holding capacity of 687 ft-lbs of torque. (Photo Courtesy Centerforce)*

*The Hays Street 650 single-disc street/strip clutch is designed to handle up to 650 hp and the stress of nitrous or forced induction. It features an 8-spring hub with encapsulated damper springs and a sintered metallic friction material to handle triple the shock loads without resorting to a solid clutch hub. Hays claims the sintered metallic material provides a degree of slippage on vehicle launch to prevent the violent engagement characteristics found in paddle-style metallic discs. (Photo Courtesy Hays)*

***The ST-246 clutches from Tilton Engineering combine high holding capacity with street-ability. They're a ground-up twin-disc clutch designed to survive the rigors of both street and racing use. The heavy-duty straps and thick floater plate reduce noise and warpage from heat soak. They're available with organic sprung hub discs for street use to hold 850 ft-lbs (left) or cerametallic solid hub discs for street/strip use and to hold 1,250 ft-lbs (right). (Photo Courtesy Tilton Engineering)***

***Exedy offers a cost-effective twin-disc solution with its Hyper Multi series twin-disc clutch (part number ET05S-RFD) that's perfect for moderately modified 2011–2014 Mustangs. It features two organic, solid hub discs that are mated to a lightweight steel flywheel. Although it's rated for 600 ft-lbs of torque, pedal effort is lower than the factory single-disc clutch. (Photo Courtesy KohR Motorsports)***

unlikely that a larger-diameter flywheel and clutch disc will fit.

Higher-friction materials are effective in increasing torque capacity, but those materials are often grabby and more difficult to drive. Original equipment manufacturers choose organic friction materials because they have smooth engagement characteristics. Other materials include metallics, carbons, and ceramics. These materials offer varying degrees of friction over organics but usually engage more harshly.

Increasing clamping load is another method of increasing torque capacity, but the corresponding increase in pedal effort can be fatiguing on a daily basis.

Exceptions to these compromises are multi-plate clutches. Street-oriented multi-plate clutches can increase holding power while maintaining good drivability and low pedal effort. Most multi-plate clutches for S197 Mustangs are of the twin-disc variety. Smaller-diameter twin-disc clutches can also reduce rotational inertia, which makes the engine more responsive to RPM changes. This can be an advantage for road-racing vehicles and lightweight drag-racing Mustangs.

Multi-plate clutches vary from street-friendly strap-drive units with sprung hubs to race-oriented setups with exotic friction materials and solid hubs. When selecting a clutch for your Mustang, select a unit with a torque capacity just above what you need because a heavy, aggressive clutch can make driving a chore.

## Shifters

Aftermarket shifters are a common upgrade for the factory MT82 transmission. Rather than mount directly to the transmission, the 2011–2014 Mustang's MT82 transmission uses a semi-remote shifter, where the back half mounts to the chassis and the front half mounts to the transmission. While this design reduces noise and vibration, it also presents a problem: missed shifts during heavy acceleration.

At rest, the factory shifter works well, but when under heavy load, the engine and transmission twist in their mounts. This movement misaligns the front of the shifter mechanism, which makes shifting inaccurate or impossible, especially when shifting from second to third gear.

While some aftermarket shifters can improve shifting accuracy through more rigid components and revised bushing materials, there are only two ways to completely solve the problem: 1) Stop the engine from moving with stiffer or solid mounts or 2) Do away with the semi-remote shifter design and mount the shifter directly to the transmission. The latter option is much more practical.

This is a side note on short-throw shifter mechanisms: in contrast to other transmissions, the MT82's front-to-back throw is much longer than its left-to-right throw. Some

*If you want better shift feel, shorter shift throws, and simple installation without the noise and vibration from transmission-mounted shifters, the Ford Performance Parts shifter (part number M-7210-MGTB) is an excellent choice. It features a dual-pivot trunnion to maintain accurate left-to-right action but reduces front-to-back throws 40 percent. The included two-post shifter mount reduces flex without causing bind, and the shifter mechanism maintains the factory-style reverse lockout. (Photo Courtesy Ford Performance Parts)*

*For those who want a full-on retro look and feel, the Hurst Competition/Plus shifter for MT82 reduces the throw by 18 percent and uses a unique T-handle mechanism to lock out reverse. The chrome flat-blade lever engraved with the classic Hurst text completes the look. The shifter is compatible with the factory boot. (Photo Courtesy Hurst)*

*MGW's Race Spec short-throw shifter for 2011–2014 MT82-equipped Mustangs is a "clean sheet" transmission-mounted shifter. Billet strut arms mount the shifter solidly to the transmission, and a solid linkage rod connects the shifter to the transmission. The result is a more conventional shifter feel and higher accuracy. (Photo Courtesy MGW Ltd.)*

early and primitive short-throw shifters effectively reduced the throws by moving the lever pivot to reduce mechanical advantage equally in all directions. Consequently, feeling the difference between the 1-2, 3-4, and 5-6 gates became more difficult.

More sophisticated designs use different fulcrums for front-to-back and left-to-right movement to make front-to-back shifter throws shorter without affecting the left-to-right accuracy.

## Manual Transmissions

Since the 1980s, Tremec (formerly BorgWarner) transmissions lived in the tunnels of Mustangs and were generally robust and reliable, even if they a bit clunky and crude. For whatever reason (perhaps cost, production capacity, and/or design) Ford moved from longtime supplier and partner Tremec to Getrag for the 2011 Mustang.

For daily use, the Getrag MT82 is a very smooth-shifting, 6-speed transmission. However, add more torque to the crankshaft or rush a high-RPM shift, and the shortcomings of the MT82 quickly surface. The Getrag gearbox's issues stem from the semi-remote shifter design, center-to-center distance, and gear ratios.

Missed shifts from the semi-remote shifter design can be addressed with an aftermarket shifter solution, but the center-to-center distance and gear ratios fundamentally limit the MT82's torque capacity. The center-to-center distance defines the maximum diameter of the gears, and the steep first gear ratio limits how much torque the gearset can take. Unlike Tremec transmissions of old, no aftermarket parts exist to increase the MT82's marginal 375 ft-lbs torque handling capability.

Ironically, if you outgrow your MT82 transmission, Tremec offers an aftermarket solution in the Magnum XL. Based upon the venerable Tremec T-56, the Tremec Magnum XL is a transmission-swap-friendly version of the company's TR-6060 6-speed transmission. (The TR-6060 was used in 2007–2014 Mustang GT500s but used a semi-remote shifter just like Coyote-powered Mustangs.)

The Tremec Magnum XL addresses the three major complaints with the MT82: missed shifts, strength, and gear-ratio spread.

A unique tail housing on the Magnum XL incorporates a conventional top-loader shifting mechanism that does away with the maladies of the semi-remote design. The included shifter is a billet-aluminum, short-throw design.

At 700 ft-lbs, the Tremec Magnum XL's torque capacity is nearly double that of the MT82. Credit an 85-mm center-to-center distance, wider gears, and taller gear ratios for the durability increase.

*The Magnum XL is a bolt-in swap with the included SFI-approved steel bellhousing, crossmember, transmission mount, isolated shifter, and shift ball. It also reuses the OEM hydraulic clutch release system. All that's required is a 26-spline clutch disc and one-piece driveshaft with a 31-spline slip yoke. (Photo Courtesy Tremec)*

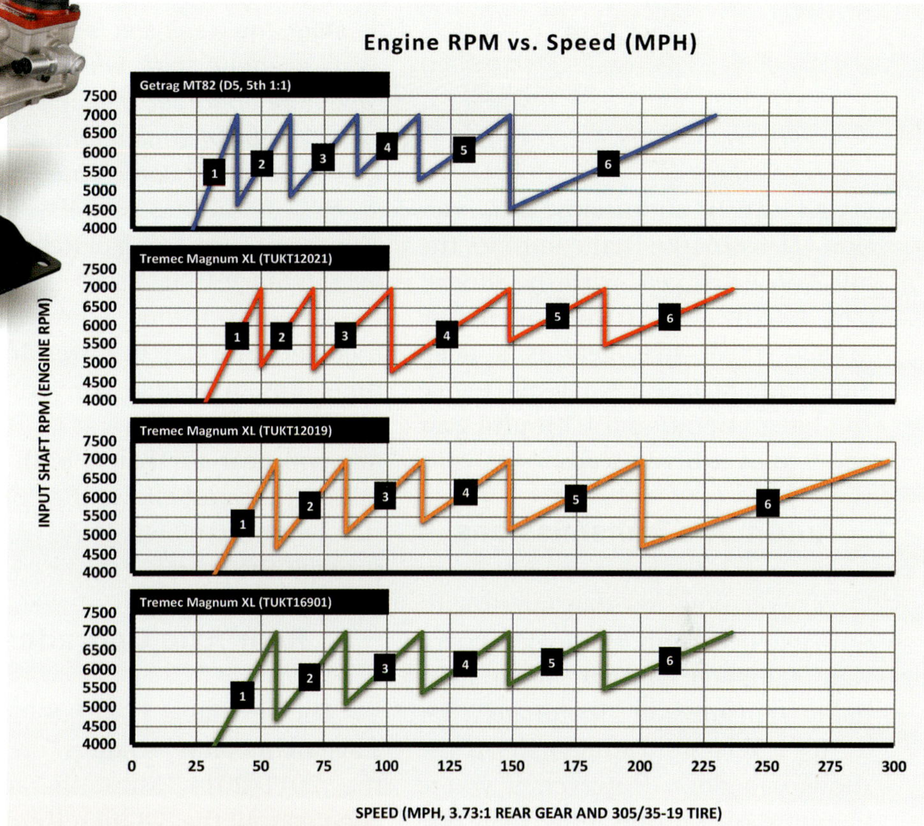


*This illustration compares the ratios of the MT82 (top) to versions of the Tremec XL (middle to bottom). Note that MT82's design crams five ratios in the same speed range that the Magnum XL fits four. The result is a large ratio gap and corresponding RPM drop to overdrive with the MT82. In contrast, Tremec spreads all six ratios more evenly over the vehicle speed range, making them more usable, so there's less of a drop when shifting to overdrive. Magnum XLs are available with different gear spreads and ratio ranges to fit varying applications.*

**Manual Transmission Specifications**

| | | Getrag MT82 D5 | Tremec Magnum XL TUKT12019 | Tremec Magnum XL TUKT12021 | Tremec Magnum XL TUKT16901 |
|---|---|---|---|---|---|
| Gear Ratios | 1st | 3.66:1 | 2.66:1 | 2.97:1 | 2.66:1 |
| | 2nd | 2.43:1 | 1.78:1 | 2.10:1 | 1.78:1 |
| | 3rd | 1.69:1 | 1.30:1 | 1.46:1 | 1.30:1 |
| | 4th | 1.31:1 | 1.00:1 | 1.00:1 | 1.00:1 |
| | 5th | 1.00:1 | 0.74:1 | 0.80:1 | 0.80:1 |
| | 6th | 0.65:1 | 0.50:1 | 0.63:1 | 0.63:1 |
| Weight (lbs) | | 124 | 155 | 155 | 155 |
| Center Distance (mm) | | 82 | 85 | 85 | 85 |
| Torque Capacity (ft-lbs) | | 375 | 700 | 700 | 700 |
| Input | | 31T | 26T | 26T | 26T |
| Output | | Flange | 31T Slip Yoke | 31T Slip Yoke | 31T Slip Yoke |

Tremec offers bolt-in Magnum XL transmissions for 2011–2014 with three different gear-ratio options. All have nearly twice the torque capacity than the factory MT82 transmission. Note that the input and output spline counts and styles are different for Magnum XL versus the MT82.

Also, speaking of gear ratios, Tremec offers three sets of gear ratios in the Magnum XL for 2011–2014 Mustangs: a 2.97:1 first-gear ratio with a 0.63:1 sixth-gear ratio (TUKT12021), a taller 2.66:1 first-gear ratio with a 0.50:1 sixth-gear ratio

*Although the 6R80 transmission is stout, the weak link is the intermediate shaft, which should be upgraded if exceeding 600 ft-lbs of engine torque. (Photo Courtesy Boninfante Friction)*

(TUKT12019), and a close-ratio version (TUKT16109) that combines the tall 2.66:1 first gear with the shorter 0.63:1 sixth gear. In contrast to the MT82, where first gear is a deep 3.66:1 and fifth gear is 1:1, all Tremec XLs have a traditional 1:1 fourth gear and two overdrive speeds.

## Automatic Transmissions

Coyote-powered Mustangs with only two pedals under the dashboard were equipped with the 6R80 automatic transmission. Fortunately for us, it's a very stout unit right off the showroom floor. However, if you're planning on putting more than 600 ft-lbs through a 6R80, there are some items to address.

The weakest link on the 6R80 transmission is the intermediate shaft. Several aftermarket shafts are available that are good to over 1,000 hp. While you're installing the shaft, a clutch upgrade is also wise. Upgraded clutch packs increase the torque holding capacity of the 6R80 to more than 1,000 ft-lbs. Exedy sells a Stage 2 clutch kit and claims a 40-percent increase in clutch capacity over its Stage 1 kit.

A looser torque converter is a tried-and-true way to lower drag-race time slips. A torque converter with a higher stall speed acts as a lower rear-end gear in that it both multiplies torque and allows the engine to stay within its power band as it goes through the gears.

## Rear Axle Upgrades

The venerable Ford 8.8-inch rear axle architecture soldiers on under the 2011–2014 Mustang—and for good reason: the 8.8-inch third member has evolved over the decades into an extremely durable and reliable rear end. All 2011–2014 Mustangs (both V-6 and V-8) have 31-spline rear axles installed from the factory. However, every rear end has its limits, and adding significantly more engine torque and/or sticky rear tires exposes the factory rear axle's limitations. Fortunately, since the 8.8-inch design has been around since the mid-1980s, plenty of aftermarket solutions exist.

*Circle D Specialties offers a range of torque converters for the 6R80 automatic transmission. They're available in 265- to 245-mm sizes and 3,200- to 4,200-rpm stall speeds. Optional single- or triple-disc lock-up clutches maintain good street driving manners and lower parasitic loss. (Photo Courtesy Circle D Specialties)*

For drag racing, options range from stronger 31-spline axle shafts to complete replacement 9-inch rear end housings. C-clip eliminator axle kits are a wise safety measure and are often required by the rules for cars running 10.99 seconds or quicker in the quarter mile. Since the factory axles slide into the housing and are retained by C-clips inside the differential, if the axle breaks, it can slide back out of the housing and take the wheel with it. Obviously, that's a problem. Rather than use the C-clip to hold the axle inside the housing, a C-clip eliminator kit uses a pressed-on bearing on the outer end of the axle shaft to retain it to the housing.

Larger axle shafts with more splines are a further upgrade, but they require a corresponding differential to accept the larger axles.

Road racing presents unique problems for the Mustang 8.8-inch rear end. With conventional C-clips, the axle slides back and forth in the axle housing as the Mustang turns corners. Since the brake rotor is attached to the axle and the caliper is attached to the housing, the side-to-side slop knocks the brake-caliper pistons back into their bores, which leaves a gap between the rotor and the pads. This gap must be taken up before the brakes start working, which results in a squishy brake pedal at best and reduced braking performance at worst. A full-floater axle conversion's hub bearing keeps the rotor and calipers aligned, which greatly reduces pad knock back and makes braking more consistent and responsive.

Rear ring-and-pinion gearsets alter the gear ratio of the rear axle. They change the mechanical advantage that the engine and transmission have over the tires. A lower gear

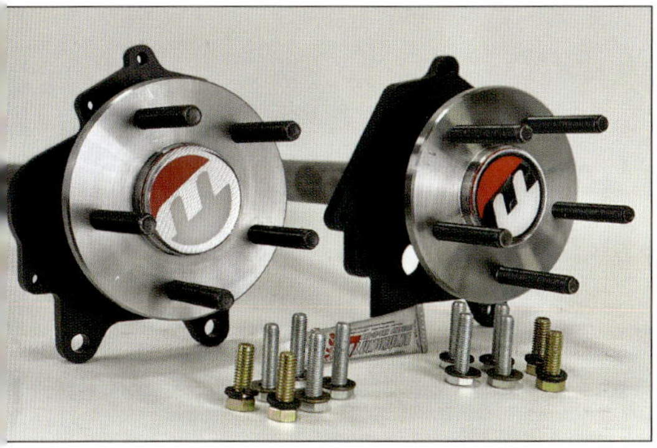

*If you're running 10.99 seconds or quicker in the quarter mile, most sanctioning bodies require C-clip eliminator axles. These axle shafts use a bearing pressed onto the axle rather than the factory C-clips. If the axle fails, the pressed-on bearing keeps the wheel attached to the car. (Most C-clip eliminator axles are not designed for road racing.) Moser Engineering's 2005–2014 Mustang GT axle and eliminator package (part number AEP-SN197) is available with 31-spline (to fit the factory differential) or larger 33- and 35-spline axles. Timken bearings, caliper brackets, and 1/2-inch wheel studs are also included. (Photo Courtesy Moser Engineering)*

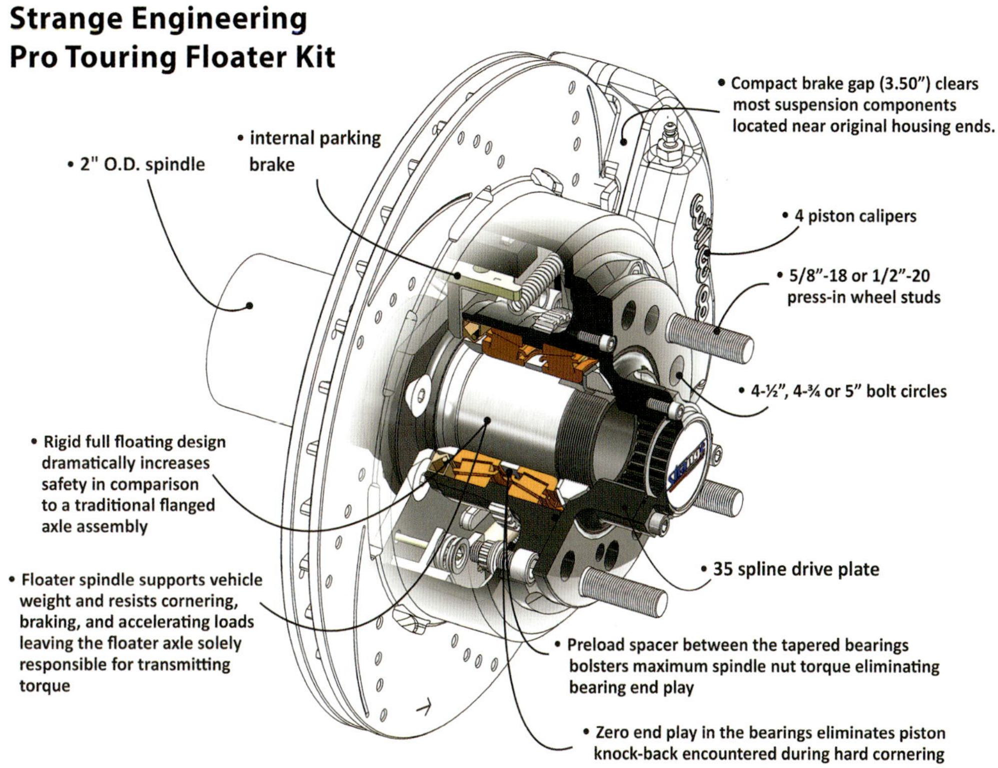


*Full-floater axle conversions use a heavy-duty hub bearing at the end of each axle tube and an axle shaft that's splined to fit the differential on one end and the hub on the other. Since the axle is splined on both ends, it floats in the housing (hence the name). For road racing, a full-floater rear axle conversion solves two problems: 1) Like a C-clip eliminator kit, the wheel stays attached to the axle housing even if the axle breaks, and 2) Rear brake pad knock-back from C-clip slop is eliminated. (Illustration Courtesy of Strange Engineering)*

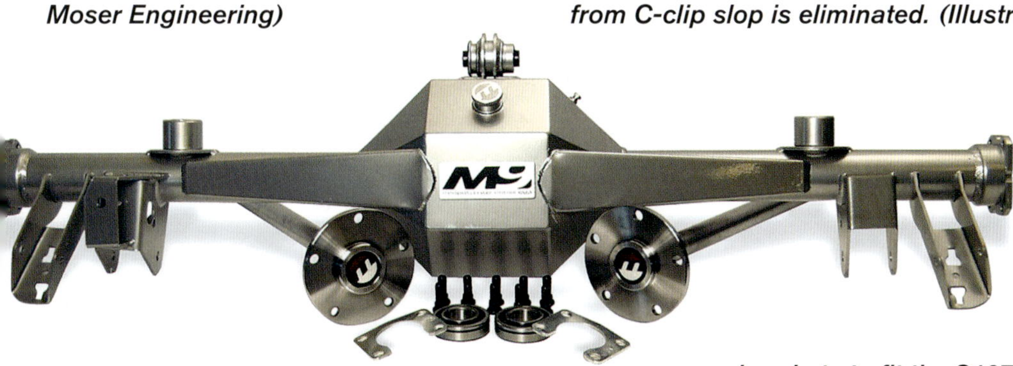

*Dedicated, drag-race-only applications are best served with a complete replacement axle assembly built on Ford's legendary 9-inch differential foundation. Moser's M9 fabricated 9-inch housing and axle package for 2005–2014 Mustangs includes spring pads and control-arm brackets to fit the S197 chassis. The Moser M9 is a serious piece with internal gussets and bulkheads. If you break one of these, you've got bigger problems. (Photo Courtesy Moser Engineering)*

*For road racing, a constraint of the traditional live axle is that the wheels are always perpendicular to the axle housing and the alignment isn't adjustable. However, a cambered rear axle housing takes the full-floater concept one step further by adding camber and toe adjustment. CorteX Racing offers a CV joint rear cambered axle conversion for serious road racing S197 Mustangs. Note how there's a wedge on the left side of the assembly that adds negative camber. These wedges can be swapped to change camber and toe.*

*Rear ring-and-pinion sets in a wide range of ratios for the Ford 8.8 are available from many manufacturers, including Motive Gear. Installing rear gears requires special tools and expertise, so it's often best left to a shop that specializes in this work. (Photo Courtesy Motive Gear)*

*The clutch pack is the most common type of limited-slip differential. Available under different names (such as Ford's Traction-Lok) the concept is similar: When torque is applied to the differential case, the load is transferred through cross-shaft and bevel gears to clutch plates behind the side gears. As more torque is applied to the cross-shaft, more force squeezes the clutch plates together. A spring (either an S spring or coil springs) applies a level of preload to the clutches to provide a baseline of traction even when one wheel is completely unloaded. (Illustration Courtesy Eaton)*

*Some clutch-pack differentials are adjustable to provide differing levels of slip on acceleration or deceleration by altering the angle of contact between the cross-shaft and pressure rings that vary the force on the clutch packs. Note the wedge angle on this Drexler Motorsport differential that loads the clutches more on acceleration than on deceleration. (Photo Courtesy Drexler Motorsport)*

*Early clutch-pack differentials didn't have the durability for high-horsepower and endurance applications, so the Detroit Locker differential was developed. Rather than use clutches to vary the amount of slip between each axle, the locker uses dog rings to completely lock the axles together under acceleration and unlock them during coast and deceleration. The result is effective, yet brutal, as the locker acts as an on-off device between locking on acceleration and unlocking on deceleration. The locking action can upset vehicle balance for road racing and is noisy on the street. (Illustration Courtesy Eaton)*

*Rather than use clutches that are subject to heat and wear, a gear-type torque-biasing differential uses worm gears and the self-locking property of gear pitch to create a limited-slip action. Examples of these differentials are the Torsen, Eaton Trutrac, and Wavetrac. Some gear-type differentials are available in different bias ratios that send different levels of torque from the unloaded to the loaded wheel. Ford installed a Torsen differential in the Boss 302 Laguna Seca and 2013–2014 GT500. (Illustration Courtesy Eaton)*

ratio (higher numerically) usually increases acceleration as the engine reaches (and stays in) the engine's sweet spot, as not only does first gear become lower but also the effective gear ratio spread of subsequent gears narrows.

However, deeper rear gears also increase engine RPM on the highway, which reduces gas mileage. They may also require another shift during a quarter-mile pass, which adds time. Cars running drag radials and taller rear tires often benefit from a lower rear-end ratio.

The differential is a critical part of the drivetrain, as it distributes the torque from the driveshaft to the rear wheels. All Mustangs come equipped with some type of limited-slip differential that preserves forward traction when the rear wheels are unevenly loaded. There are several different limited-slip differential designs, each with unique characteristics and applications.

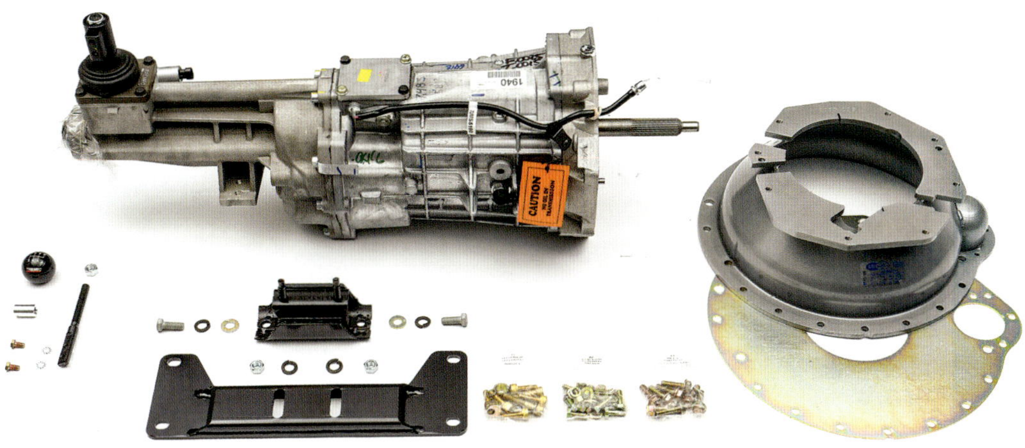

***The Tremec Magnum XL (part number TUKT12021) is a complete, bolt-in solution for 2011–2014 Mustang GTs. It includes an SFI-approved "blow proof" bellhousing, transmission crossmember, and shifter. With a 2.97:1 first gear and a 1:1 fourth gear, the 12021 transmission features a more useable gear-ratio spread than the MT82.***

## How-To Project: Clutch and Manual Transmission Upgrade

At stock power levels, the 2011–2014 Mustang's Getrag MT82 transmission is an easy-shifting gearbox. However, it's not very strong and doesn't like being shifted quickly. Add a supercharger and sticky tires to the mix, and the MT82 is on borrowed time.

Fortunately, Tremec offers a solution: the Magnum XL 6-speed transmission (part number TUKT12021). It offers a 700 ft-lbs torque rating (significantly higher than the MT82's 375 ft-lbs figure), and the shifter mounts directly to an extra-long tailhousing (hence the XL designation). The transmission-mounted shifter eliminates the missed shifts from the MT82's body-anchored shifter design.

With a few accessories, the Magnum XL transmission is a bolt-in replacement for the MT82. The Magnum XL needs a 26-spline clutch disc, a conventional 31-spline slip-yoke driveshaft, and a harness module to convert the speed signal and operate the reverse lockout.

We paired the Tremec Magnum XL transmission with an Exedy Stage 4 twin-disc clutch (part number ET05SRFC). With a 600 ft-lbs torque capacity, the Exedy twin-disc clutch is more than up to the task of holding all the torque that a supercharged Coyote engine can throw at it. However, the Exedy's twin organic discs and pressure plate make it an extremely smooth and light clutch to operate.

After installation, we were extremely pleased with this upgrade. Even though the Tremec Magnum XL is arguably the toughest street-oriented transmission on the market, the shifting action is extremely smooth and accurate, even when driving aggressively. Likewise, the drivability of the Exedy twin disc belies its monstrous torque rating. The pedal effort is significantly lower and offers more take-up feedback than the factory clutch. Right out of the box, the Exedy was the smoothest clutch we ever experienced—OEM or aftermarket.

The only drawback that we experienced was increased transmission growl in third and fourth gears between 1,500 and 2,000 rpm. This is due to the Exedy's solid-hub clutch discs. We reasoned that this was a small price to pay for how much torque this combination is designed to handle. Enthusiasts with milder power combinations and lower annoyance thresholds should opt for a sprung-hub clutch setup.

The conversion process is fairly straightforward, and the tools and supplies list is pretty limited:

- Tremec Magnum XL transmission kit (part number TUKT12021)
- Bowler Transmissions all-in-one harness module (part number T56-RLM)
- Modern Driveline/Dynotech driveshaft (part number DSA4.0-B-S197GT-XL)
- Modern Driveline shifter ball collar (part number MD-319-7001-P)
- Dexron III automatic transmission fluid (4 quarts)
- Exedy Stage 4 twin-disc clutch (part number ET05SRFC)
- Flywheel holding tool
- Basic tool kit
- Floor jack and jack stands
- Transmission jack (or fabricated transmission floor jack cradle)
- Torque wrench

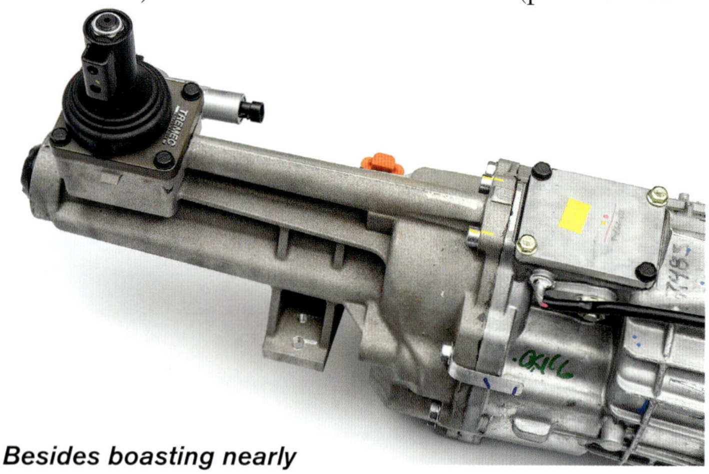

*Besides boasting nearly twice the torque capacity of the factory MT82 transmission, the Magnum XL's extra-long tail housing (hence the XL designation) mounts the shifter mechanism directly to the transmission. No more missed shifts!*

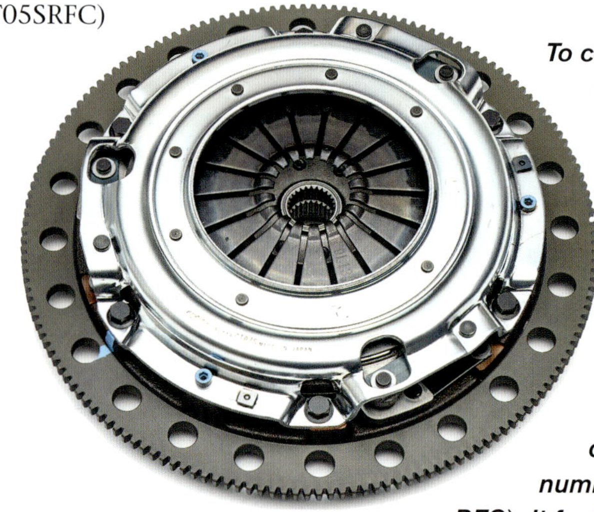

*To complement the Tremec Magnum XL's 700 ft-lbs torque rating, we opted for an Exedy Stage 4 twin-disc clutch (part number ET05S-RFC). It features a 600 ft-lbs torque capacity, twin organic discs, and a steel flywheel.*

*The Exedy twin-disc clutch has a strap drive floater and pressure plate, which minimize the clutch noise and rattle that are often associated with other multi-plate clutches. The steel flywheel is also lightened around the perimeter to reduce rotating inertia.*

*The Exedy Stage 4 twin-disc clutch features twin solid-hub, 26-spline clutch discs to match the input shaft of the Magnum XL.*

## Clutch and Manual Transmission Upgrade

**1** *Begin the conversion process by removing the shifter knob and console. The knob simply spins off and the console comes straight out.*

**2** *Next, remove the driveshaft.*

**3** *Remove the starter. The top bolt is a challenge but can be reached using the right length of extensions and a stubby ratchet wrench.*

**4** *Disconnect the three electrical plugs from the transmission and the hydraulic clutch line at the firewall.*

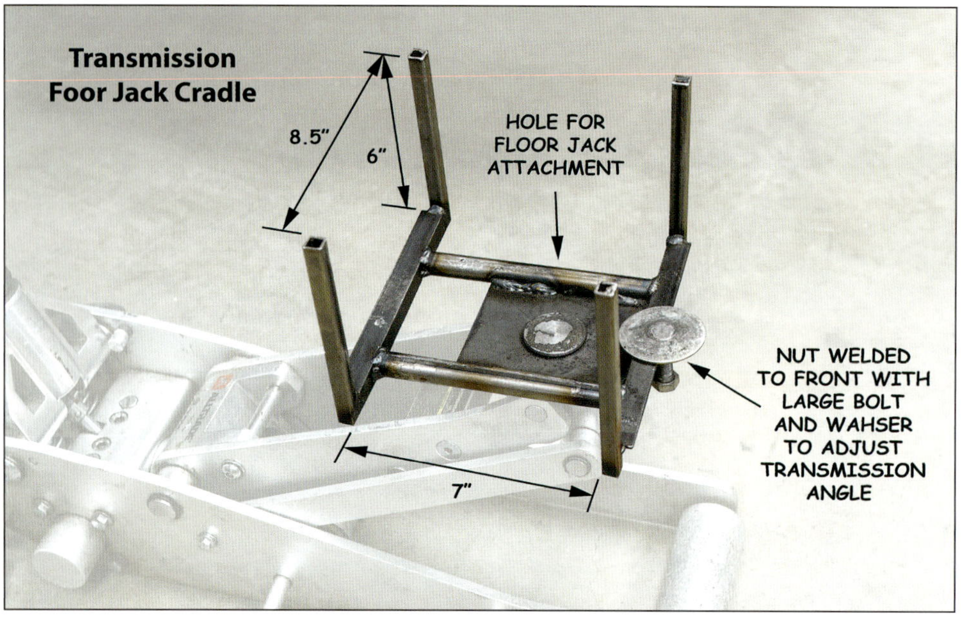


**5** *We fabricated this handy transmission cradle that fits a floor jack. If you want to use this instead of a transmission jack, here are the basic dimensions.*

**6** *We supported the transmission with our floor-jack cradle. A block of wood between the cradle and the MT82 transmission netted a little bit of extra height to support the transmission.*

**7** *Use various sockets, extensions, and wrenches to remove all the bolts fastening the MT82 to the Coyote engine. The two top bolts can be accessed by reaching behind the engine from the top.*

**8** *Remove the rear mount from the chassis and the back of the transmission.*

**9** *With the mount and driveshaft out of the way, unbolt the remote shifter mechanism from the body and the transmission arm.*

**10** *With everything disconnected, carefully lower the MT82 down and out from under the car. It helps to tip the engine back as far as possible to aid in removal.*

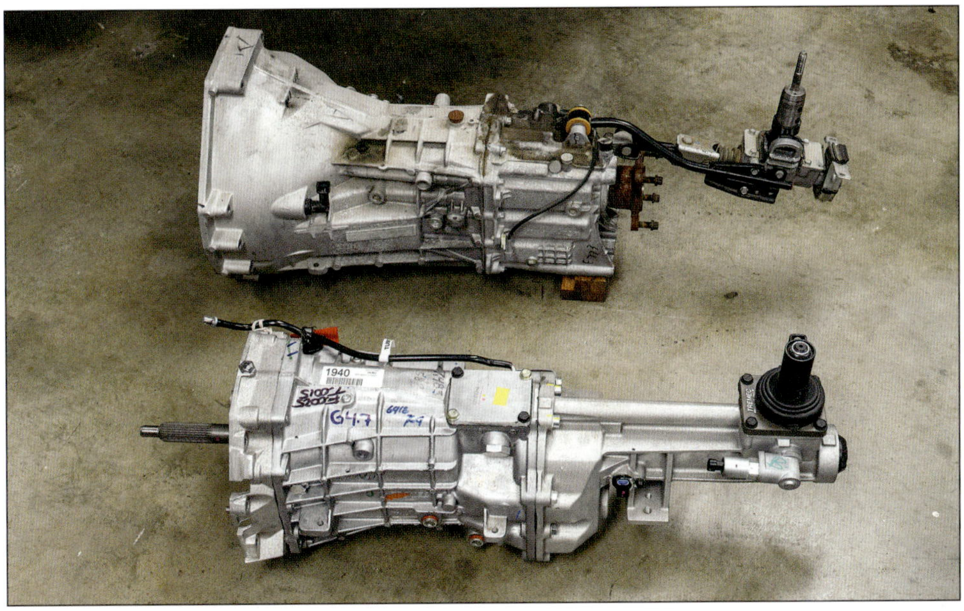

**11** *With the MT82 (top) removed, the physical differences between it and the Tremec Magnum XL (bottom) are clear. Note how the MT82 has an integrated aluminum bellhousing, while the Tremec Magnum uses a separate bellhousing. The separate bellhousing eases installation and means a safer steel housing is an option. Also, the troublesome remote shifter on the MT82 is easily distinguishable from the fully transmission-mounted Magnum shifter.*

**12** *Continue the process by removing the factory clutch assembly.*

**13** *Next, remove the factory nodular-iron flywheel.*

**14** *The OEM clutch and flywheel assembly (left) weighs 47.4 pounds, while the Exedy twin disc (right) weighs 40.0 pounds. Besides weighing less, the Exedy clutch assembly's diameter is slightly smaller than the factory clutch, which makes the moment of inertia of the Exedy clutch lower than the factory setup. This benefits throttle response and aids engine acceleration.*

**15** *Replace the factory bellhousing plate with the laser-cut steel piece that Tremec includes with the Magnum XL kit.*

**16** *Next, install the Exedy steel flywheel using the factory bolts, which are torqued to 63 ft-lbs. Note that you can use a scrap piece of metal and a bellhousing bolt to keep the flywheel from spinning during assembly.*

**17** *Using the supplied alignment tool to center the disc, bolt the Exedy twin-disc clutch to the flywheel and sequentially tighten the cover bolts in a crisscross pattern. The final torque specification is 17 to 24 ft-lbs.*

**18** *Next, install the steel bellhousing. The kit includes spacers that go over the dowel pins on either side. The left spacer is drilled on-center.*

**19** *On the right side, the offset spacer fits over the dowel to clear the bellhousing.*

**20** *Torque the bellhousing bolts to 31 to 40 ft-lbs.*

**21** *Pour three of the four required quarts of Dexron III automatic transmission fluid into the transmission before installing it to minimize how much fluid you will have to pump once the transmission is installed.*

**22** *Transfer the clutch slave cylinder and spacer from the MT82 transmission to the Tremec Magnum XL using the factory bolts.*

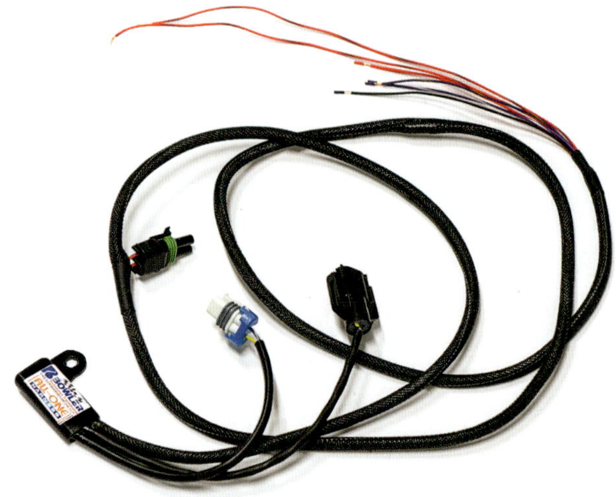

**23** *To get the Magnum XL to communicate with the 2012 Mustang's electrical system, use Bowler Transmissions' all-in-one harness module (part number T56-RLM). The Bowler harness module converts the signal from the Magnum XL's 12 pulses-per-revolution speed sensor to the MT82's 34 pulses-per-revolution output. It also uses the speed signal to operate the reverse lock-out solenoid. The outputs and functions are configurable using a free smartphone app.*

**24** *Plug the Bowler Transmissions all-in-one harness into the speed sensor, reverse lock-out solenoid, and backup light switch. The module mounts to the speed-sensor retaining bolt.*

**25** *Load the Magnum XL transmission on the transmission cradle, roll it under the car, and raise it up into place.*

**26** *The top bolt on the right side can be challenging to access. An option is to use two swivels so that the tool can jog around the transmission case.*

**27** *Torque the transmission-to-bellhousing bolts to 31 to 40 ft-lbs.*

**28** *Next, install the included transmission mount.*

**29** *Modern Driveline sent us a one-piece aluminum driveshaft made by Dynotech. It features a billet steel slip yoke and is 57-percent lighter than the factory steel shaft.*

**30** *The Dynotech driveshaft attaches to the differential with this one-piece, precision-machined flange adapter.*

**31** *Snap the center console cover back into place and install the Tremec shifter handle and knob.*

## 2011-2014 Mustang GT
## Bowler All-In-One Module for Tremec Magnum XL Conversion Wiring

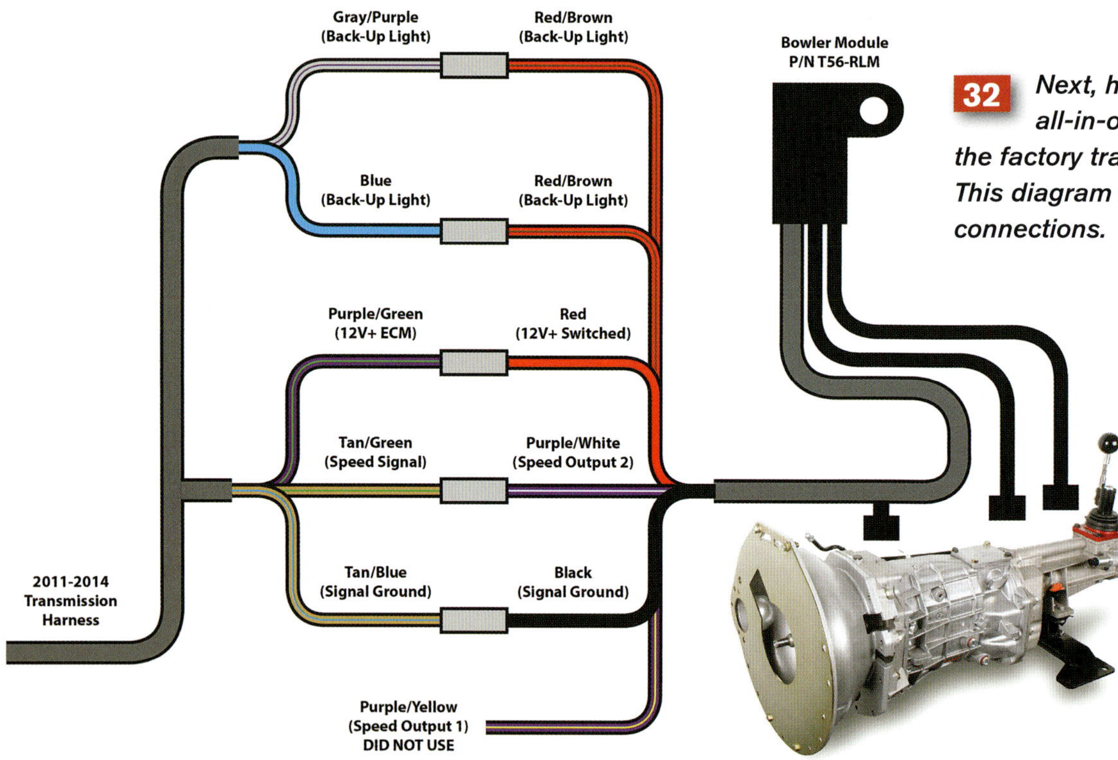


**32** *Next, hook up the Bowler all-in-one harness module to the factory transmission harness. This diagram shows the connections.*

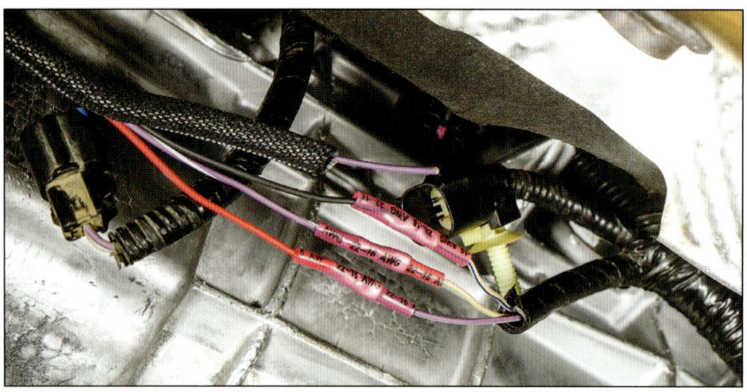

**33** *Cut the factory speed sensor connector off and splice the wires from the Bowler module to the factory harness using heat-shrink butt connectors. Use a harness loom and tape to tidy up the wiring.*

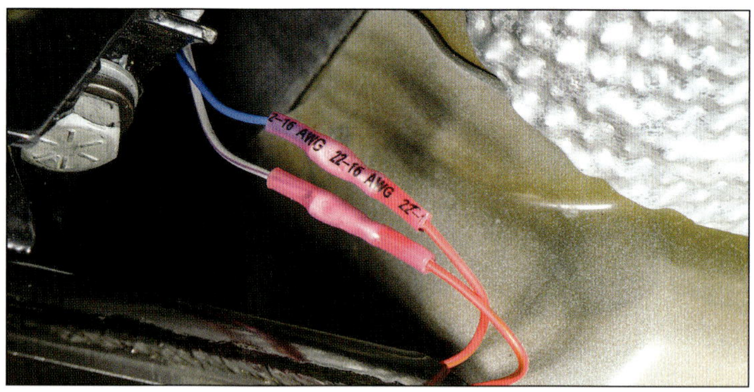

**34** *The backup light switch wiring is a simple affair. Cut off the factory switch connector and splice it to the appropriate wires on the Bowler harness. It's a simple switch, so there's no wrong way to connect the wires.*

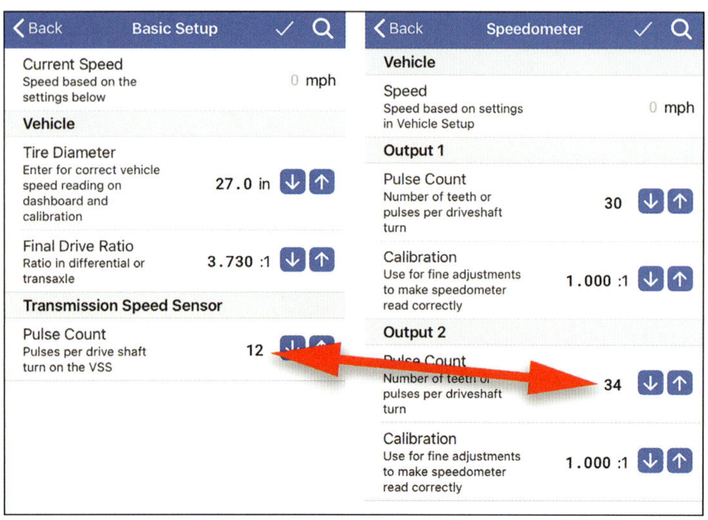


**35** *With the car back together, we connected our smart phone to the Bowler module using the module's WiFi feature. Note how we set the transmission speed sensor to 12 counts in the basic setup tab and configured Output 2 to 34 pulses per revolution. This made our speedometer read correctly.*

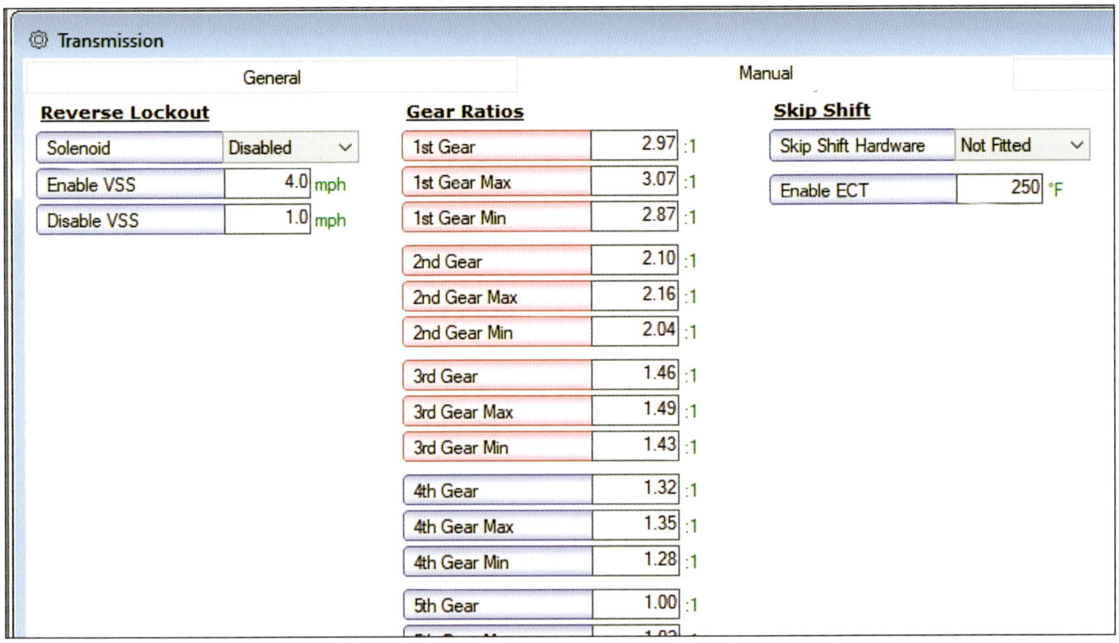


**36** *The PCM also uses the gear ratios for calculations, including cruise control, so we used the HPtuners VCM Editor to revise the ratios to reflect our Magnum XL transmission.*

| PCM Transmission Ratios | | | | |
|---|---|---|---|---|
| | **MT 82** | **Tolerance** | **Magnum XL (TUKT12021)** | **Tolerance** |
| **1st Gear** | 3.66 | 1.000 | 2.970 | 1.000 |
| 1st Gear Max | 3.81 | 1.041 | 3.074 | 1.035 |
| 1st Gear Min | 3.51 | 0.959 | 2.866 | 0.965 |
| **2nd Gear** | 2.43 | 1.000 | 2.100 | 1.000 |
| 2nd Gear Max | 2.51 | 1.033 | 2.163 | 1.030 |
| 2nd Gear Min | 2.35 | 0.967 | 2.037 | 0.970 |
| **3rd Gear** | 1.69 | 1.000 | 1.460 | 1.000 |
| 3rd Gear Max | 1.73 | 1.024 | 1.489 | 1.020 |
| 3rd Gear Min | 1.64 | 0.970 | 1.431 | 0.980 |
| **4th Gear** | 1.32 | 1.000 | 1.000 | 1.000 |
| 4th Gear Max | 1.35 | 1.023 | 1.020 | 1.020 |
| 4th Gear Min | 1.28 | 0.970 | 0.980 | 0.980 |
| **5th Gear** | 1.00 | 1.000 | 0.800 | 1.000 |
| 5th Gear Max | 1.02 | 1.020 | 0.812 | 1.015 |
| 5th Gear Min | 0.98 | 0.980 | 0.788 | 0.985 |
| **6th Gear** | 0.65 | 1.000 | 0.630 | 1.000 |
| 6th Gear Max | 0.66 | 1.015 | 0.643 | 1.020 |
| 6th Gear Min | 0.64 | 0.985 | 0.617 | 0.980 |
| **Reverse** | 3.32 | 1.000 | 2.900 | 1.000 |
| Reverse Max | 3.43 | 1.033 | 2.987 | 1.030 |
| Reverse Min | 3.20 | 0.964 | 2.813 | 0.970 |

Each ratio has a minimum and maximum value in the PCM, so we used a spreadsheet to apply the factory ratio tolerance to the Magnum XL gear-ratio values and enter them into the PCM.

CHAPTER 6

# Bolt-On Power Upgrades

Since factors including noise, long-term durability, and (most notably) cost, can compromise ultimate performance, Ford engineers did a great job squeezing a lot of performance from the 3.7- and 5.0-liter engines. Consider that the same five liters of displacement in a 1993 Mustang yields nearly twice the horsepower in 2011. While the powerplants of modern Mustangs aren't as handicapped from the factory as their older brethren, there's still low-hanging fruit for performance aftermarket companies to pluck.

All engines are glorified air pumps, so most bolt-on performance upgrades strive to increase cylinder filling by removing restrictions from the intake and exhaust. However, bigger isn't always better, especially when it comes to exhaust systems.

## Air Intake Systems

Engines need to breathe, so if there's a restriction in the intake system, performance suffers. There are a few reasons why most factory Mustang intake systems have restrictions. First, reducing the intrusion of dust, debris, and water is essential to extend air filter change intervals. Second, intake noise can be a problem for factory engineers, so stock intake systems are often designed to minimize intake growl.

These factors often compromise factory intake systems to the point where installing a freer-breathing intake setup can yield significant results. A note of clarification: "intake systems" generally refers to ducting upstream of the throttle body, whereas "intake manifolds" distribute the air downstream of the throttle body to each cylinder.

Because intake systems are fairly simple and relatively inexpensive, there are dozens of air-intake manufacturers. Air-intake systems are available for both 3.7L V-6 and 5.0L V-8 engines. While no one manufacturer is a standout in this field, there are a few things to consider when choosing an intake system.

### *Filter Shape and Material*

There are many different filter shapes, including cone, flat panel, and cylindrical. No shape is better than another, as the airflow restriction of a filter is only a function of its material and surface area. Some conical and cylindrical filters incorporate a velocity stack that smooths airflow into the tube.

Filters are made from paper, foam, and fabric gauze. Paper is the most restrictive and therefore requires more surface area to flow comparably to foam or fabric gauze.

Under no circumstances should no filter be used. Taking a look at the debris in the bottom of a factory air box demonstrates what an engine can ingest if run without a filter! If the filter is too much of a restriction, use a better-flowing filter.

### *Cold-Air Intakes*

Cooler air is denser air, which increases horsepower. Avoid systems that don't shield the air filter from engine-compartment heat.

### *Tuning*

Some intake systems increase the cross-sectional area at the mass airflow (MAF) sensor location over factory specifications, which increases the ultimate flow capacity of the tube. As long as the additional flow is within a certain limit, the Mustang's powertrain control module (PCM) will read the wideband oxygen sensors and inject additional fuel to compensate. However, if the fuel needed exceeds the window of adjustment,

Steeda's intake system (part number 555-3190) includes a sleeve that reduces the throat diameter past the MAF, so a tune isn't required. The sleeve is removed when the owner is ready to retune the PCM for additional power gains. (Photo Courtesy Steeda)

The iNTECH system from Holley for the 2011–2014 Mustang GT (part number 223-04) features a unique downward-facing conical filter housed in an enclosure that utilizes the factory cold-air feed and is completely sealed from the engine compartment. The tubing is sized so that it doesn't require tuning of the PCM. (Photo Courtesy Holley)

the PCM must be retuned. Most intake system makers will specify if a tune is required, but if in doubt, check with the manufacturer.

### Gains

Air-intake systems that don't require a tune add about 15 hp and 15 ft-lbs of torque over a broad range. Adding a tune to the mix muddies the waters on intake-only gains, but nearly 30 hp is typical on 5.0L V-8s. Gains for V-6 systems that don't require a tune are more modest.

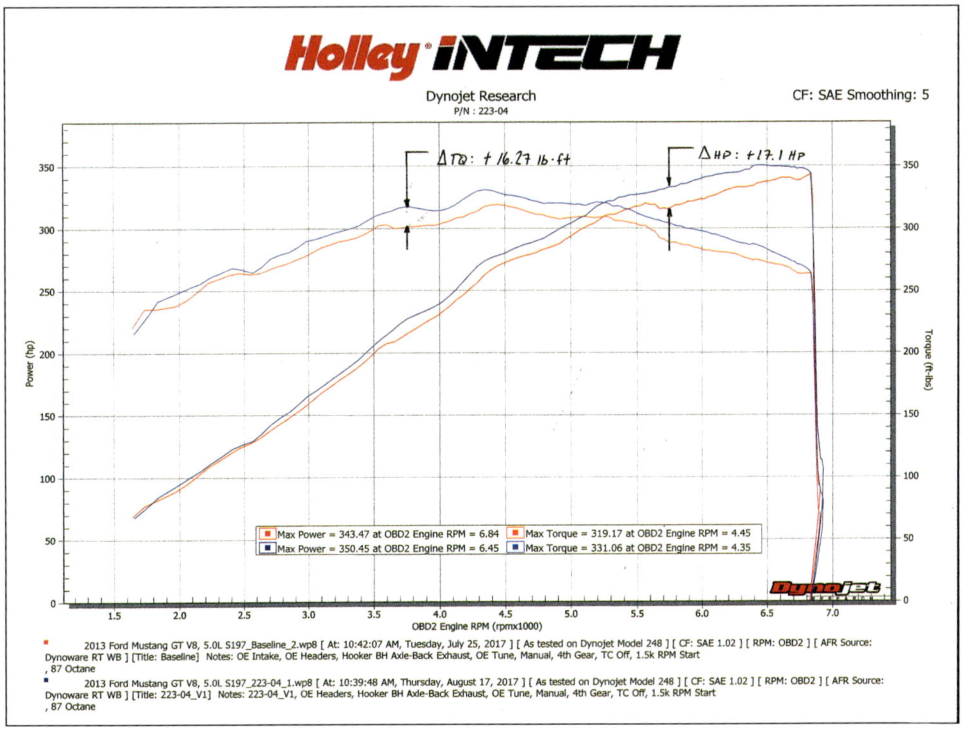


The performance gains from the Holley iNTECH intake system (part number 223-04) are pretty solid for a system that doesn't require a tune. Holley's testing found maximum gains of 17 hp and 16 ft-lbs of torque to the rear wheels. (Photo Courtesy Holley)

Mustangs equipped with the 3.7L V-6 can also benefit from a performance-minded air-intake system, such as this Delta Force Performance air intake (part number 615146) from Flowmaster, which adds about 10 hp and doesn't require a PCM tune. (Photo Courtesy Flowmaster)

*Ford Performance Parts' 90-mm throttle body for 2011–2014 5.0L V-8s (part number M-9926-M5090) is a direct replacement for the factory 80-mm unit. Ford claims it flows 1,132 cfm, whereas the stock unit flows 913 cfm. Installation on a factory GT or Boss 302 manifold requires a spacer specific to each manifold (also available from Ford Performance Parts) because the manifolds' openings are designed for 80-mm throttle bodies. (Photo Courtesy Ford Performance Parts)*

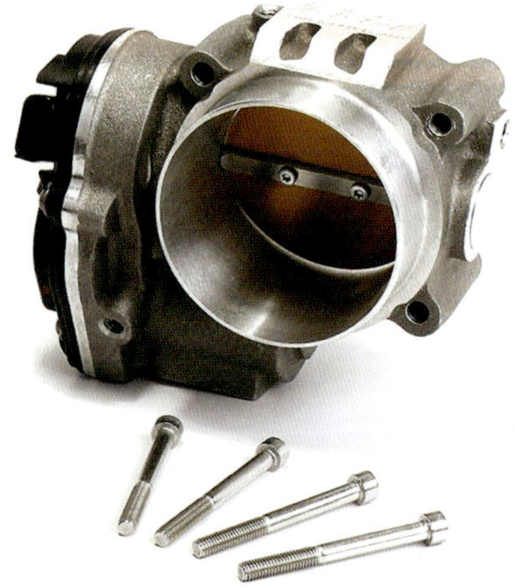

*Larger throttle bodies are also available for 3.7L V-6 engines. BBK claims that its 73-mm throttle body (part number 1822) adds 15 hp, is 50-state legal, and doesn't require any tuning or PCM modifications. (Photo Courtesy BBK)*

## Throttle Bodies

The throttle body controls the air entering the engine. All 2005-to-current Mustang throttle bodies are "drive by wire", which means that there is no mechanical linkage between the gas pedal and the throttle body. Rather, the PCM controls the throttle body based upon inputs from the throttle pedal. This method has several benefits, including eliminating the idle-control circuit, reduced emissions, and throttle response that can be tuned via the PCM.

The factory throttle bodies on 3.7L V-6 and 5.0L V-8 engines are 68 mm and 80 mm, respectively. They easily support most naturally aspirated horsepower levels and most blow-through boosted combinations. Draw-through (most positive-displacement superchargers) applications are the main ones that benefit from larger throttle bodies.

### Size

Throttle-body size is limited by the throat of the intake manifold and the diameter of the intake tube. Adding a throttle body that's larger than the intake manifold or the intake tube can negate the bigger throttle body's benefits. In addition, installing an unnecessarily large throttle body can make the throttle response touchy (just off idle) because the larger throttle blade flows significantly more air than a smaller one when first cracked open. This makes the larger throttle body feel faster, but the dynamometer may say otherwise.

### Shape

All factory 3.7L and 5.0L Mustang manifolds have round throttle-body openings, although the Ford Racing Performance Parts Cobra Jet manifold requires an oval throttle body.

### Throttle Body Spacers

Adding plenum volume via a throttle-body spacer sometimes yields a few horsepower. Some spacers have features that are designed to tumble or twist the incoming air to increase airflow. However, the actual effects are subtle and hard to quantify.

### Gains

Larger throttle bodies vary in effectiveness with different intake and/or boosted applications, but don't expect gains over 10 hp on mostly stock naturally aspirated engines. Because the PCM's electronic throttle control is specific to the factory throttle body, the engine's PCM must be tuned for any aftermarket throttle body.

*Steeda offers a throttle-body spacer (part number 555 3163) for 5.0L-equipped Mustangs. Besides adding plenum volume, the spacer is shaped to break the aerodynamic surface boundary layer to increase airflow into the intake manifold. (Photo Courtesy Steeda)*

## Intake Manifolds

Factory intake-manifold designs have improved by leaps and bounds in recent decades—so much so that

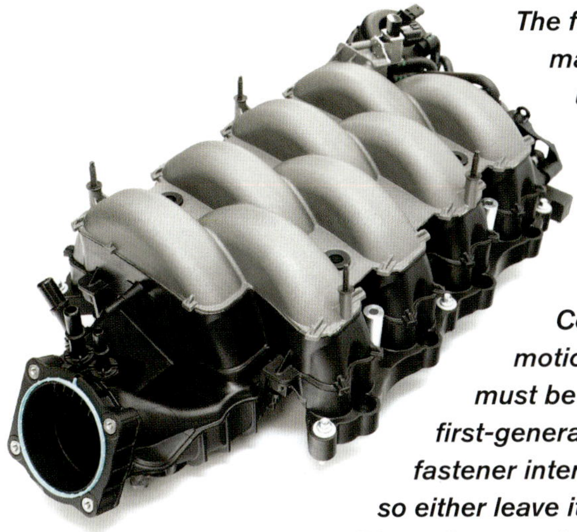

The factory 2018 Mustang GT intake manifold is a surprisingly effective upgrade from the 2011–2014 Mustang GT manifold. Even though it's a spitting image for the stocker, power and torque rival that of the best aftermarket intakes. To fit on 2011–2014 Coyotes, the 2018's intake-charge motion-control valve actuators must be removed and locked out. The first-generation Coyote's back water-neck fastener interferes with the manifold slightly, so either leave it out or install a 2015–2017 water neck. (Photo Courtesy Late Model Restoration)

The Boss 302 intake manifold (part number M-9424-M50BR) is a race-inspired piece from Ford, and it looks the part. Where the factory manifold is tuned for power below 6,000 rpm, the Boss 302's shorter runners enhance power past 6,000 rpm (albeit at the expense of some low-RPM torque). It's a direct replacement for the factory manifold. (Photo Courtesy Late Model Restoration)

it's hard to beat the stock manifold's broad torque curve for everyday road use. That's not to say that higher peak gains can't be made or that the engine's usable RPM range can't be extended.

Provided that the factory manifold isn't restrictive, different manifold designs involve trade-offs. Peak power gains are often made at the expense of low-end torque and response, and vice versa. The goal of a well-designed intake manifold is to enhance cylinder filling over the RPM range desired.

### Runner Size

One variable that impacts cylinder filling is the velocity of the air moving through the intake manifold runner. A skinny runner will have a faster rushing column of air to fill the cylinder. This promotes mixture swirl and enhances pressure-wave tuning, both of which add power. However, a runner that's too small can restrict airflow at high RPM. In general, intake manifolds with smaller runners make better low-end power than manifolds with large runners. Good intake manifolds have runners that gradually taper down in cross section from their entrance to where they approach the intake valve.

### Runner Length

When the intake valves open and close, they create a pressure wave that travels back up the intake runner. When that wave reaches the end of the runner, it bounces back toward the intake valve. Like waves in a Slinky, these waves bounce back and forth, and if the pressure waves reach the intake valves at the right time, these waves help to ram more air into the cylinders.

As with a musical instrument, an intake manifold's runners have a resonant frequency related to their length that affects the timing of the pressure waves. Longer runners resonate at lower frequencies, which increases low-end power, and shorter runners resonate at higher frequencies, which adds power higher in the RPM range. Even if ultimate power isn't improved, shorter-runner intake manifolds can extend the usability of a road-race engine as torque doesn't fall off as quickly after peak power,

Ford's Cobra Jet manifold (part number M-9424-M50CJA) improves on the Boss 302 design by increasing high-RPM power without sacrificing low-end torque. It's the hot ticket for serious Coyote performance. However, its oval throttle-body flange requires a matching throttle body and intake tube, which adds to the upgrade cost.

*Edelbrock's Victor 2 Modular Ford 5.0L Coyote intake manifold (part number 7180) offers similar gains to the Cobra Jet but uses stock or aftermarket round throttle bodies. Edelbrock claims 27 ft-lbs of torque over the Boss 302 manifold and 16 hp over the stock manifold. It's cast from aluminum and features nitrous nozzle bosses and withstands high boost pressures. The factory fuel rails and all emissions provisions are retained. (Photo Courtesy Edelbrock)*

*Once reserved for custom race applications, Holley offers its Sniper EFI Race Series intake as a direct replacement for the factory manifold on 2011–2014 Mustang GTs. The sheet-metal construction opens up possibilities, such as nitrous injector installation, burst plates, and other custom inlet options. It features a 90-mm throttle bore opening and a large intake plenum for serious naturally aspirated and high boost applications and includes 3/8-inch billet fuel rails. Holley advertises an operating range of 2,100–8,200 rpm. (Photo Courtesy Holley)*

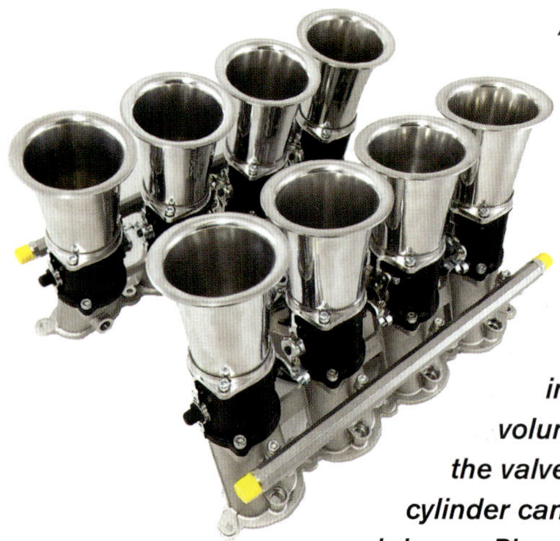

*An individual throttle body (ITB) system, such as this one from Jenvey Dynamics, offers nearly instant throttle response. In a single throttle body and plenum arrangement, air entering the throttle body must first fill the plenum before reaching each cylinder. In contrast, an ITB system places a throttle body inside each cylinder's runner, which greatly reduces the volume that the air must fill before reaching the valve. In addition, the runner length of each cylinder can be tuned individually via replaceable air horns. Plenums can be added for forced-induction applications. (Photo Courtesy Jenvey Dynamics Ltd.)*

and drivers can "hold a gear" longer rather than upshifting and then downshifting through certain sections of the race track.

#### *Plenum Volume*

Most intake manifolds have a single plenum from which each intake runner draws. The plenum is fed by the throttle body. Although it's not to the degree that runner length affects power, plenum volume also impacts performance: more plenum volume enhances top-end power, and less plenum volume boosts low-end torque. Individual throttle body (ITB) intakes, where each cylinder has its own throttle body, have an infinitely large plenum volume in that each runner draws from open atmosphere.

### Headers

In their simplest form, exhaust manifolds (headers) collect the exhaust gasses from each cylinder and combine them into a single exhaust tube for each cylinder bank. However, there's a lot of unused energy in each exhaust pulse, and if designed correctly, headers can harness the energy from these pulses to increase volumetric efficiency and, consequently, engine power. This effect is called scavenging, which is using the exhaust pulse energy from each cylinder to pull the exhaust from it and other cylinders. There are two components to effective exhaust scavenging: inertia and tuning. Exhaust-header design leverages these factors via primary tube length, primary tube diameter, and collector design.

#### *Primary Tube Length*

Rather than a constant stream, the exhaust gasses from each cylinder travel down the primary tube in pulses. Behind each exhaust pulse is negative pressure (recall the Slinky?). The inertia of the exhaust pulse traveling down the tube can help draw a fresh intake charge into the cylinder before the exhaust valve closes and after the intake valve opens (valve overlap).

Besides inertia, exhaust pulses produce a sonic wave, which is what makes them loud. These waves travel down the tube faster than the speed of sound, and when they reach the end of the primary tube, they produce a reflective wave that travels back up to the exhaust valve. If timed correctly, this wave reaches the exhaust valve as it reopens for the next cycle, further drawing exhaust from the cylinder.

Like a pipe organ, the length of the primary tubes from each cylinder to the collector determine the resonant frequency (RPM) at which both inertial and sonic waves scavenge exhaust from the cylinder. In practical terms, primary tubes should be around 30 inches for most applications. In the real world, a header primary that's too long will perform better than a header that's too short.

Header designers will try and equalize the primary tube lengths to maximize performance at a specific engine speed. However, primary tubes that are slightly different lengths can help broaden the torque curve as each cylinder operates at peak scavenging at a slightly different engine speed. So, headers don't have to be perfectly equal length to work well.

Headers for Mustangs are often lumped into two categories: shorty and long tube. The terms refer to the length of the primary tubes as a result of the design. Shorty headers are usually designed as a direct replacement for the factory manifolds, whereas long-tube headers have primary tubes that are of the proper length to provide inertial and wave-tuned scavenging. However, long-tube headers eliminate or replace the factory catalytic converters, which makes them a race-only upgrade.

### *Primary Tube Diameter*

Choosing a primary-tube diameter is striking a balance between inertial scavenging and resistance to flow. Small tubes increase the velocity of each exhaust pulse, which increases inertial scavenging, but a primary tube that's too small can restrict exhaust flow. Larger-displacement and higher-horsepower engines respond better to larger primary tubes, while smaller primary tubes are more effective on smaller-displacement engines. Tuners have found that 1¾-inch primary headers work best on most naturally aspirated and mildly supercharged engines, whereas larger-displacement and highly-boosted engines can benefit from a 1⅞-inch, or in extreme cases, a 2-inch primary header. With header primary diameter, it's better to err on the side of a smaller diameter than a larger one.

Just as the negative pressure wave is reflected back up the primary tube when the exhaust pulse reaches the collector, more waves can be generated if the primary tube diameter steps up along the way to the collector. Stepped primaries increase the primary tube diameter in small increments once or twice before the end of the tube to affect scavenging. If the steps are placed so that their refracted waves amplify the large wave, scavenging at that engine speed is enhanced. Alternatively, the steps can be positioned so that their refracted waves enhance scavenging at other engine speeds, which can broaden an engine's torque curve.

### *Collector Size and Design*

The scavenging effects of each primary tube can be enhanced when they're gathered together. That's where the header collector comes in. The inertia from the exhaust gas pulse from one cylinder creates a negative pressure ahead of the exhaust pulses in surrounding primaries inside the collector.

These secondary tuning effects boost low-end torque and are affected by collector size and design. Like primary tube diameter, a smaller collector diameter increases exhaust velocity (and therefore, inertial scavenging) at the risk of increasing exhaust flow restriction.

Merge collectors have an hourglass shape and further improve inertial scavenging but minimize the reflected sonic wave. This helps broaden the power curve at the expense of peak power figures.

When it comes to choosing a header, don't sweat the collector too much. For most applications, primary tube length and diameter have a greater effect on engine performance than collector size and design.

### *Material and Coatings*

Selecting a header material is mostly a balance between cost and longevity. Most headers for the Mustang aftermarket are made from mild steel or stainless steel (usually 409 or 304 grades). Uncoated mild-steel headers are susceptible to rust, but they're the least expensive. The 409 stainless-steel grade is a good step up from mild steel; 409 stainless is slightly more expensive than

*The factory tubular headers are proof positive that car guy culture is alive and well inside Ford. Legend has it that after countless tubular designs didn't meet design criteria, the Coyote team was ready to pull the trigger on a cast manifold. An engineer was determined to make a tubular manifold work, so he fabricated a prototype of this concept over a weekend in his home garage. It passed the tests and made it to production. Astute enthusiasts will recognize that the Coyote's horsepower rating was increased from 412 to 425 in 2013. The tubular headers were such a late addition that they weren't used on the 2011-model-year test engines, which had cast exhaust manifolds. Ford's bean counters wanted to keep the cast manifolds, but the Mustang's chief engineer told them to pound sand, and the tubular shorty headers were used. Not only did the headers add 13 hp but they also were a hit with the media, which was more than worth the cost hit.*

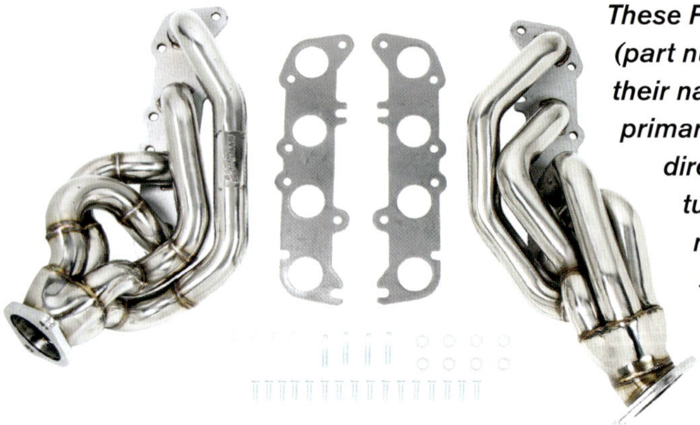

*These Flowtech shorty headers (part number 12141FLT) derive their name from their short primary tubes. Shorty headers directly replace the factory tubular manifolds and connect to the stock exhaust system. Although the short primaries compromise scavenging benefits, Flowtech's design does an admirable job of equalizing the tube lengths within the packaging constraints. The $1\frac{7}{8}$-inch primaries feed a true 4-into-1 collector, which is an improvement over the factory manifold. Expect gains of around 10 hp from shorty headers. (Photo Courtesy Flowtech)*

*Long-tube headers utilize longer primary tubes that provide inertial and wave tuning benefits in the RPM range where most engines operate. However, since most eliminate or replace the factory catalytic converters, they're not designed for road use. These Flowtech long-tube headers (part number 32139FLT) feature primaries that step from $1\frac{3}{4}$ inch to $1\frac{7}{8}$ inch to further enhance wave tuning effects. Increases of 20 hp and 20 ft-lbs of torque with long-tube headers is common. (Photo Courtesy Flowtech)*

mild steel but only develops surface rust, which doesn't affect the structural integrity of the part. (Automotive manufacturers recognized this and now use cost-effective stainless steels, such as 409, to increase exhaust-system life while minimizing cost.) The 304 stainless-steel grade is popular in the aftermarket because, although it's more expensive than other materials, it maintains its shiny appearance after years of use.

Most header tubing is made from 16-gauge and 18-gauge material. The thinner 18-gauge tubing is lighter but harder to weld and bend.

Ceramic coating is a popular option for headers and can dramatically increase the corrosion resistance of mild steel headers. Ceramic coating has insulative proprieties, purportedly lowering under-hood temperatures and increasing power by keeping heat energy inside the header. While most ceramic coatings are applied more for appearance, some thick coatings (popularized by Swain Tech Coatings) are thicker to increase the coating's effects.

### Tuning

The S197's Copperhead PCM utilizes wideband oxygen sensors that monitor the air/fuel ratio and allow the PCM to make adjustments—even at wide-open throttle. Historically, long-tube headers required the PCM to be reprogrammed because the

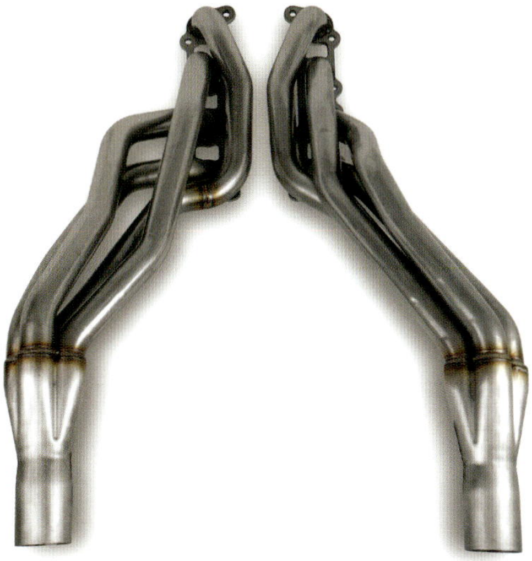

*An example of higher-end headers are these Hooker offerings. They feature 1¾ 4-inch primaries (70103303-RHKR) or 1⅞-inch primaries (70103302-RHKR) and are constructed of 304 stainless steel in a lighter, 18-gauge thickness. The 3 inch incorporates a merge-style hourglass shape to improve exhaust velocity. They mate to Hooker's exhaust systems. (Photo Courtesy Hooker)*

*V-6 Mustangs benefit from headers just like their V-8 brethren. JBA's shorty headers for V-6 Mustangs (part number 1618S) feature 1⅝-inch primaries and a large fire-cone collector to increase flow over the factory manifolds. (Photo Courtesy JBA)*

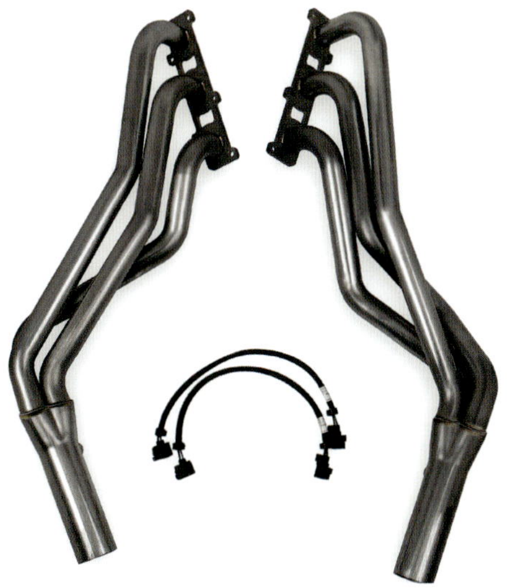

*Hooker's long-tube headers for 3.7L Mustangs (part number 70103306-RHKR) bring the benefits of proper-length primaries to V-6 Mustangs. They're made from 304 stainless steel and feature 1⅝-inch primary tubes and 18-gauge construction. Note the included oxygen sensor harness extensions since the oxygen sensors are located in the 2½-inch collectors. (Photo Courtesy Hooker)*

oxygen sensors are usually located in the collector, which is farther away from the engine than with the factory manifolds. This delayed the feedback to the mixture changes that the oxygen sensors provided, which confused the PCM. The 2011–2014 Mustang's PCM learns this delay, so generally exhaust changes don't require PCM changes, even with long-tube headers.

## Mid-Pipes

Connecting the headers to the rest of the exhaust system is a section that many call the mid-pipe. Besides the catalysts, the mid-pipe usually incorporates a crossover, or balance tube, and a resonator. Resonators mellow out the exhaust tone and reduce interior resonance.

### *Design*

The exhaust pulses from each cylinder bank on a V-8 engine alternate as the engine rotates. On a cross-plane crank V-8, the left (L) and right (R) cylinder banks fire in this order: R, R, L, R, L, L, R, L. Just as with a header, exhaust pulses from one cylinder bank can be used to scavenge the exhaust from the other bank. The shape of the crossover, or balance tube, usually contributes to the nickname of the mid-pipe (such as H-pipe, X-pipe, or Y-pipe).

**Exhaust Tube Diameters**

| Tubing Diameter (inches) | Single-Exhaust Recommended Horsepower Limit | Dual-Exhaust Recommended Horsepower Limit |
|---|---|---|
| 2.25 | 150 | 250 |
| 2.50 | 200 | 400 |
| 3.00 | 250 | 500 |
| 3.50 | 350 | 700 |
| 4.00 | 425 | 850 |
| 4.50 | 500 | 1,000 |
| 5.00 | More than 500 | More than 1,000 |

This is a guide for selecting the minimum exhaust system tubing diameter based upon engine horsepower. (Note that the Coyote's factory horsepower rating is 412, and the stock exhaust system is made from 2.75-inch tubing.)

#### *Tubing Diameter*

The primary concern regarding exhaust tubing diameter is resistance to flow (commonly called back pressure). However, choosing an exhaust system that's too large can reduce exhaust velocity and hurt low-end power. (Turbocharged exhaust systems are the exception to this rule, as the pressure differential across the turbine directly affects boost. From a performance standpoint, an ideal exhaust system after a turbo is no exhaust system.) Besides torque loss, clearance between the ground and other components is a concern with large-diameter exhaust tubing.

## Axle-Back Exhaust

S197-chassis Mustangs have a joint between the exhaust system's over-axle bends and the mufflers, which makes a muffler swap a simple bolt-on affair. Many aftermarket companies offer replacement mufflers as "axle-back" exhaust systems that replace everything from the axle back to the exhaust tip.

#### *Design*

Two major strategies reduce exhaust noise: cancellation and absorption. Cancellation mufflers use geometry and acoustics to cancel out undesirable sound frequencies, while absorption mufflers use packing material to soak up unwanted noise. Factory mufflers usually use a combination of absorption and cancellation technology to achieve their sound goals.

#### *Tubing Diameter*

Just as in the design of the rest of the exhaust system, muffler diameter affects velocity and back pressure. The rule of thumb shown in the Exhaust Tube Diameters table still applies. However, if the muffler is restrictive, placing it as far downstream from the engine as possible minimizes performance loss.

#### *Gains*

Most modern axle-back systems are minimally restrictive, so gains between 10 and 20 hp and a like amount of torque are typical.

*An absorption muffler, such as this Flowmaster FlowFX, uses packing material to soak up unwanted sound frequencies. Exhaust flows through a perforated tube that is surrounded by wads of small fibers. Attenuation is directly related to the surface area exposed to the exhaust (size and number of holes in the tube) and amount of packing (size of the muffler case). By nature, these straight-through mufflers absorb higher frequencies and let lower tones pass. (Photo Courtesy Flowmaster)*

*The factory mufflers are very effective, meaning that they are very quiet. They also weigh a lot (22 pounds each). Replacing the factory mufflers is usually the first modification that most Mustang owners make.*

*The ubiquitous chambered Flowmaster muffler uses sound-cancellation technology to reduce unwanted noise. The exhaust flows through chambers and around plates that reflect specific sound waves that crash together and cancel each other out. The result is a distinctive, metallic tone that is unique to this type of muffler. (Photo Courtesy Flowmaster)*

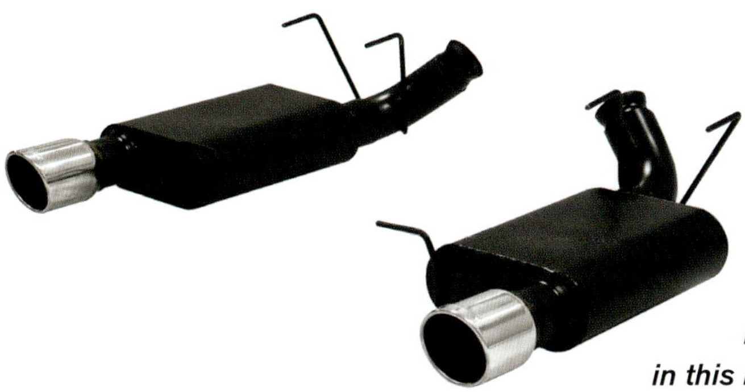

*Flowmaster's American Thunder axle-back exhaust system for 2011–2014 Mustang GTs (part number 817496) features its classic chambered mufflers (Super 44 series in this kit) with 3-inch tubing and polished 4-inch tips. The V-6 Mustangs are served via Flowmaster part number 817497. (Photo Courtesy Flowmaster)*

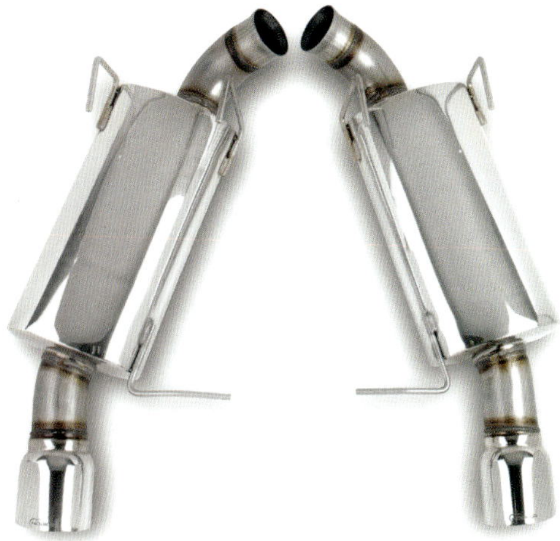

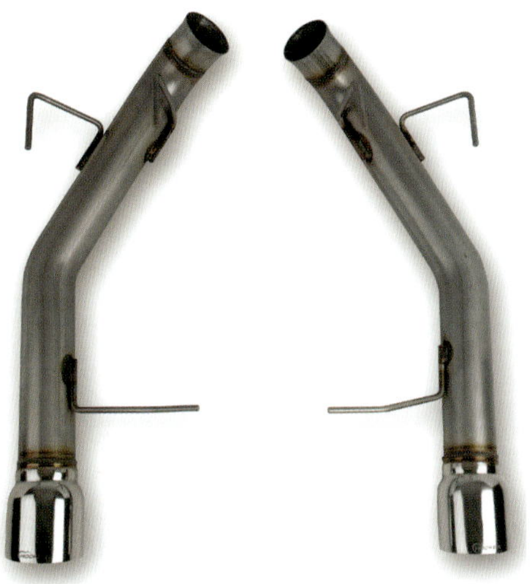

*Another option for a muffler is to have none at all. Hooker Blackheart's non-muffled axle-back system (part number 70403301-RHKR for the GT, part number 70403310-RHKR for the V-6) eliminates the rear mufflers entirely. If the factory catalytic converters and exhaust system remain in place, the result isn't as loud as one might expect.*

*The most common type of axle-back system for 2011–2014 Mustangs features absorption mufflers, such as this Hooker Blackheart system (part number 70403302-RHKR). Hooker's offering features 3-inch tubing, a 4-inch tip, and 304 stainless-steel construction. The V-6 systems have 2½-inch tubing and are available as part number 70403311-RHKR. (Photo Courtesy Hooker)*

## Handheld Tuners

The PCM orchestrates all aspects of the engine and transmission operation. Known internally as the Copperhead PCM, it's an extremely sophisticated system. To make sure that all Mustangs that roll off the assembly line work properly and safely under a wide range of conditions and scenarios, Ford's calibration engineers must make compromises. While these compromises provide a safety factor for the manufacturer, they create opportunities for individual tuners to change the performance characteristics of the engine to better meet the expectations of enthusiasts. There's usually some wiggle room in the calibration where tuners can nudge the fuel mixture, spark advance, and camshaft position closer to optimum performance. This is especially true with tunes calibrated for fuel higher than 87 octane.

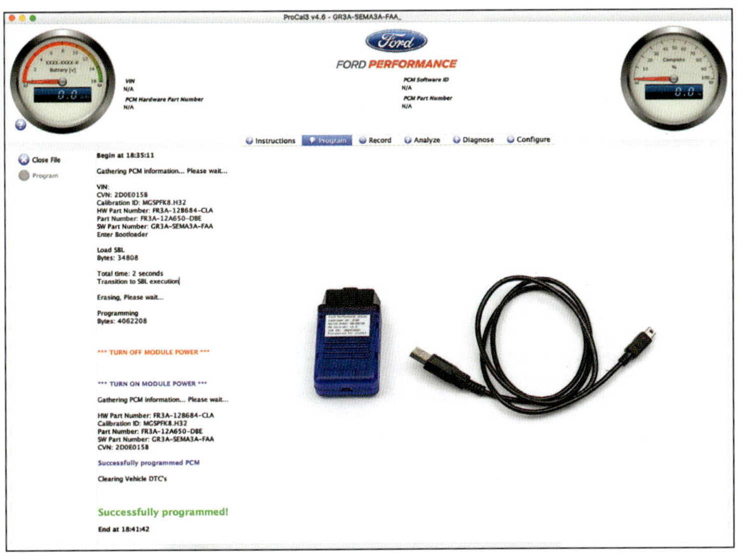


*Arguably, no one knows Ford's Copperhead PCM better than those who created it. While it's pretty straightforward to add power at wide-open-throttle, the sophisticated torque-based calculations severely complicate part-throttle drivability results. Ford Performance Parts unleashed Ford's skilled calibrators and extensive engineering resources to optimize the performance of its vehicles without shortcutting drivability, catalytic-converter longevity, or emissions compliance. Some of Ford Performance Parts' ProCal tunes are 50-state legal and even come with a warranty when installed by a Ford dealer.*

*DiabloSport's Trinity T2 Platinum is an advanced performance programmer and monitor that can write preloaded tunes to the PCM, display and log data, and make basic tuning tweaks, including wide-open throttle (WOT) fuel, spark, and camshaft position adjustments. Shift point and firmness changes are also possible on automatic-transmission-equipped cars. The Trinity T2 includes a windshield mount to monitor data in real time. Data logs can be used to transmit results to remote tuners, whose custom tunes can be loaded using the Trinity T2. (Photo Courtesy DiabloSport)*

Several companies offer devices that are preloaded with tunes that are written to the PCM via the on-board diagnostics (OBD-II) port. Ranging from simple loading devices to complex diagnostic tools, these handheld devices don't require a standard laptop computer to operate. Some devices tap into the information available at the OBD-II port to monitor and record the PCM's vital signs. Not only does this allow users to keep tabs on the PCM's inputs and outputs but also recorded information can be sent to remote tuners who modify their calibrations based upon the information gathered.

Besides performance gains, many handheld devices can perform other functions, such as recalibrating the speedometer to compensate for different rear-axle ratios or tire sizes, changing the electronic throttle-control response, modifying cooling-fan operation, disabling traction control, and clearing diagnostic trouble codes.

Peak gains from most preloaded tunes are modest (about 5 percent more horsepower and torque depending upon the fuel octane required).

## How-To Project: Long-Tube Headers and Exhaust System Installation

To maximize horsepower at the track on a high-revving Coyote-powered Mustang, long-tube headers and a free-flowing exhaust are essential. Hooker Blackheart offers headers with 1¾-inch or 1⅞-inch primaries and a complete 3-inch exhaust system for 2011–2014 Mustang GTs. Although they're designed for no-compromise racing applications, the headers and exhaust fit like an OEM setup. The last thing you want when you're elbows deep in a header install is to realize that the headers don't fit well.

We installed Hooker's 1¾-inch headers and 3-inch exhaust (sold as a complete kit via part number VK050006) on an otherwise 100-percent stock 2012 GT. You don't need a fancy lift or exotic tools; we completed the installation with the Mustang on jack stands. The following photos and captions hit the high points and pass along tricks that we learned.

Overall, we were thrilled how well not only the headers fit but also the entire 3-inch exhaust system. Hooker clearly did its homework. The collectors and exhaust tuck up higher than the frame rails so that ground clearance is unaffected, which is welcome

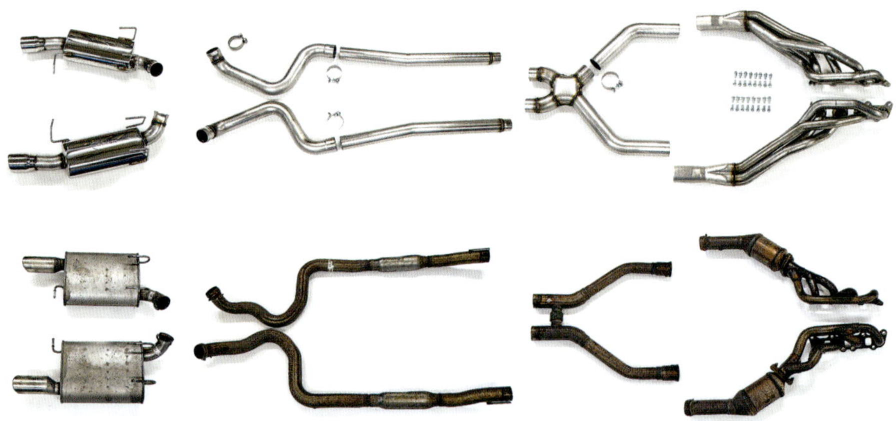

*Designed specifically for racing applications, Hooker's Blackheart exhaust kit (part number VK050006, top) for 2011–2014 Mustang GTs is a complete system that replaces the entire factory exhaust system (bottom) from the cylinder head to the muffler tip. Where the factory system is mainly comprised of 409 stainless steel, the Hooker system is fashioned from 304 lightweight, 18-guage stainless steel. The headers feature 1-3/4-inch primaries and 3-inch collectors that mate to a full 3-inch exhaust system that includes an X-pipe and straight-through mufflers.*

*The headers' thick, one-piece flanges feature TIG welds and hand-blended ports.*

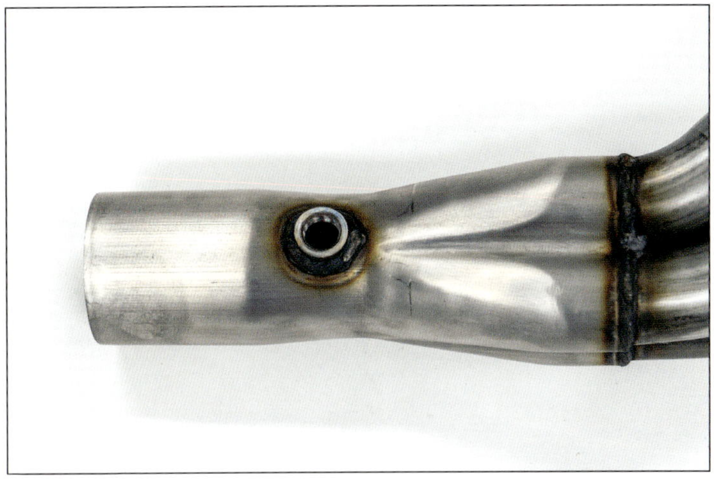

*A merged 3-inch collector features an internal spike and a bung for the factory wideband oxygen sensor.*

news for lowered cars. Even though this system is designed for competition vehicles, the exhaust doesn't sound obnoxious and the dreaded 2,000-rpm interior drone has been eliminated. Back-to-back dyno comparisons showed solid gains of 27 hp and 25 ft-lbs of torque over the factory exhaust system.

Besides a basic tool set, here are some helpful tools and supplies:

- Hooker Blackheart 1¾-inch long-tube header and exhaust kit (part number VK050006)
- Basic tool kit
- Floor jack and jack stands
- 13- and 15-mm flex-head ratcheting combination wrenches
- 24-inch long, 3/8- and 1/2-inch-drive extension bars
- 8-inch long, 3/8-inch-drive extension bar
- 3/8-inch-drive swivel-head ratchet
- 10-, 13-, and 15-mm swivel sockets
- Spray penetrating lubricant
- Anti-seize compound
- MT82 bellhousing lift block (details on this later)

*The polished Hooker Blackheart mufflers use absorption technology and are surprisingly effective for their small size and weight.*

## Installing Long-Tube Headers and Exhaust

**1** *Because the power wire for the starter is hot at all times, start the installation process by disconnecting the negative side of the battery.*

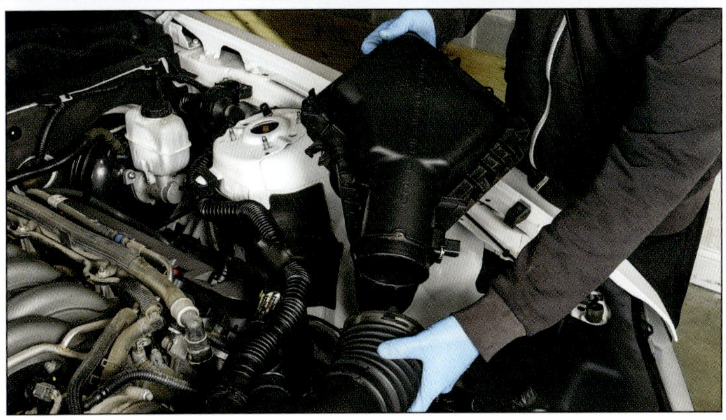

**2** *While in the engine compartment, remove the factory air box to improve access to the driver-side header fasteners.*

**3** *With the car securely supported by jack stands, loosen the clamps and remove the factory mid-pipe.*

**4** *After unbolting the vibration isolator brackets from the chassis, remove the factory mufflers and over-axle pipes.*

**5** *Before unscrewing the factory oxygen sensors, disconnect all four oxygen sensors from the wiring harness. The left-side upstream oxygen sensor connector is located on top of the bellhousing behind the intake manifold.*

**6** *With all four oxygen sensors disconnected, unscrew the downstream sensors from the exhaust system.*

**7** *After soaking the fasteners with penetrating oil, remove the nuts securing the factory catalysts to the exhaust manifolds. A long extension helps to access the top nuts from the engine compartment.*

**8** *Next, disconnect the steering shaft from the rack.*

**9** *The other end of the steering shaft is disconnected from the steering column under the dashboard.*

**10** *To improve access, remove the lower crossmember brace.*

**11** *Next, disconnect the wires from the starter and remove it.*

**12** *Before removing the engine mounts, support the engine securely. Using this block makes supporting and jacking the engine extremely easy.*

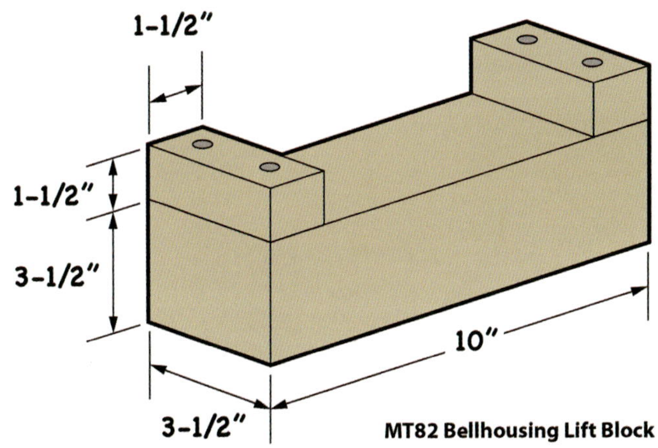


**13** *You can make this bellhousing support from a wood 4x4 block cut 10 inches long and a 2x4 cut into two 1½-inch pieces. This block supported the engine via the cast-in bellhousing bolt bosses rather than the thin fins on the bottom.*

**14** *With the engine supported, remove the left-side engine mount.*

**15** *A wiring harness makes removing the right-side mount trickier. To give the needed working room, unbolt the harness support bracket from the air-conditioning compressor. Note that there's a ground wire attached to one of the engine-mount studs that needs to be removed first.*

**16** *A range of extensions, sockets, wrenches, and swivels come in handy when accessing all the nuts securing the factory headers to the heads. With creativity, patience, and perseverance, you will eventually get them all.*

**17** *With all the nuts removed, the factory headers can be pulled from the car.*

**18** *Next, remove the factory wideband oxygen sensors from the shorty headers.*

**19** *The factory header and catalyst setup (top) fits within a footprint surprisingly similar to the Hooker Blackheart long-tube header (below). This means the Hooker headers can connect to the factory exhaust system with minimal modification if desired.*

**20** *The factory multilayer steel exhaust gaskets are so effective and durable that they can be reused if they are in good condition. Sealing technology has come such a long way from the leaky paper gaskets of the past.*

**21** *To ease header installation, use a Torx socket and remove all of the factory studs except the upper-front stud.*

**22** *The steering shaft needs to slip between the header tubes, so remove the universal joint from the end of the steering shaft.*

**23** *After hanging the gasket from the front stud and rear bolt, thread the header up into position and hang it by the front stud.*

**24** *While the Hooker headers come with a full set of fasteners for the headers, you can reuse the factory studs and all-metal locking nuts wherever possible. On the right side, you don't have to remove any of the studs and can reuse them all. On the left side, however, you need to remove all of the studs except for the front to install the headers. Then, hang the gasket and the header by the fasteners before installing the combination.*

**25** *Here's a view of the left-side header installed with the factory studs reinstalled along the bottom and three bolts along the top.*

**26** *With the headers bolted up, reinstall the engine mounts.*

**27** *Then, reinstall the easily accessible starter bolts.*

**28** *The top starter bolt takes a special combination of tools to reach. We attached a 10-mm swivel socket to an 8-inch-long, 3/8-inch-drive extension and a swivel-head ratchet.*

**29** *With the extension and swivel socket routed under cylinder number-1's tube, hold the socket on the bolt from the bottom and have someone operate the ratchet from the top. It's tedious, but it works.*

**30** *Next, reconnect the steering shaft on both ends.*

**31** *Then, reinstall the factory's wideband oxygen sensors. Note how tightly the headers tuck up to the floor for ground clearance. Impressive.*

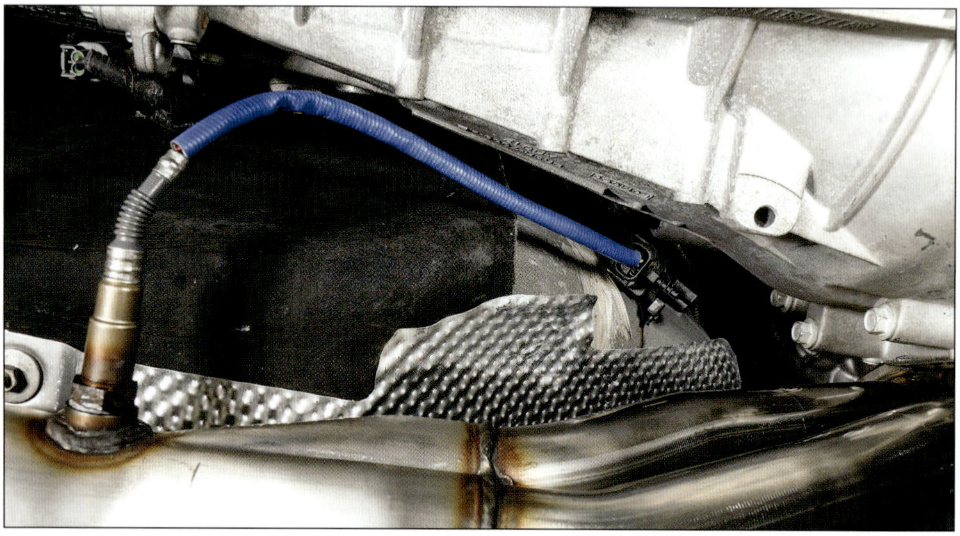

**32** *Even though the oxygen sensors are relocated farther downstream from the headers, harness extensions aren't required. Instead, you can unanchor the connectors from the main electrical harness and route them farther down on each side of the transmission until they reach the oxygen sensor connector.*

**33** *After slipping the factory and supplied butt-joint clamps over all four ends, lift the X-pipe into position.*

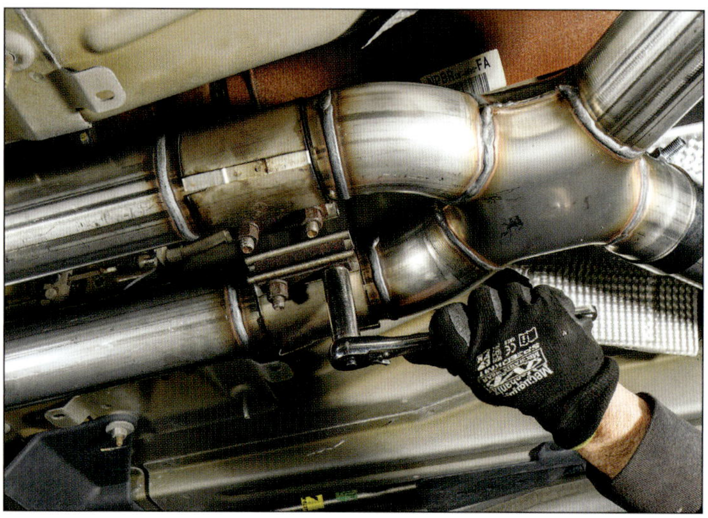

**34** *The Hooker Blackheart kit uses the factory clamps behind the X-pipe.*

**35** *With everything in position, loosely install the clamps to hold the system together.*

**36** *The over-axle pipes are a two-piece design to ease installation as well as allow adjustment.*

**37** *Besides being quieter, the Hooker muffler (right) is 11 pounds, while the factory muffler (left) is 22 pounds.*

**38** *You can transfer the vibration isolator brackets from the factory mufflers to the Hooker mufflers.*

**39** *Next, lift the Hooker mufflers into position and reinstall the isolator bracket fasteners. You can wrap the mufflers in plastic to avoid scratching their polished surface during installation.*

**40** *Once satisfied with the alignment of all the components, tighten all the clamps.*

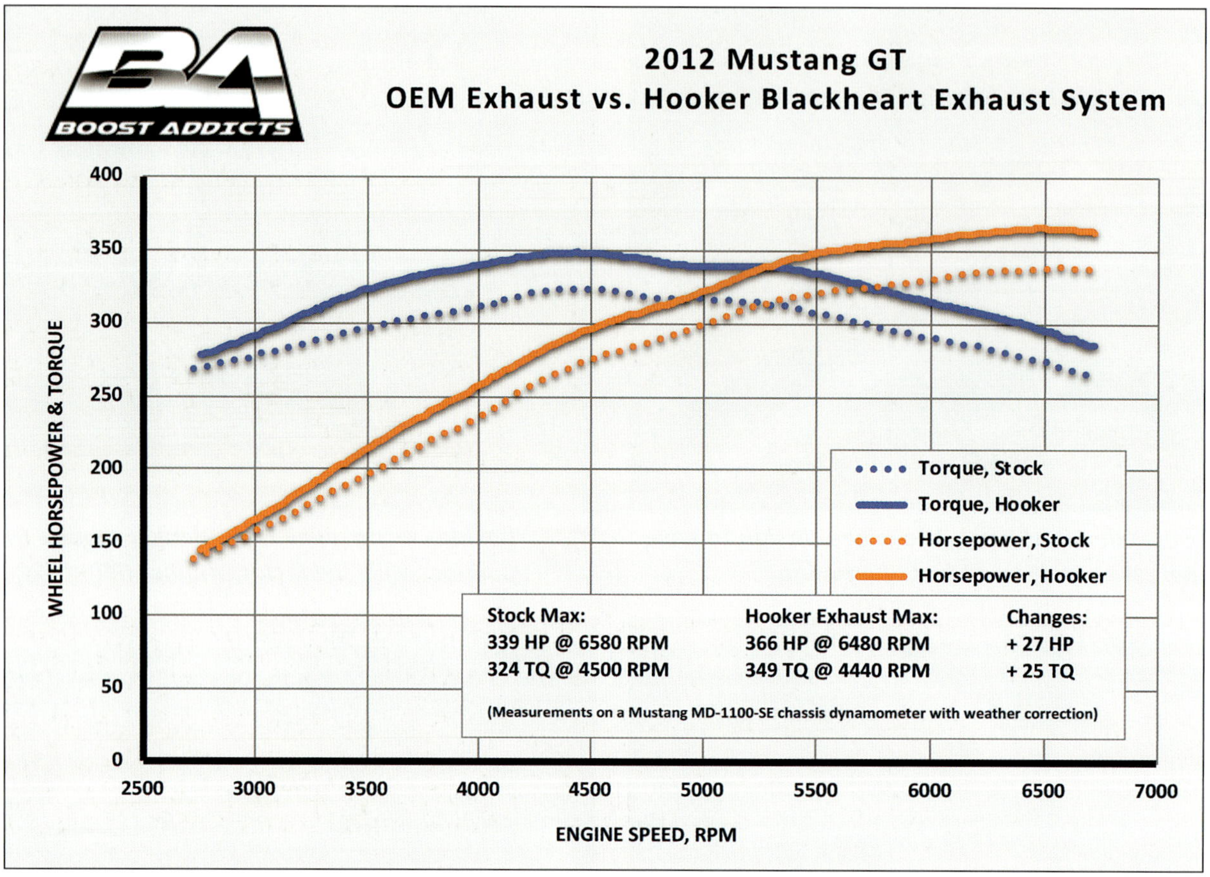


***Not only were we pleased with the no-hassle fitment of the Hooker exhaust but the power gains were also impressive. We gained a solid 27 hp and 25 ft-lbs of torque to the rear wheels on the chassis dyno at Boost Addicts in Gallatin, Tennessee. The results weren't just at the peaks, as evidenced by a thick torque gain from 3,500–6,700 rpm.***

***Intake Manifold System Installation***

The Cobra Jet intake from Ford Performance enjoys a stellar reputation as the go-to intake for extracting maximum performance from a Coyote engine, and for good reason: it was developed as a no-holds-barred intake manifold for Ford's naturally aspirated Cobra Jet factory drag racing program. Its short runners and large plenum volume are designed to capitalize on the Coyote's high-RPM breathing capabilities.

Gains on otherwise-stock Coyote engines are modest, but it's in the upper reaches of the RPM range where the Cobra Jet intake manifold shines. Because Ford Performance Parts offers virtually everything needed for this swap, installing it in place of a factory 2011–2014 intake is very straightforward, although ECM tuning is required. Refer to the following photos and illustrations for details.

Here's what you'll need:

- Ford Performance Parts Cobra Jet intake manifold kit (part number M-9424-M50CJA)
- Ford Performance Parts Cobra Jet twin 65-mm throttle body (part number M-9926-CJ65)
- Ford Performance Parts intake manifold install kit (part number M-9444-M50B)
- Ford Performance Parts Cobra Jet cold-air kit (part number M-9603-M50CJ)
- Basic tool kit
- Floor jack and jack stands
- Torque wrench (in-lbs)
- 6 x 25–mm bolts (4)
- ECM tuner and/or software

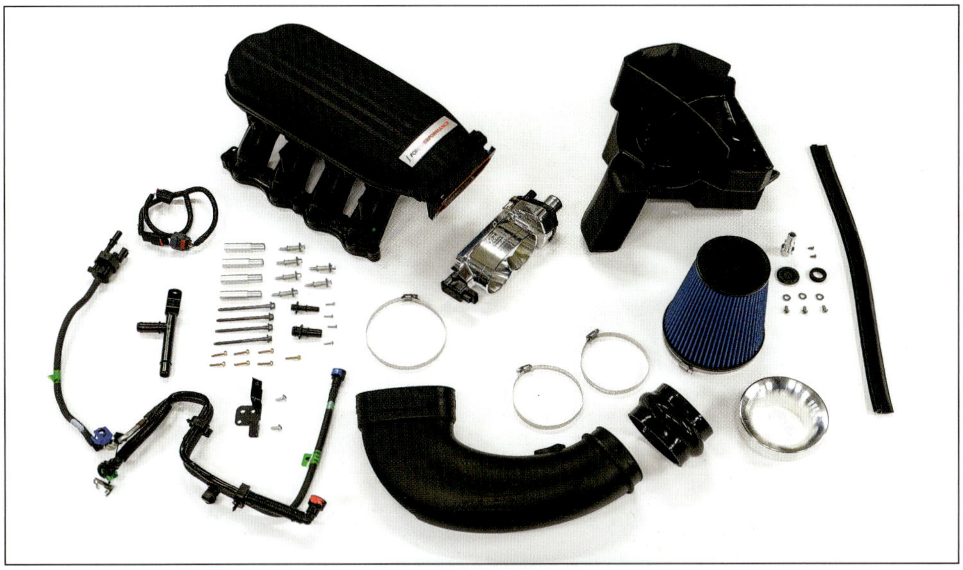

*Ford Performance Parts includes virtually everything needed to install a Cobra Jet intake manifold on a 2011–2014 Mustang GT via four part numbers: M-9424-M50CJA, M-9926-CJ65, M-9444-M50B, and M-9603-M50CJ. We were extremely impressed with the fit and finish of all the parts. Even the installation instructions downloaded from the Ford Performance Parts website (not shown) are detailed and excellent.*

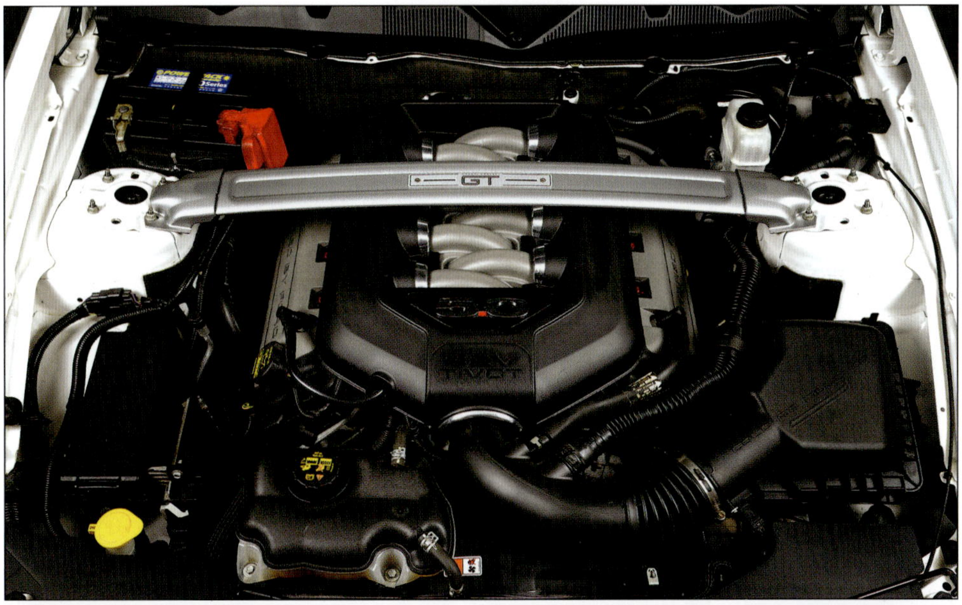


*Here's where we started: a completely stock 2012 Mustang GT.*

## Installing an Intake Manifold System

**1** *Remove the fuel-pump relay and fuse from the under-hood electrical panel and run the engine out of fuel to depressurize the fuel system.*

2 Next, remove the stock cold-air intake system.

3 The factory sound tube is also removed and will not be reused.

4 The Ford Performance Parts Cobra Jet cold-air kit includes this rubber plug to fill the hole vacated by the sound tube.

5 With a rag underneath to catch any dripping fuel, disconnect the fuel supply line from the fuel rail.

6 Next, disconnect all of the hoses and electrical connections at the front of the intake manifold.

7 Use compressed air to blow out the debris that collected on the intake manifold so that it doesn't fall down in the intake ports during removal.

**8** *Next, remove the fuel rail insulators.*

**9** *Unplug all of the fuel-injector harness connectors.*

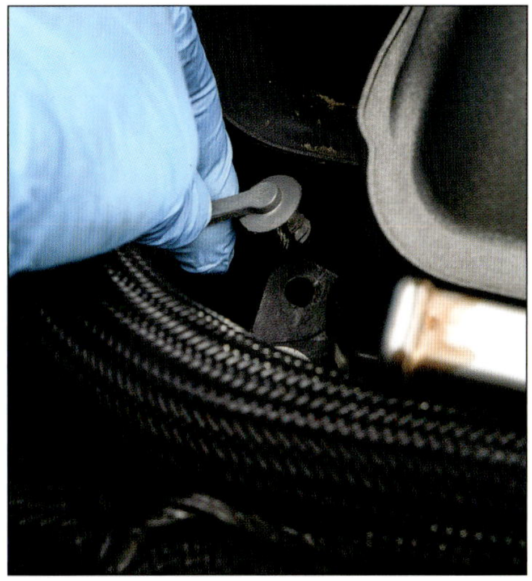

**10** *Free the electrical harness where it is anchored to the back side of the manifold.*

**11** *After removing all the manifold bolts, pull the manifold from the engine.*

**12** *With the factory GT manifold removed (left), compare it to the Cobra Jet intake manifold (right). Note how the stock manifold's plenum fills the valley and the longer runners run from the plenum up and around the top of the manifold on their way to the cylinder-head intake ports. The Cobra Jet manifold is a more traditional ram design with a larger plenum on top and runners that are essentially a straight shot to the intake ports. The Cobra Jet's throttle body opening is also considerably larger than the factory part.*

**13** *Prep the Cobra Jet manifold by installing the supplied vacuum fittings and transferring the fuel rails from the factory manifold to the Cobra Jet.*

**14** *After ensuring that the cylinder head's sealing surfaces are clean, drop the Cobra Jet intake manifold in place.*

**15** *Use a torque wrench to tighten the intake manifold bolts in the specified sequence in the instructions to 89 in-lbs plus 45 degrees. (Note that 89 in-lbs is about 7.4 ft-lbs.)*

**16** *After connecting all of the fuel injectors, replace the factory fuel and vapor lines with the Ford Performance Parts–supplied versions.*

**17** *Use a short length of vacuum hose to reconnect the brake booster to the Cobra Jet intake manifold.*

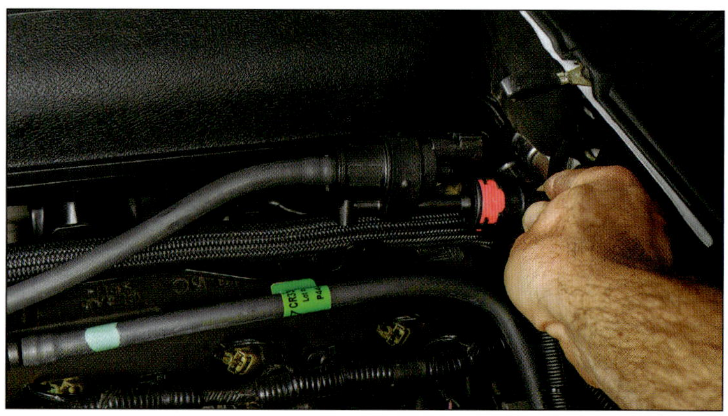

**18** *The purge solenoid is in a different spot for the Cobra Jet and Boss 302 intake manifold. Connect the supplied purge line to the new solenoid.*

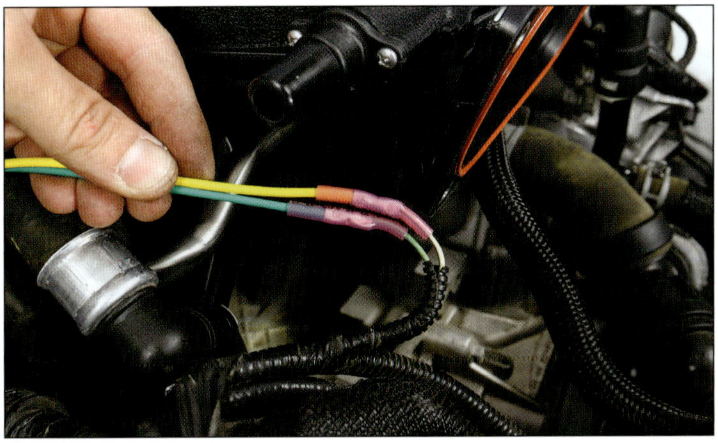

**19** *Since the purge solenoid is relocated to the opposite corner of the intake manifold, extend the wires for the solenoid using heat-shrink butt-splice connectors and about 40 inches of wire.*

**20** *Connect the extended harness to the solenoid.*

**21** *Ford Performance Parts incudes this handy throttle-body jumper harness that converts the factory harness to the Cobra Jet twin 65-mm throttle body. Connect it as indicated.*

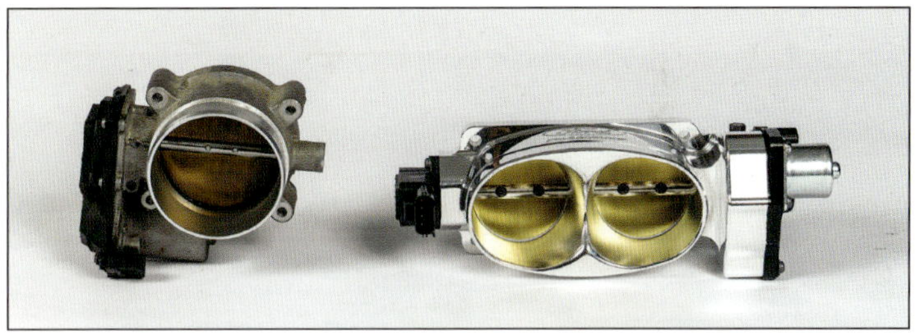

**22** *Speaking of throttle bodies, the size difference between the 80-mm stocker (left) and the Cobra Jet twin 65-mm unit (right) is staggering. We'll split the Coyote's block in half before this throttle body becomes a restriction.*

**23** *The Cobra Jet twin 65-mm throttle body's motor interferes with the factory heater-hose tube (left), so Ford Performance Parts includes a revised replacement (right).*

**24** *After draining enough coolant so that it is below the mid-line of the block, replace the factory heater tube with the included tube.*

**25** *Use four 6 x 25–mm screws to secure the Cobra Jet Twin 65-mm throttle body to the Cobra Jet intake manifold.*

**26** *Next, turn your attention to the Cobra Jet cold-air system by installing the supplied fittings and transferring the MAF sensor from the factory intake tube to the Cobra Jet piece using the supplied hardware.*

**27** *After transferring the rubber mounting grommet from the factory air box to the Cobra Jet air box, install the supplied aluminum filter adapter and box assembly into the engine compartment and hook it up to the factory cold-air feed duct.*

**28** *Next, connect the Cobra Jet air tube assembly between the throttle body and filter adapter and secure it with the supplied clamps.*

**29** *The Cobra Jet Cold Air kit includes this seal to insulate the filter and air box from the under-hood heat.*

*The Ford Performance Parts Cobra Jet intake manifold singlehandedly transformed our engine compartment from ho-hum to race ready.*

*With the GT back up and running, we headed to Boost Addicts in Gallatin, Tennessee, to see how our Mustang fared with the Cobra Jet intake manifold.*

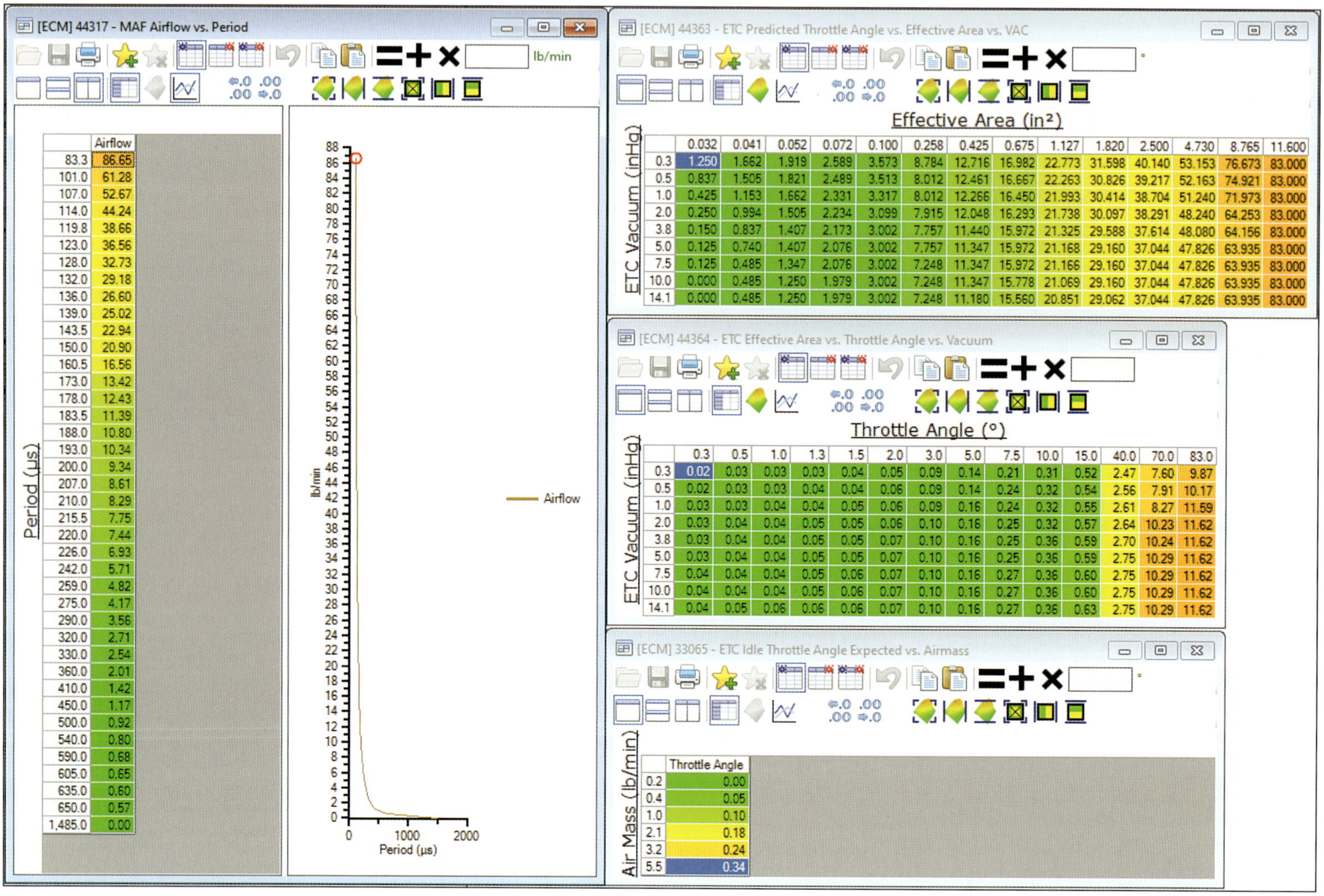


| Period (µs) | Airflow |
|---|---|
| 83.3 | 86.65 |
| 101.0 | 61.28 |
| 107.0 | 52.67 |
| 114.0 | 44.24 |
| 119.8 | 38.66 |
| 123.0 | 36.56 |
| 128.0 | 32.73 |
| 132.0 | 29.18 |
| 136.0 | 26.60 |
| 139.0 | 25.02 |
| 143.5 | 22.94 |
| 150.0 | 20.90 |
| 160.5 | 16.56 |
| 173.0 | 13.42 |
| 178.0 | 12.43 |
| 183.5 | 11.39 |
| 188.0 | 10.80 |
| 193.0 | 10.34 |
| 200.0 | 9.34 |
| 207.0 | 8.61 |
| 210.0 | 8.29 |
| 215.5 | 7.75 |
| 220.0 | 7.44 |
| 226.0 | 6.93 |
| 242.0 | 5.71 |
| 259.0 | 4.82 |
| 275.0 | 4.17 |
| 290.0 | 3.56 |
| 320.0 | 2.71 |
| 330.0 | 2.54 |
| 360.0 | 2.01 |
| 410.0 | 1.42 |
| 450.0 | 1.17 |
| 500.0 | 0.92 |
| 540.0 | 0.80 |
| 590.0 | 0.68 |
| 605.0 | 0.65 |
| 635.0 | 0.60 |
| 650.0 | 0.57 |
| 1,485.0 | 0.00 |

| ETC Vacuum (inHg) \ Effective Area (in²) | 0.032 | 0.041 | 0.052 | 0.072 | 0.100 | 0.258 | 0.425 | 0.675 | 1.127 | 1.820 | 2.500 | 4.730 | 8.765 | 11.600 |
|---|---|---|---|---|---|---|---|---|---|---|---|---|---|---|
| 0.3 | 1.250 | 1.662 | 1.919 | 2.589 | 3.573 | 8.784 | 12.716 | 16.982 | 22.773 | 31.598 | 40.140 | 53.153 | 76.673 | 83.000 |
| 0.5 | 0.837 | 1.505 | 1.821 | 2.489 | 3.513 | 8.012 | 12.461 | 16.667 | 22.263 | 30.826 | 39.217 | 52.163 | 74.921 | 83.000 |
| 1.0 | 0.425 | 1.153 | 1.662 | 2.331 | 3.317 | 8.012 | 12.266 | 16.450 | 21.993 | 30.414 | 38.704 | 51.240 | 71.973 | 83.000 |
| 2.0 | 0.250 | 0.994 | 1.505 | 2.234 | 3.099 | 7.915 | 12.048 | 16.293 | 21.738 | 30.097 | 38.291 | 48.240 | 64.253 | 83.000 |
| 3.8 | 0.150 | 0.837 | 1.407 | 2.173 | 3.002 | 7.757 | 11.440 | 15.972 | 21.325 | 29.588 | 37.614 | 48.080 | 64.156 | 83.000 |
| 5.0 | 0.125 | 0.740 | 1.407 | 2.076 | 3.002 | 7.757 | 11.347 | 15.972 | 21.168 | 29.160 | 37.044 | 47.826 | 63.935 | 83.000 |
| 7.5 | 0.125 | 0.485 | 1.347 | 2.076 | 3.002 | 7.248 | 11.347 | 15.972 | 21.166 | 29.160 | 37.044 | 47.826 | 63.935 | 83.000 |
| 10.0 | 0.000 | 0.485 | 1.250 | 1.979 | 3.002 | 7.248 | 11.347 | 15.778 | 21.069 | 29.160 | 37.044 | 47.826 | 63.935 | 83.000 |
| 14.1 | 0.000 | 0.485 | 1.250 | 1.979 | 3.002 | 7.248 | 11.180 | 15.560 | 20.851 | 29.062 | 37.044 | 47.826 | 63.935 | 83.000 |

| ETC Vacuum (inHg) \ Throttle Angle (°) | 0.3 | 0.5 | 1.0 | 1.3 | 1.5 | 2.0 | 3.0 | 5.0 | 7.5 | 10.0 | 15.0 | 40.0 | 70.0 | 83.0 |
|---|---|---|---|---|---|---|---|---|---|---|---|---|---|---|
| 0.3 | 0.02 | 0.03 | 0.03 | 0.03 | 0.04 | 0.05 | 0.09 | 0.14 | 0.21 | 0.31 | 0.52 | 2.47 | 7.60 | 9.87 |
| 0.5 | 0.02 | 0.03 | 0.03 | 0.04 | 0.04 | 0.06 | 0.09 | 0.14 | 0.24 | 0.32 | 0.54 | 2.56 | 7.91 | 10.17 |
| 1.0 | 0.03 | 0.03 | 0.04 | 0.04 | 0.05 | 0.06 | 0.09 | 0.16 | 0.24 | 0.32 | 0.55 | 2.61 | 8.27 | 11.59 |
| 2.0 | 0.03 | 0.04 | 0.04 | 0.05 | 0.05 | 0.06 | 0.10 | 0.16 | 0.25 | 0.32 | 0.57 | 2.64 | 10.23 | 11.62 |
| 3.8 | 0.03 | 0.04 | 0.04 | 0.05 | 0.05 | 0.07 | 0.10 | 0.16 | 0.25 | 0.36 | 0.59 | 2.70 | 10.24 | 11.62 |
| 5.0 | 0.03 | 0.04 | 0.04 | 0.05 | 0.05 | 0.07 | 0.10 | 0.16 | 0.25 | 0.36 | 0.59 | 2.75 | 10.29 | 11.62 |
| 7.5 | 0.04 | 0.04 | 0.04 | 0.05 | 0.06 | 0.07 | 0.10 | 0.16 | 0.27 | 0.36 | 0.60 | 2.75 | 10.29 | 11.62 |
| 10.0 | 0.04 | 0.04 | 0.04 | 0.05 | 0.06 | 0.07 | 0.10 | 0.16 | 0.27 | 0.36 | 0.60 | 2.75 | 10.29 | 11.62 |
| 14.1 | 0.04 | 0.05 | 0.06 | 0.06 | 0.06 | 0.07 | 0.10 | 0.16 | 0.27 | 0.36 | 0.63 | 2.75 | 10.29 | 11.62 |

| Air Mass (lb/min) | Throttle Angle |
|---|---|
| 0.2 | 0.00 |
| 0.4 | 0.05 |
| 1.0 | 0.10 |
| 2.1 | 0.18 |
| 3.2 | 0.24 |
| 5.5 | 0.34 |

*Thanks to the extensive experience of the HPtuners' online community, we made the required changes and got our Cobra Jet intake manifold up and running fairly easily. Three aspects comprised the required ECM changes: 1) increased "MAF Airflow vs. Period" about 35 percent over stock (to compensate for the larger cold-air inlet tube in which the MAF sensor is installed), 2) changed predicted throttle angle and effective area (because of the larger twin 65-mm throttle body), and 3) increased manifold volume 15 percent (to compensate for the Cobra Jet's larger plenum volume). Unless you're a dedicated do-it-yourselfer, enlist the help of an experienced professional for this part.*

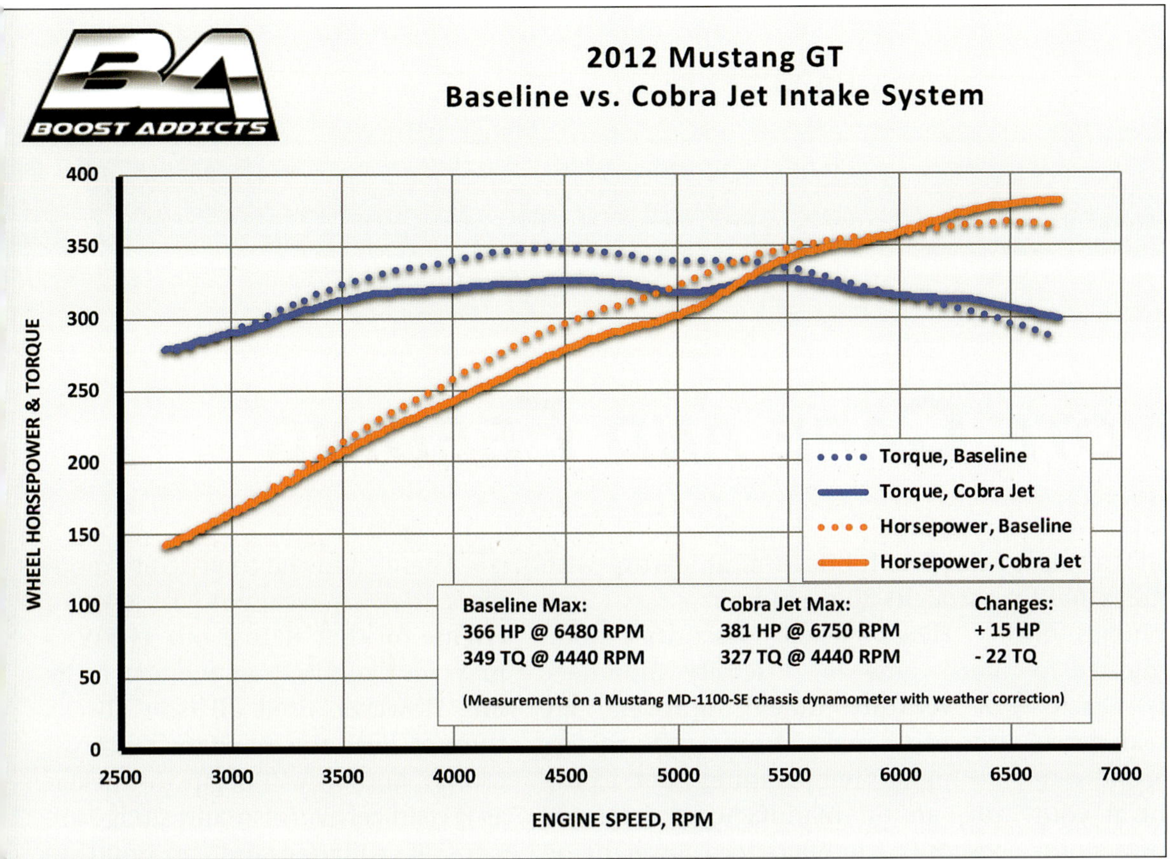


*Still running the factory spark programming, camshaft-timing strategy, and rev limit, the GT picked up 15 hp but lost 22 ft-lbs of torque. One can see how the stock intake manifold rules below 6,000 rpm, but the Cobra Jet starts to come alive just before the factory rev limit crashes the party. Data logging revealed that the ignition and camshaft timing were too conservative for the Cobra Jet manifold.*

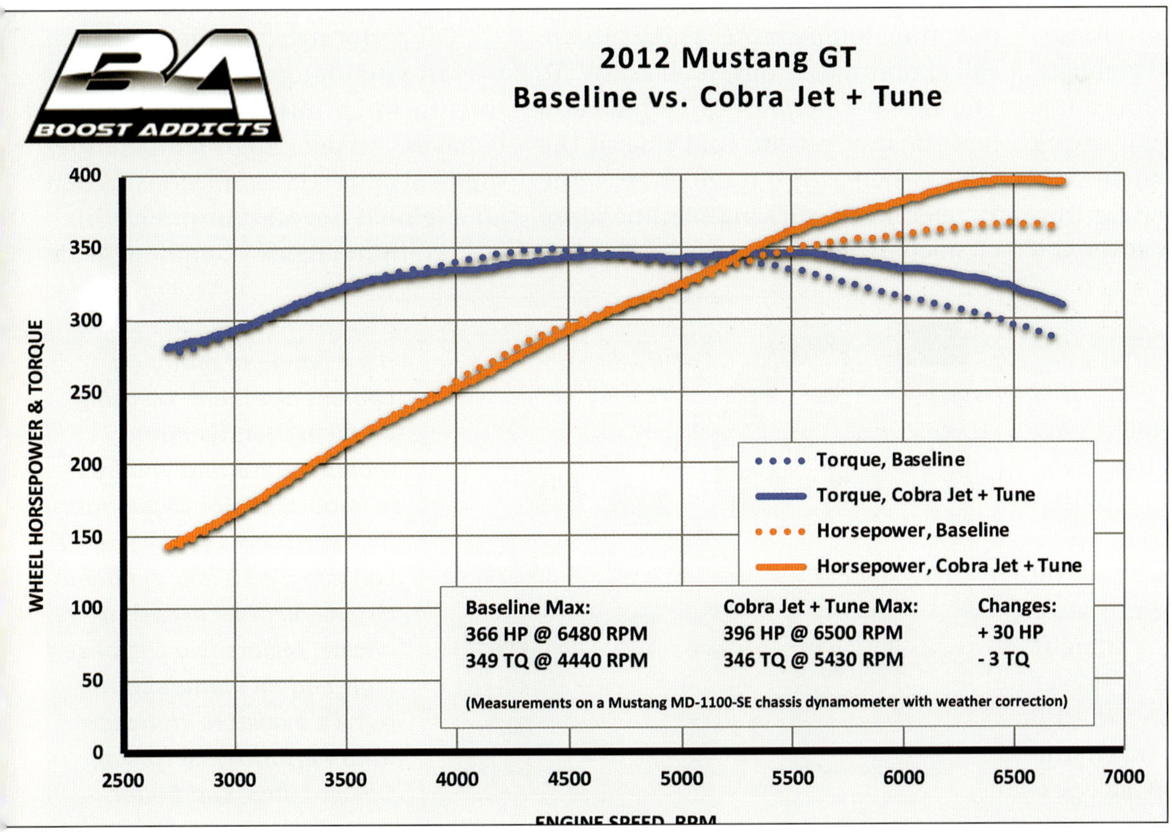


*With some more-aggressive spark and camshaft timing to take advantage of the Cobra Jet intake manifold's characteristics, we ran another dyno test. We picked up nearly all the low-end torque we lost and gained 15 additional horsepower over the factory tune. In total, we gained 30 hp and lost only 3 ft-lbs of torque over the factory intake manifold and tune. There may be more performance locked inside the Copperhead ECM, but with nearly 400 naturally aspirated hp to the rear wheels, we were satisfied and ready to move on.*

# Coyote Care and Feeding

The science of motor oil is a continually evolving and complex field of engineering. Entire volumes of books (and careers) are dedicated to understanding engine oils. Discussions of engine oil brands can get as heated as those of politics and religion. Want to start a fight at your next car event? Start debating motor oil brands.

Fortunately for us enthusiasts, the motor oil market is so competitive that as long as you follow a few guidelines, it's hard to go wrong with any of today's reputable oil brands. Without getting too far into the weeds, we're going to cover the basics.

## Lubrication

Engine oils are a complex cocktail of base oils, viscosity modifiers, and other ingredients that help keep the engine clean and prevent wear. Oil, by nature, gets thicker as the temperature decreases. Resistance to flow is called viscosity. A straight 20-weight oil will flow at a slower rate (have a higher viscosity) at 40°F than it would at 200°F. An engine designed for 20-weight oil at operating temperature may not receive adequate lubrication at startup with a straight 20-weight oil.

Here's where viscosity modifiers come in. Viscosity modifiers, or viscosity index improvers, are added to make thinner oils thicker at higher temperatures. For example, an oil manufacturer may add viscosity modifiers to a 5-weight oil so that it acts like a 50-weight oil at operating temperature. These oils are called multigrade oils, such as 5W50. The number before the W indicates performance on the cold side of the scale, whereas the number after the W refers to the oil's high-temperature characteristics.

There's a caveat to viscosity modifiers: they can wear out with use. An engine oil that started out as 5W50 may act like 5W20 at the end of its life. However, used oil isn't always thinner. Push the oil-change interval too far, and oil will begin to thicken as it oxidizes. Varnish and sludge are signs of oxidation and can build up over time.

Oil performance is more than an overall viscosity grade. Of particular interest to enthusiasts is how an oil behaves under high-temperature/high-shear (HTHS) conditions. When an engine is hot and running at high RPM, critical engine components are

*It's a jungle of motor oil choices out there, so using an oil from a reputable manufacturer that you trust is important. For Mustangs that see hard use, Millers XF Longlife 5W50 fully synthetic engine oil is an excellent choice. Millers is a UK-based high-end oil manufacturer, but it's available stateside from Performance Racing Oils in 1-liter and 5-liter containers.*

moving past each other at alarming speeds (shear forces) and at high temperatures (both from combustion and friction within the oil itself). HTHS testing simulates this condition by measuring the viscosity of an oil at 150°C (302°F) under constant shear. An oil with higher HTHS performance will maintain the necessary oil film under severe conditions when compared to one with lower HTHS performance. Keep in mind that HTHS performance is more relevant than overall viscosity because it's possible for one brand of 5W40 oil to have higher HTHS viscosity than a different brand of 5W50 oil. Accordingly, higher HTHS performance in a given viscosity range is indicative of a higher-quality base stock oil.

Base oil types are categorized in groups. Group I, II, and III oils are derived from crude oil, although Group III is referred to as synthetic, because it is extremely highly refined, and the process to refine it is longer and more intense than Groups I and II. Group IV and Group V base oils include polyalphaolefins and esters that are not extracted but synthesized from uniform particles, which is why they're called synthetics.

In cases where high heat and stress are a concern, synthetic oils usually perform better than conventional oils, although not all oils are created equal. Lubrication, detergents, and other additives affect ultimate performance. The viscosities of synthetic oils are more stable versus temperature (they have a higher viscosity index), which means that synthetic oils need fewer viscosity modifiers to hit their target viscosity range.

So, what oil should you use? If you feel the need to use a different oil than Ford specifies, it's important to do some research and gain an understanding of what differentiates various oils. Consider how you use your Mustang. The biggest factor when choosing an oil is the duty cycle.

Think of the duty cycle in terms of how much time your Mustang spends at wide-open throttle, high RPM, and at high engine temperatures during an oil-change interval. To your engine's oil, the daily commute, drag strip, and road track are distinctly different environments. A daily commute involves many cold starts and minimal load. A drag strip has short wide-open-throttle bursts between relatively long cool-down periods. A track day at a road course is the most grueling environment because the engine spends a significant time at full throttle and high RPM for long periods.

If you primarily use your Mustang for daily driving, choosing a good synthetic oil in the factory-recommended specification is a solid choice. Drag racing with cool-down periods between rounds and where squeezing every last horsepower out of the engine can be the difference between advancing to the next round or packing up and going home may also be well-suited to the factory-specification oil. However, if you're doing road-course track days with your Mustang, choosing an oil with a higher HTHS viscosity rating than the factory specification is worth considering.

Regarding zinc, or more specifically, Zinc Dialkyl Dithiophosphates (ZDDP), zinc oil additives protect against metal-to-metal contact by adding a sacrificial layer of zinc to engine parts that is wiped away before component damage occurs, such as engines with flat-tappet cams or when a thin oil is used that increases the risk of metal-to-metal contact. However, zinc poisons catalytic converters when oil is burned,

<table>
<tr><th colspan="4">Ford Intelligent Oil Life Monitor Logic</th></tr>
<tr><th>3,000 Miles</th><th>5,000 Miles</th><th>7,500 Miles</th><th>10,000 Miles</th></tr>
<tr><td colspan="2">Severe Duty<br>Short Trips in Extreme Hot or Cold Weather or Mostly High Load Driving</td><td></td><td></td></tr>
<tr><td></td><td colspan="2">Moderate Duty<br>Mountainous Driving or Extended Idling</td><td></td></tr>
<tr><td></td><td></td><td colspan="2">Light Duty<br>Normal Commuting with Highway Driving</td></tr>
<tr><td colspan="4">1 Year Maximum Oil Change Interval</td></tr>
<tr><td colspan="4">Ford's intelligent oil-life monitor on 2011–2014 Mustangs uses PCM data to determine when the oil on your Mustang should be changed. It's a handy tool that provides peace of mind and can save you money by avoiding unnecessary oil changes.</td></tr>
</table>

*If you really want to geek out about your oil, have your old engine oil analyzed when you change it. The test reads the oil to help you choose your ideal engine oil, receive warning about abnormal engine wear, and fine-tune your oil-change interval.*

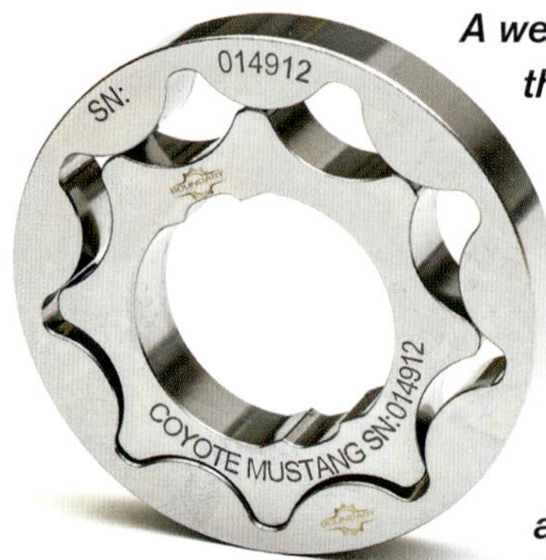


*A well-known Achilles heel of the Coyote engine is the powdered-metal oil-pump rotor gears. As the RPM and horsepower levels increase, undamped harmonics rattle the gears, and they can break into pieces, especially if a non-stock crank damper is fitted. Billet-steel oil-pump gears are good insurance. They even developed a Black series gearset that features unique ports to increase the aspiration of the oil-pump gear at high RPM. Boundary Racing Pumps offers both individual oil-pump gears as well as complete, assembled pumps and pump accessories for Coyote engines.*

*While addressing the oil pump, install a billet timing gear, such as this one from Boundary Racing Pumps.*

*It's critical that the oil-pump pickup is fully submerged and sucking oil at all times. That may seem simple, but it can be a big ask during high RPMs and big lateral accelerations. Several oil pans are available on the market that feature tricks to direct and retain oil near the pump pickup, such as this 7-quart oil pan from Canton (part number 15-734). It uses a diamond-shaped sump with trap doors that keep oil from sloshing away from the pickup during hard cornering, acceleration, and braking. (Photo Courtesy Canton Racing Products)*

*An oil-air separator keeps oil vapors from the PCV system from reentering the engine via the air intake. This is especially useful on supercharged engines with intercoolers, as oil vapor reduces intercooler efficiency. Plumbing and mounting an air-oil separator can often be a challenge, but Ford Performance Parts' M-6766-A50 air-oil separator addresses both issues by using OEM-designed hoses and conveniently mounts the canister on the cam cover. (Photo Courtesy Ford Performance Parts)*

and since the Coyote uses roller finger followers, there's less of a benefit to a special high-zinc oil.

What about oil change intervals? Luckily, the 2011–2014 Mustang PCM includes the Ford intelligent oil-life monitor. The PCM continually monitors engine use (for example, duty cycle) and determines when the oil likely needs to be changed. The intelligent oil life monitor is a great rule of thumb, but if you're really into oil technology, opt for an oil analysis at each change to help you determine engine wear and refine your oil choice and change interval.

*A straightforward way to increase cooling performance is with a larger, higher-capacity radiator. Ford Performance Parts offers a direct-fit radiator (part number M-8005-MGT) plucked from the Boss 302S and Boss 302R racing programs that offers a massive increase in cooling capacity. It features provisions for the air-conditioning condenser and the factory automatic transmission cooler (if equipped). Since it's thicker than the factory radiator, the cooling fan is moved closer to the engine, which is a potential complication for applications with front-mount centrifugal superchargers.*

*Higher engine speeds and pressure on bearing surfaces increase oil temperature. An oil cooler is an excellent way to stabilize oil temperatures and maximize oil and engine life. The Boss 302 oil cooler from Ford Performance Parts (part number M-6642-MB) was factory-installed on the 2011–2014 Boss 302 and later-model Track Pack–equipped Mustang GTs. It's a direct fit for 2011–2014 Mustang GTs. It's a liquid-to-liquid cooler that transfers heat from the oil to the coolant.*

*Mishimoto takes the guesswork out of fitting a liquid-to-air oil cooler to 2011–2014 Mustang GTs with a convenient bolt-on kit that features premade hoses and a cooler mount. Available as part number MMOC-MUS-11T, the Mishimoto claims that its oil cooler lowers temperatures by 35°F and increases capacity by 0.75 quarts. (Photo Courtesy American Muscle)*

## Cooling

Only about 25 percent of a gasoline engine's energy is used to turn the crankshaft—the remaining 75 percent is released as heat. The engine's cooling system keeps the engine operating temperatures in check so that the tight fitment tolerances and materials aren't affected. Adding engine power consequently adds more heat, so cooling capacity and rejection rates need to be addressed on modified engines.

*Selecting the right coolant for your Mustang is extremely important. Over the past few decades, manufacturers have transitioned from traditional green coolant to newer, long-life coolants. Some are incompatible with each other, so it's important to use the coolant specified in your owners' manual. It's important to mix concentrated coolant in a 50/50 mixture with distilled water to prevent corrosion and prevent freezing that will damage the engine and other components. Overheating issues are best addressed with a larger radiator rather than relying on coolant tricks that might increase corrosion.*

## How-To Project: Cooling Upgrade

With more horsepower comes more heat. Add a summer day and extensive track use, and the factory cooling system can quickly become overwhelmed. When it comes to cooling, there aren't any hacks or shortcuts. The only way to improve cooling is to increase cooling-system capacity and airflow. Fortunately, Ford offers a suite of bolt-in components that trickled down from Ford's factory racing programs to the Ford Performance Parts catalog.

The beauty of these parts is that they've been battle tested in both competition and thousands of production vehicles. Not only were we impressed with the results but also the fit and finish made installation a breeze. The radiator bolted in just like stock, and the oil cooler's quick-connect fluid couplings were foolproof.

Besides basic hand tools, here's what we used for this project:

- M-6642-MB - Mustang Boss 302 engine oil cooler
- M-6731-FL820 - high-performance oil filter
- M-8005-MGT - FR500S/Boss 302S aluminum radiator
- M-8200-MBR - Boss 302S front grille
- 8R3Z-16228-A - Boss 302 pony grille emblem
- M-5025-MBR - Boss 302 manual transmission cooler air scoop
- VC-13-G - Motorcraft yellow concentrated coolant (if replacing coolant)
- Distilled water if replacing coolant (1 gallon)
- Millers XF Longlife 5W-50 synthetic motor oil
- M6 x 1.0 x 20-mm-long bolts (2)
- 14-mm hex impact socket

***Ford Performance Parts offers a wide range of battle-tested and production-proven components to increase cooling on 2011–2014 Mustang GTs. They include the Boss 302 manual transmission cooler air scoop (left, part number M-5025-MBR), the FR500S/Boss 302S aluminum radiator (top, part number M-8005-MGT), the Mustang Boss 302 engine oil cooler (right, part number M-6642-MB), and the Boss 302S front grille (bottom, part number M-8200-MBR).***

### Upgrading the Cooling System

**1** ***Begin by removing the lower radiator cover and swinging the lower engine cover out of the way.***

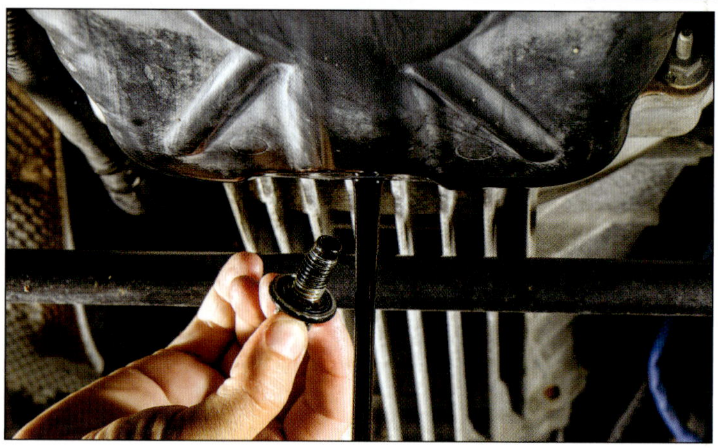

**2** ***Then, drain the oil.***

3 *Drain the coolant into a clean container to reuse or recycle.*

4 *While the oil and coolant finished draining, remove the upper radiator cover.*

5 *Next, remove the air-intake tube and air-filter box.*

6 *Remove the coolant reservoir.*

**7** *The cold-air duct is retained to the cooling fan shroud, so remove it as well.*

**8** *Disconnect the fog lights and remove the grille.*

**9** *With the grille removed, you can access the bolts holding the air-conditioning condenser to the radiator.*

**10** *This nifty coupler connects the upper radiator hose to the thermostat housing. Pry the retaining clip away and disconnect the hose.*

**11** *With the hoses and fan harness disconnected, remove the factory radiator and fan together.*

**12** *It's easy to see how the Boss 302S radiator (right) offers a sizable increase in cooling capacity over the factory radiator (left).*

**13** *What's really great about the Boss 302S radiator is how it's a direct replacement for the factory radiator. The craftsmanship is also top-notch.*

**14** *Transfer the nut clips from the factory radiator to the Boss 302S unit. The Boss 302S radiator has provisions to mount all factory coolers, including the power-steering cooler, transmission cooler, and air-conditioning.*

**15** *Once the radiator is prepped, slide it into the Mustang's engine compartment and bolt it into place.*

**16** *To install the Boss 302 oil cooler, you need a long-shank, 14-mm impact hex socket to reach the oil filter fitting's hex flats.*

**18** *The quick-connect fluid couplers make assembling the oil cooler a snap . . . literally.*

**20** *Connect the oil cooler to the lower radiator hose, noting the hose and fittings with the dots match.*

**17** *Use the 14-mm hex socket to remove the factory oil-filter fitting from the engine block.*

**19** *Using the long-shank 14-mm impact hex socket, fasten the Boss 302 oil cooler to the engine block and torque the fitting to 43 ft-lbs.*

**21** *To secure the bottom of the air-conditioning condenser to the radiator, the factory studs (top) are too long to insert, so use two M6 x 1.0 x 20-mm-long bolts instead.*

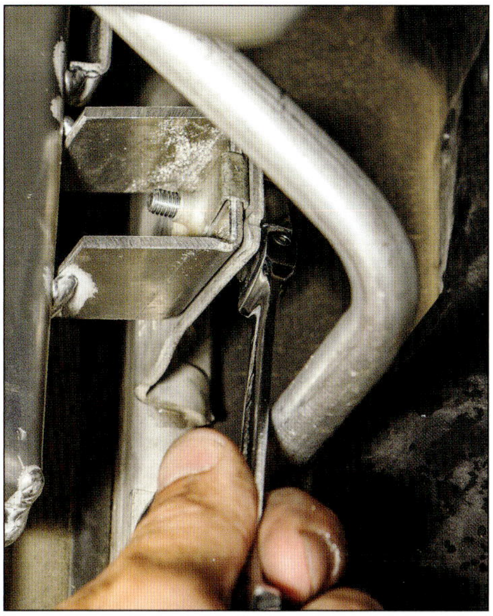

**22** *The shorter bolts make the installation easier.*

**23** *Reinstall the fan and reconnect the hoses to the radiator.*

**24** *Next, reinstall the coolant reservoir.*

**25** *Because the Boss 302S radiator is thicker than the factory radiator, this tab on the cold-air duct doesn't match up anymore, so just cut it off and reinstall the cold-air duct.*

26 The Boss 302S grille features substantially more open area, including coarse wire mesh that replaces the fog lights to feed more air to the radiator.

27 The backside of the Boss 302S grille is milled to open up more cooling paths to the radiator.

28 The Boss 302 grille simply snaps in place of the factory part. Easy!

29 As a finishing touch, we stuck a factory Boss 302 pony emblem on the Boss grille.

**30** *Installing the Boss 302 transmission cooling scoop is simple. First, remove the factory pencil brace.*

**31** *Then, simply use the factory nuts to install the Boss 302 transmission cooling scoop and torque the nuts to 35 ft-lbs.*

**32** *We chose to fill our crankcase with 8 quarts of Millers 5W50 oil. We've had great results using this top-quality synthetic oil from Millers.*

**33** *Considering that our test subject was 8 years old, we chose to refill the cooling system with fresh coolant. We mixed Ford's concentrated VC-13-G coolant 1:1 with distilled water for maximum temperature and corrosion protection. We refilled the cooling system and started the engine. After letting the engine run for a few minutes, we topped off the reservoir and screwed on the radiator cap. It's important to check the coolant level periodically as trapped air is purged from the system.*

# Power Adders

It's often said that an engine is just a glorified air pump. That's true to a point, as finding ways to fill the cylinders with more air adds power. More accurately, filling the cylinders with denser oxygen molecules and adding the requisite fuel increases torque. There are three popular power adders that fill the cylinders with more oxygen than the engine can ingest on its own: nitrous oxide, supercharging, and turbocharging.

## Nitrous Oxide

Injecting nitrous oxide into the engine is arguably the simplest way to increase power on a Mustang. As a compound that's comprised of two nitrogen molecules and one oxygen molecule, nitrous oxide carries more oxygen (33 percent) than normal air (21 percent). As a consequence, nitrous oxide is a convenient way to increase the oxygen in the cylinders.

Nitrous oxide is an oxidizer, in that it makes things burn faster. When heated in the combustion chamber (above 570°F), the nitrogen and oxygen separate, and the oxygen that is present reacts with added fuel to produce more power. As the nitrous oxide vaporizes, it also has a large cooling effect, which makes nitrous oxide significantly denser than ambient air.

The hit of nitrous is essentially instantaneous, and all of the additional torque is available as soon as the nitrous system is enabled. In fact, the nitrous hit can often overwhelm the tires, so progressive controllers that "ramp in" the nitrous delivery by pulsing the solenoids are popular with drag racers. Nitrous oxide increases the burn rate of the fuel, so combined with increased combustion temperatures, higher-octane fuel or spark advance should be reduced to avoid knock. The beauty of nitrous-oxide injection for street-driven cars is that

***Nitrous Oxide Systems (NOS) offers a single-fogger EFI nitrous system for the 2011–2014 5.0L Coyote Ford Mustang (part number 06017BNOS). It also fits 2012–2014 3.7L V-6 models. It's the easiest and least expensive way to add a wet nitrous system to your V-6- or V-8-powered Mustang. The system is centered around a NOS fogger soft plume nozzle for smooth power delivery and easy jet changes. The kit includes a 10-pound black bottle and jetting to add 50, 100, and 150 hp. An adapter fitting is installed between the fuel hose and fuel rail to ease installation. (Photo Courtesy Nitrous Oxide Systems)***

For those looking to step up, NOS offers a wet-plate nitrous system for 2011–2014 Mustang GTs (part number 02125BNOS). The kit includes an injector plate that installs behind the throttle body. The included mini two-stage progressive controller smooths power delivery, and a window switch sets the minimum and maximum RPM for nitrous system operation to minimize engine damage potential. Jetting for 75, 100, 125, and 150 rear-wheel hp is included, although the kit supports 250-hp jetting if your engine and fuel system are up to the task. (Photo Courtesy Nitrous Oxide Systems)

everyday drivability is unaffected. The extra power is only available when you want it.

Nitrous kits fall into three major categories: dry, wet, and direct port. There are advantages and compromises to all three.

Dry kits only inject nitrous and fuel through the factory injectors (either through increasing pulse width or increasing fuel pressure). Dry systems are considered safer because the intake manifold is already designed to flow air, so nitrous distribution is usually good. The popular method to add the extra fuel is to increase fuel pressure. However, since the 2011–2012 Mustang uses a returnless fuel system with the fuel-pressure regulator inside the tank, it's difficult to manipulate the fuel pressure. Adding pulse width via the factory PCM is also complex.

| Configuration | $N_2O$ Jetting | Fuel Jetting | Configuration | $N_2O$ Jetting | Fuel Jetting |
|---|---|---|---|---|---|
| 75 RWHP* | 35* | 18* | 150 RWHP* | 57* | 31* |
| 100 RWHP* | 40* | 21* | 175 RWHP** | 60 | 36 |
| 125 RWHP* | 50* | 27* | 200 RWHP** | 65 | 39 |

*Jetting Included in kit

**Will require an upgraded fuel system

NOTE: It is recommended to install one to two steps colder, non-Iridium or other fine wire spark plugs when using Nitrous Oxide.

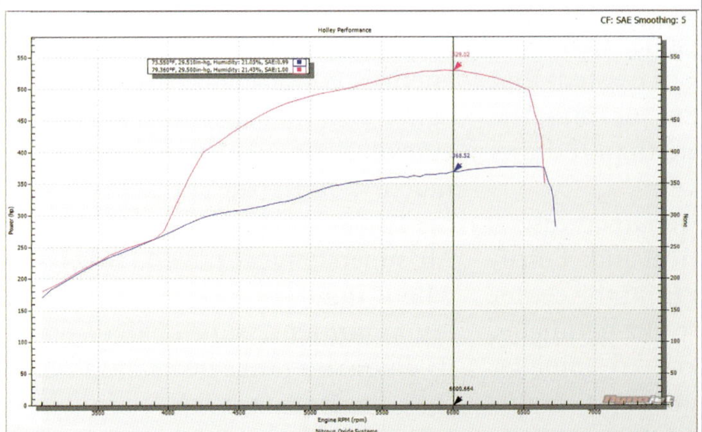

Here are jetting suggestions and a power graph for the NOS wet-plate nitrous system. Note how the horsepower gain is instantly available when the system is activated. This sudden power delivery is typical of nitrous systems and explains why they're popular. (Photo Courtesy Nitrous Oxide Systems)

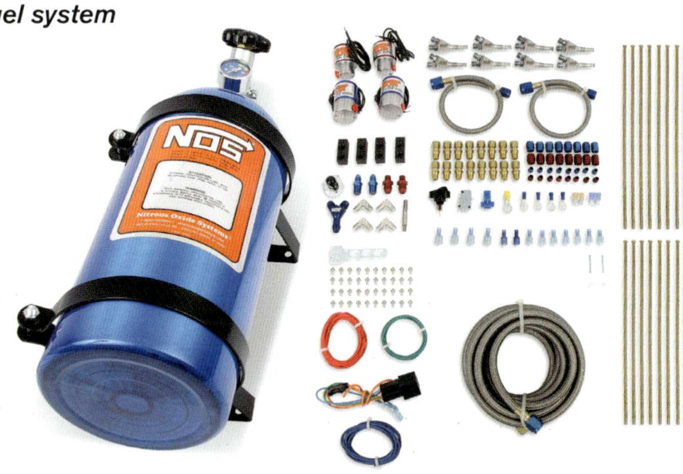

A direct port fogger system is the ultimate nitrous setup because not only is the fuel and nitrous injected closer to the cylinders (improving fuel and nitrous distribution) but also the amount of fuel and nitrous that each cylinder receives can be tailored for maximum power. The plumbing and setup of direct-port systems is more complex than single wet-fogger nozzle systems and plate systems, so most direct-port systems are used on dedicated race applications for engines built specifically to maximize the power from nitrous injection. (Photo Courtesy Nitrous Oxide Systems)

Wet systems inject both nitrous and fuel at the same point, which is usually a nozzle upstream of the throttle body or a plate behind the throttle body. Direct-port setups use individual wet nozzles at each intake port. Wet systems simplify adding the necessary fuel, as the fuel is tapped from the fuel rails and the in-tank fuel pump and regulator compensate for the drop in fuel pressure. However, unlike a carbureted intake manifold, a Mustang's intake isn't designed to flow fuel, so uneven fuel distribution (and consequently rich and lean cylinders) is a risk.

Direct-port systems address the fuel distribution problem by inserting nozzles in the individual intake ports where fuel and nitrous are injected together, bypassing the intake manifold plenum entirely. However, direct-port systems are complex and more costly than their single-nozzle counterparts.

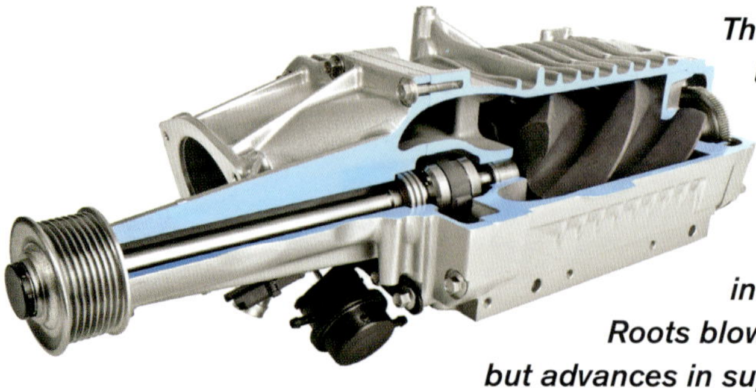

*This cutaway shows an Eaton R1900 supercharger that is a Roots-type design with two rotors that mesh together to squeeze air into the engine. The first Roots blowers used straight rotors, but advances in supercharger design and manufacturing have found twisted rotors to be advantageous. As the pulley spins clockwise, the rotors unmesh, which draws air through the front inlet and to the top of the supercharger. Each rotor grabs onto a pocket of air and carries it around the sides of the case to the bottom of the supercharger, where the air is squeezed into the engine as the rotors mesh back together. Clearances are tight to improve efficiency, but the rotors never touch each other or the case. (Photo Courtesy Eaton)*

*This cutaway of a Vortech V-2 supercharger shows the inner workings of a typical centrifugal supercharger. Note the gear drive that steps up the speed of the impeller faster than the drive pulley. This V-2's helical gearset is quieter than the company's earlier V-1 straight-cut gears and is lubricated by engine oil. Later V-3 Vortech superchargers have a self-contained oiling system, which negates the need to run an oil feed and return line and simplifies installation. (Photo Courtesy Vortech Superchargers)*

## Supercharging

Although supercharging is a term that covers any system that adds denser air into an engine's cylinders, supercharging informally refers to engine-driven air compressors, or blowers. Superchargers fall into one of two common categories: positive displacement and centrifugal.

Positive-displacement superchargers pump a set volume of air per each revolution of their input shaft. Air output is directly proportional to supercharger speed, so a positive-displacement supercharger makes the engine larger, as boost is relatively constant regardless of engine speed. The result is instant torque when the throttle is opened from idle to redline. The most common positive-displacement supercharger is a Roots-style that uses rotors (either straight or twisted) that are driven to squeeze air into the engine at a higher rate than it draws on its own.

Centrifugal superchargers use a spinning impeller wheel and centrifugal force to draw air from the center of the impeller and out its perimeter. Airflow is exponential to impeller speed, meaning that boost builds with engine speed. While maximum boost isn't available at lower engine speeds, centrifugal superchargers are generally more efficient than positive-displacement superchargers.

A note on efficiency: according to the ideal gas law, as air is compressed, it gets hotter. Hot air is the enemy of horsepower, as it is less dense and increases knock risk. The efficiency of a supercharger is how much it heats the air above what's necessary per the laws of physics. All superchargers have a sweet spot where they are most efficient. Simply spinning a supercharger out of its efficiency range heats the air more than necessary while requiring more horsepower to spin. Both are detrimental to ultimate power output.

Because the Coyote engine's factory compression ratio is a relatively high 11:1, keeping air inlet temperatures low when supercharging is critical to avoid knocking the engine

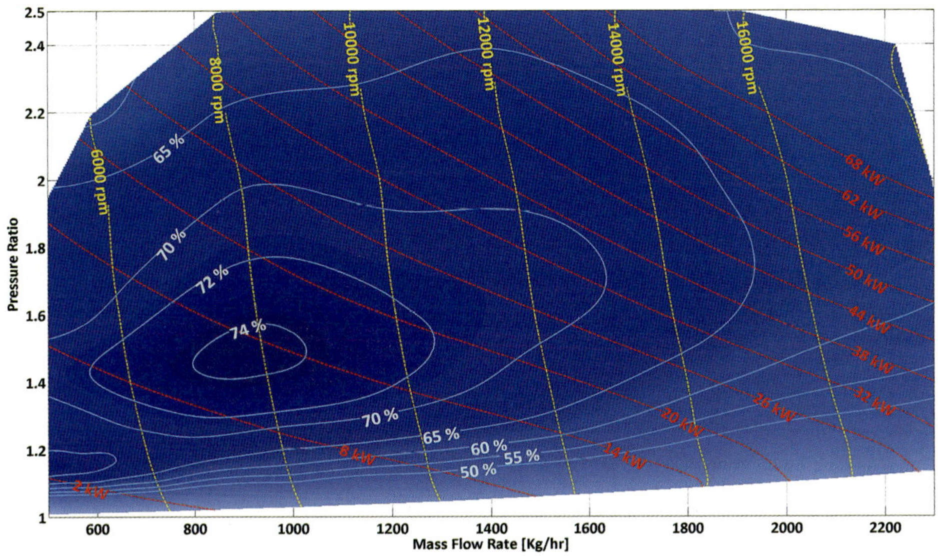


*The performance characteristics of a supercharger are described with a compressor map. A compressor map is used to match a supercharger's performance to the intended application (engine size and target boost). While Roots superchargers should provide airflow in a linear fashion under most conditions, porting and other thermodynamic effects mean that even Roots superchargers have a sweet spot. This compressor map is for the Eaton R1900 supercharger shown in the previous cutaway. Note how the Eaton supercharger is around 74-percent efficient when spun 8,000 rpm and operating at a pressure ratio between 1.4 and 1.6 (5.8 and 8.8 psi of boost). (Illustration Courtesy Eaton)*

into oblivion. Most supercharger systems for 2011–2014 Mustangs use an intercooler that is a heat exchanger between the supercharged air and either liquid coolant (liquid to air) or ambient air (air to air). Packaging makes liquid-to-air intercoolers common with positive-displacement blowers and air-to-air intercoolers often used with centrifugal superchargers.

## Turbocharging

Technically a type of supercharger, turbochargers use exhaust heat and pressure to spin an

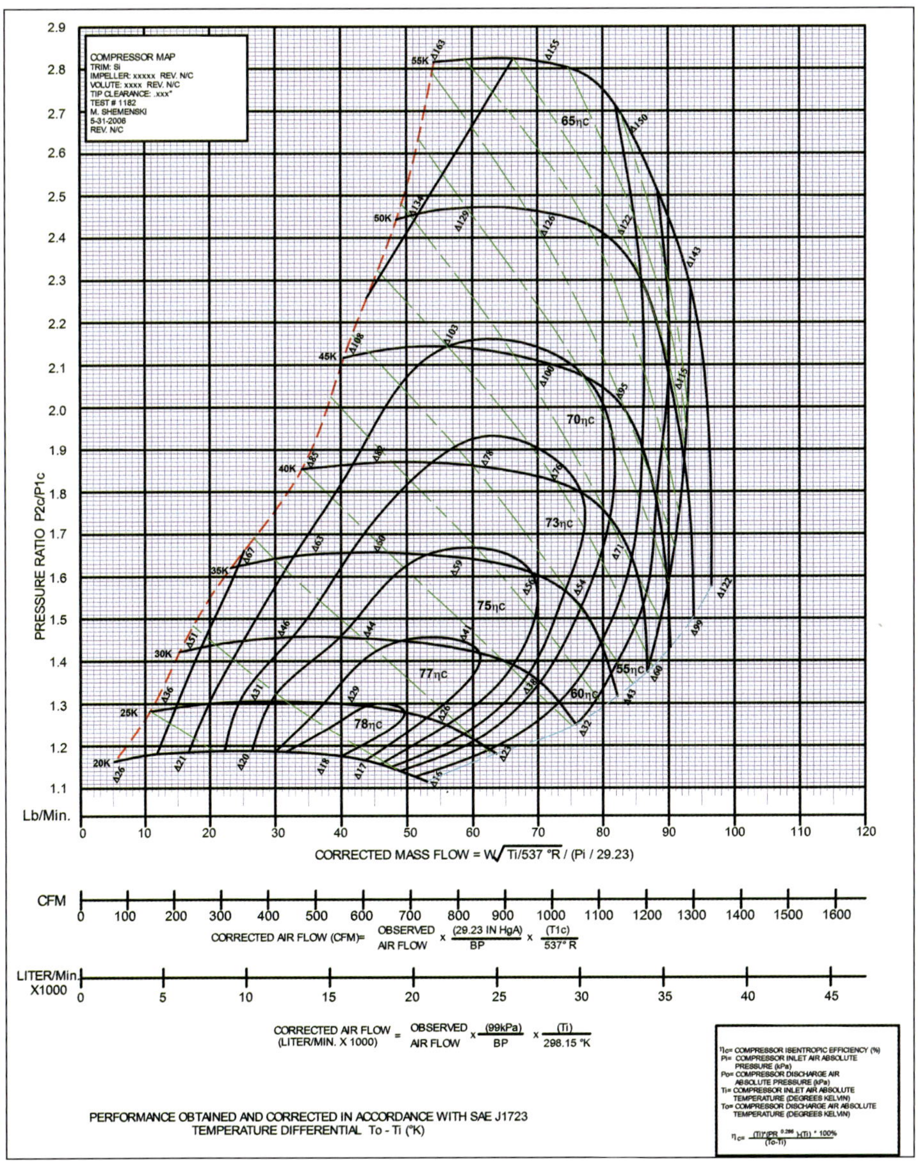


*The compressor map for Vortech's Si trim supercharger reveals a few things about this centrifugal supercharger: 1) The Vortech Si supercharger is extremely efficient (78 percent) at low boost levels (between 3 and 5 psi of boost and 30 to 50 lbs/min of airflow), and 2) the supercharger is still over 70-percent efficient at 16 psi of boost. (Illustration Courtesy Vortech Superchargers)*

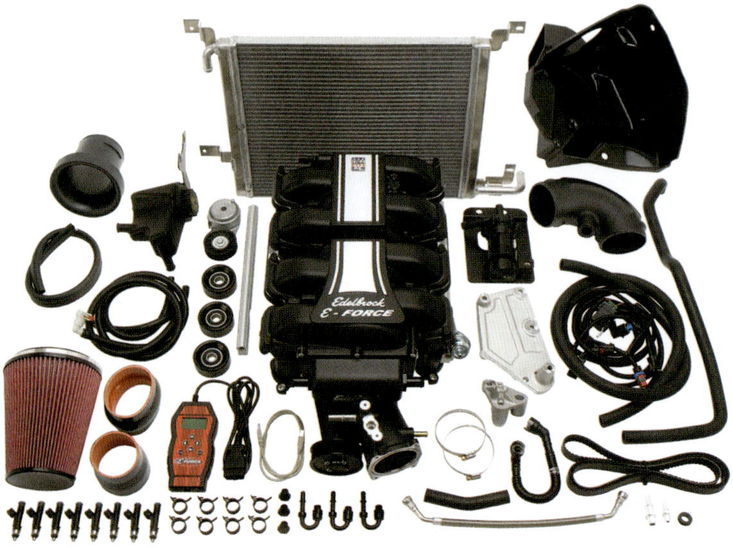


*The success of Eaton's positive-displacement superchargers on vehicles such as Ford's SVT Lightning F150 truck and the 2003–2004 "Terminator" Mustang Cobra has undoubtedly made Roots-style supercharging a popular aftermarket approach. Edelbrock combines Eaton's Gen VI 2300 TVS rotor package in a unique inverted arrangement that places the supercharger low in the engine valley. Longer, generously curved intake runners improve airflow for torque from less boost. Edelbrock offers various stages of kits for 2011–2014 Mustang GTs. The Stage 1 system (part number 1588) nets 559 hp and 503 ft-lbs of torque from a completely stock Mustang GT and is 50-state emissions legal. Stage 2 (part number 15896, shown) ups the ante to 636 hp and 538 ft-lbs of torque. Both systems include an air-to-water intercooler and come complete with a PCM tune. (Photo Courtesy Edelbrock)*

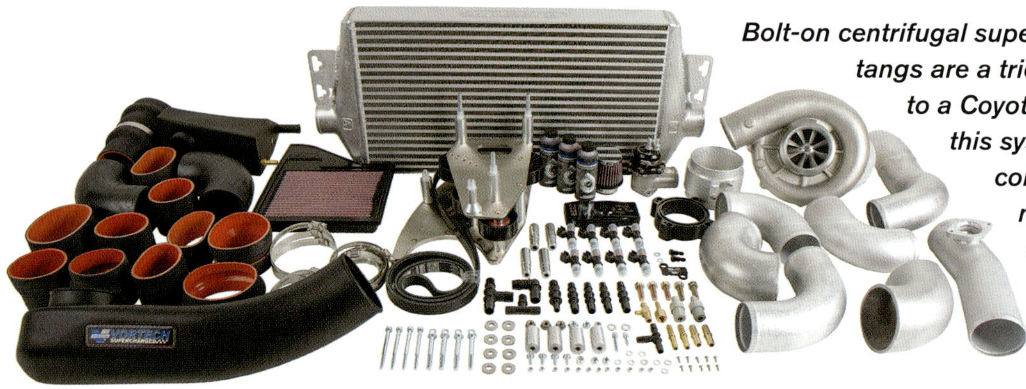


*Bolt-on centrifugal supercharger kits for 2011–2014 Mustangs are a tried-and-true method to add boost to a Coyote-powered Mustang. Kits such as this system from Vortech Superchargers come complete with everything you need to force feed your Mustang, including fuel-system upgrades and tuning already sorted. Some are even 50-state emissions legal. This system from Vortech features the company's V-3 Si-trim centrifugal supercharger with air-to-air charge cooler. The result is 605 hp and 483 ft-lbs of torque from a mild 7.5 psi of boost. (Photo Courtesy Vortech Superchargers)*

*A turbocharger is similar to a centrifugal supercharger in that the compressor's impeller uses centrifugal force to increase the density of the air. However, the engine's exhaust energy drives the compressor instead of the engine's crankshaft. (Photo Courtesy STS Turbo)*

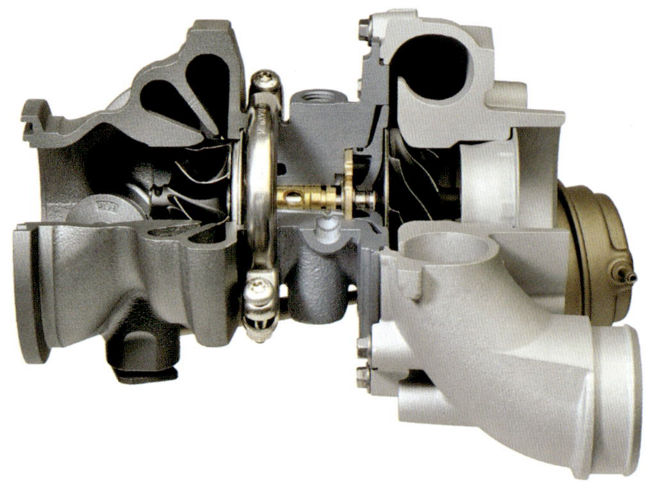

*A turbocharger is a supercharger driven by exhaust energy. Exhaust is fed to the perimeter of the turbine housing (left side), which spins the turbine and is expelled out the center. The turbine is connected to the compressor's impeller (right side) via a shaft that is lubricated with engine oil. Some turbos support the shaft with ball bearings to reduce friction). As the impeller spins, it draws air through the center of the compressor housing and is forced out through the perimeter. (Photo Courtesy Garrett Motion)*

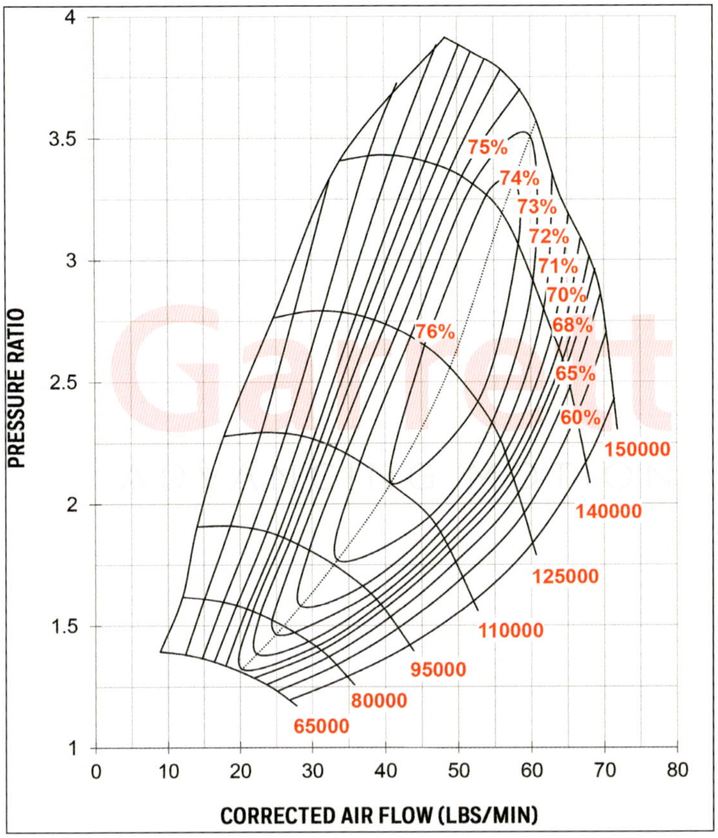


*If the compressor map for the Garrett G30-770 compressor looks similar to an engine-driven centrifugal supercharger, it's not an accident, since both increase air density in a similar fashion. Note how the turbocharger is most efficient when the impeller spins between 110,000 and 140,000 rpm. This is nearly three times that of a typical engine-driven centrifugal supercharger and 15 times as fast as a Roots-type blower's rotors. (Photo Courtesy Garrett Motion)*

*Hellion Power Systems offers both "tuner" and "complete" twin-turbo systems for 2011–2014 Mustang GTs. Boost can be set from 5 psi to more than 25 psi. Hellion claims that its 5-psi setting will yield more than 600 hp to the wheels on a completely stock car, but the kit can support over 1,200 rear-wheel hp with a fortified engine, fuel system, etc. The kit includes Precision 6266 CEA turbos, Turbosmart 44-mm wastegates and bypass valves, stainless-steel headers, a large vertical-flow dual-inlet intercooler, and dual 3-inch downpipes that can connect to aftermarket or factory exhaust systems. (Photo Courtesy Hellion Power Systems)*

impeller to blow more air into the engine. Because they don't rely on the engine to mechanically spin the compressor, turbochargers are sometimes called free power, in that the parasitic losses are much lower than mechanically driven superchargers.

Increasing intake boost adds exhaust flow, which in turn spins the compressor faster, which creates a feedback loop that is controlled by a wastegate that bleeds off exhaust pressure when intake boost reaches a set point. The rate that a boost feedback loop intensifies is called turbo lag. This is the main disadvantage of turbocharged systems, and designing a turbocharger system is dominated by a compromise between ultimate power and turbo lag.

## How-To Project: Supercharger System Installation

When choosing a supercharger system for 2011–2014 Mustangs, ease of installation can be a major factor. Even though the S197 chassis has more real estate available under the hood than its SN-95 predecessor, finding space for a centrifugal supercharger or turbocharger(s) can be challenging. Oftentimes, other components need to be modified or relocated to accommodate the power adder. In contrast, the positive-displacement supercharger systems on the market occupy space vacated by the intake manifold, which presents fewer packaging hurdles.

Additionally, complete kits that are 50-state legal offer further peace of mind and convenience in that they include the necessary computer tuning and fuel system upgrades. Edelbrock's E-Force Supercharger for 2011–2014 Mustangs is one such kit. It's pretty clear that Edelbrock did its

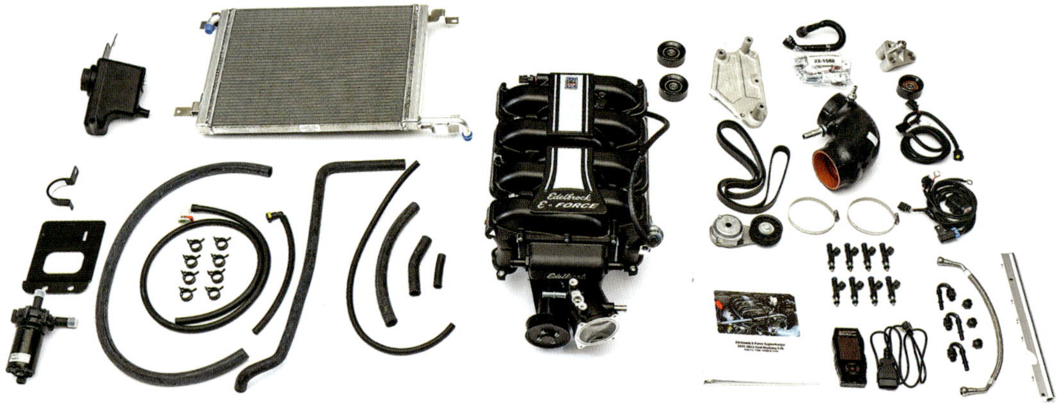

*The Edelbrock E-Force Stage 1 supercharger system for 2011–2014 Mustang GTs (part number 1588) is a complete bolt-on supercharger system. It includes everything needed for a thorough installation: the supercharger, plumbing, hardware, OBD-II flash tuner, 47-lb/hr fuel injectors, an intercooler heat exchanger system, and detailed instructions and documentation in a handy binder.*

*The Edelbrock E-Force supercharger integrates the supercharger, intercooler, and manifold into one unit. It is centered around an Eaton Gen VI 2300 TVS rotating assembly with four-lobe, 160-degree twisted rotors. The short, front-feed arrangement eliminates the long, torturous intake path of rear-feed superchargers or a jack shaft to drive the blower.*

*Before beginning the installation, we used the provided OBD-II flash tool to gather some required vehicle information and send it off to Edelbrock. Edelbrock emailed us a tune file that we loaded into this 2012 Mustang GT using the flash tool. (Doing this step first minimizes downtime after the under-hood work is complete.)*

*When viewing the Edelbrock E-force supercharger from the bottom, you can see the blower housing and how it sits below the intake manifold flange.*

*The rear view shows the intercooler housing and the long intake runners that maximize torque (runner length impacts torque even in supercharged applications).*

homework. The instructions are very thorough, the components are beautifully manufactured, and permanent modifications to the vehicle are few and minor. It's a turnkey package that doesn't require a trip to the auto parts store or the tuner to complete. Edelbrock even includes the necessary drill bit and tap. To demonstrate the benefits of such a kit, we installed Edelbrock's Stage 1 supercharger kit (part number 1588) on a 2012 Mustang GT. We only needed basic hand tools and a couple of things that some installers may not have:

- Right-angle drill
- $1^1/_8$-inch hole saw
- Spark-plug gapping tool
- Yellow coolant (for supercharger intercooler)

## Installing a Supercharger System

**1** *With the car supported on jack stands, remove the bottom radiator close-out panel.*

**2** *Next, remove the front half of each inner wheel housing.*

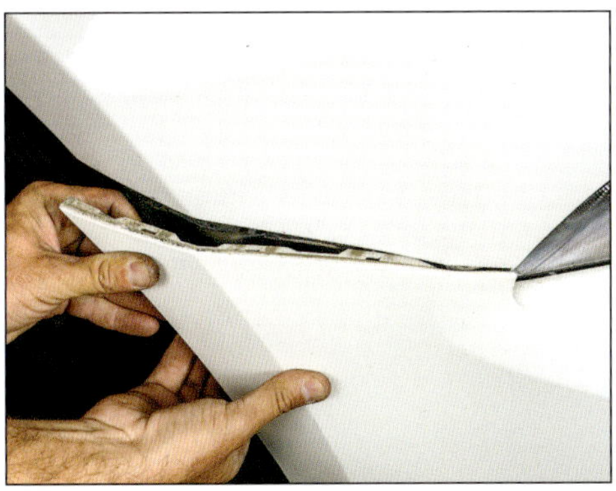

**3** *Then, after removing the necessary hardware, carefully pry the front bumper cover away from the fender.*

**4** *After releasing the front bumper cover from the header panel, slide the bumper cover away from the car.*

**5** *While the car is in the air, drain the coolant into a clean bucket if you intend to reuse it later.*

**6** *After removing the intake manifold, cover the intake ports with tape. (To see a detailed rundown of how to remove the factory intake manifold, refer to the procedure outlined in Chapter 6.)*

**7** *Next, use a panel puller to remove the foam bumper filler.*

**8** *Remove both radiator deflector panels and the cold-air intake duct on the driver's side.*

**9** *With wood blocks supporting the air-conditioning condenser, remove the four bolts that fasten the condenser to the radiator.*

**10** *Next, slide the Edelbrock intercooler heat exchanger into position ahead of the air-conditioning condenser and fasten it using the OEM condenser bolts.*

**11** *Assemble the intercooler pump as shown, and mount it behind the bumper using the supplied hardware.*

**12** *Then, connect the pump's output hose to the intercooler heat exchanger using the supplied spring clamps.*

**13** *Use a $1^1/_8$-inch hole saw to drill a clearance hole in the passenger-side radiator deflector for the intercooler pump inlet hose.*

**14** *Here's the finished intercooler pump installation.*

**15** *Modify the driver-side radiator deflector to clear for the intercooler heat exchanger's outlet tubing.*

**16** *Next, turn your attention to installing the tensioner bracket. First, remove the timing cover fasteners as indicated in the instructions.*

**17** *Then, use a spacer and adjust the length of the drill bit the required depths as indicated in the instructions.*

**18** *Using a right-angle drill and the included drill bit, enlarge the holes on the timing cover before tapping.*

**19** *Use the provided tap to cut the necessary M8 x 1.25 threads into the timing cover. (Note: a short 1/4-inch extension was used here so that the tap handle cleared the water-pump pulley.)*

**20** *After bolting the bracket to the timing cover, install the supplied idlers and tensioner.*

**21** *On the other side of the engine, remove the factory serpentine-belt tensioner.*

**22** *The tensioner was replaced with an idler pulley that attached to this cast bracket that Edelbrock supplies.*

**23** *To clear the supercharger, bend the bleed tube at the top of the driver's side head slightly outward with a deep 10-mm socket.*

**24** *Remove and gap all the spark plugs to 0.035 inch.*

**25** *Install the intercooler wiring harness by attaching the power to the under-hood fuse box and the ground to the radiator support, and tee into the wiring harness at the purge valve. The fuse-box ground is also relocated to make room for the intercooler reservoir.*

**26** *The fuel injectors will interfere with some of the harness anchor tabs on the cam covers, so you can trim them with an air saw.*

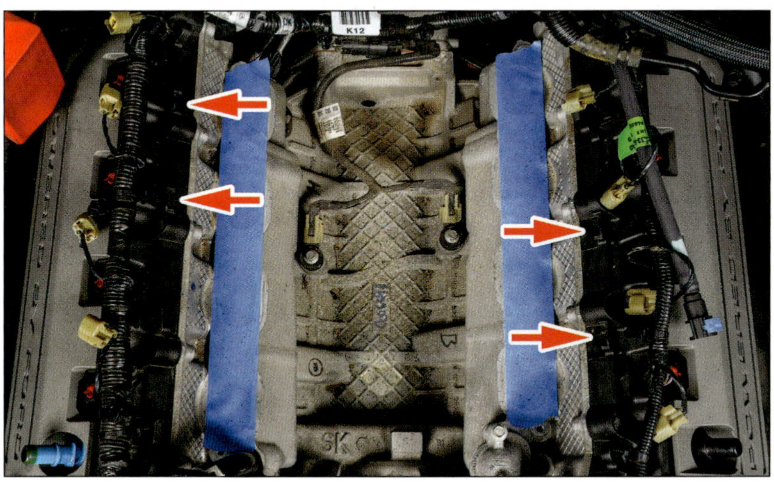

**27** *These are the four tabs that were trimmed.*

**28** *Clean and transfer the intake manifold seals from the factory intake manifold to the supercharger.*

**29** *The supercharger is heavy, so enlist an extra pair of hands to help lower it into position on the engine.*

**30** *Once you are sure that the supercharger is lined up on the heads, install and torque the supplied bolts following the sequence and specifications in the instructions.*

**31** *Prep the fuel rails by installing the supplied hardware, plumbing adapters, and 47-lb/hr injectors.*

**32** *After lubricating the fuel-injector O-rings, press the fuel rails into place and install the supplied fuel crossover hose.*

**33** *Using a breaker bar on the belt tensioner, install the supplied serpentine belt. The Edelbrock supercharger is driven by the accessory drive system and not a separate crank pulley.*

**34** *We scavenged the 90-degree brake booster fitting from the factory brake booster hose and combined it with the supplied hoses and clamps to connect the brake booster to the supercharger inlet.*

**35** *Then, transfer the purge valve from the factory intake manifold to the Edelbrock supercharger.*

**36** *Using a sharp utility knife, carefully slit and separate the purge-valve fitting from the factory purge valve and use the supplied hose to hook up the fuel tank vent to the purge valve.*

**37** *Interestingly, the driver-side PCV hose is reused and transferred to the passenger's side.*

**38** *Next, transfer the factory throttle body from the factory manifold to the Edelbrock supercharger inlet.*

**39** *Then, install the intercooler reservoir and plumbing using the supplied hoses and clamps.*

**40** *Next, attach the supplied silicone inlet elbow to the factory mass air meter/air box and connect it to the throttle body.*

**41** *With the OEM air box installed, attach the driver-side intercooler hose to the supercharger.*

**42** *The air-temperature sensor is relocated from the MAF sensor to the top of the intake manifold, so Edelbrock includes a wiring harness for this. One end attaches to the air-temperature sensor.*

**43** *The other end tees in between the MAF sensor and the MAF sensor connector next to the air box.*

**44** *We plugged the bottom fitting on the elbow (it was not used on our manual-transmission car) and connected the supplied PCV tube to the valve cover and intake elbow.*

**45** *Close the radiator drain petcock, reinstall the hoses and reservoir, and refill the cooling system.*

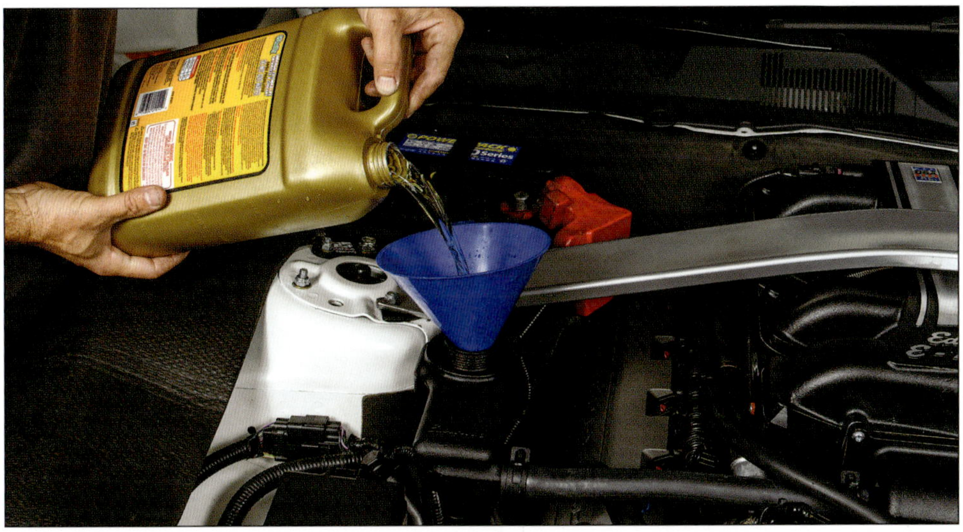

**46** *Using fresh coolant, fill the intercooler system and turn the key to Run to turn on the pump and bleed the system of air.*

**47** *To make sure our dirty paper air filter wasn't choking our Edelbrock Supercharger, we installed an AFE filter (part number 30-80179). Note the unique shape of the AFE filter that increases surface area similar to a conical filter.*

*The Edelbrock E-Force Stage 1 fits perfectly (visually and physically) in the engine compartment of this 2012 Mustang GT. The supercharger fits under this Boss 302 strut tower brace as well!*

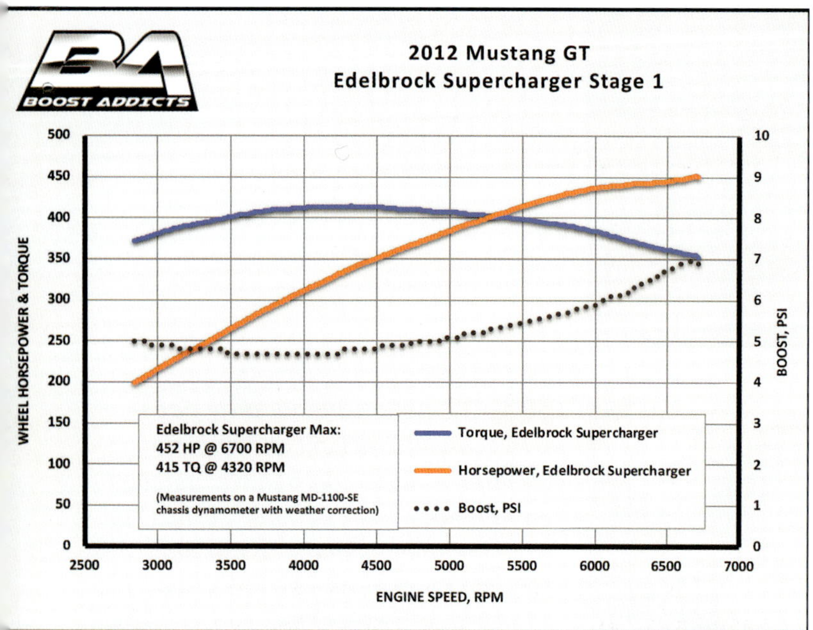


*While we expected solid gains, what we didn't expect was the boost curve. Rather than starting strong and running out of steam like a typical Roots blower, the Eaton 2300 TVS rotors in the Edelbrock supercharger build boost as the revs climb, starting from a little under 5 psi and finishing at 7 psi. At this boost level, the Edelbrock blower is barely breaking a sweat.*

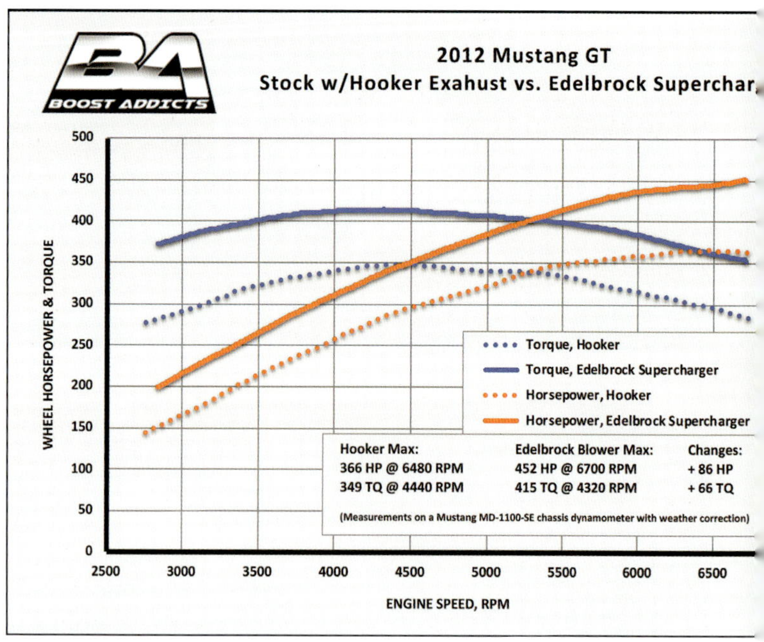


*Our baseline (stock engine with Hooker 1¾-inch long-tube headers and 3-inch exhaust system) made 366 hp and 349 ft-lbs of torque on Boost Addicts' Mustang dynamometer. The Coyote loved the Edelbrock boost, putting 452 hp and 415 ft-lbs of torque to the wheels. That's a solid 86 hp and 66 ft-lbs of torque improvement over the baseline. The force-fed Coyote never makes less than 350 ft-lbs from 2,800 rpm to redline. That's what we call a fat torque curve!*

# PCM Tuning

The S197 Mustang's Coyote is controlled by the Copperhead powertrain control module (PCM). It's a powerful, sophisticated piece of kit that controls all aspects of the powertrain.

*The Copperhead PCM is located in the engine compartment between the fuse box and the upper radiator hose.*

## Innovations

The Coyote engine and Copperhead PCM bring some noteworthy innovations under the hood of the Mustang of interest to enthusiasts.

### *Electronic Throttle Control*

Rather than using a cable to control the throttle, the Coyote uses a drive-by-wire throttle body where the driver makes a torque request via the throttle pedal and the Copperhead PCM determines the throttle, camshaft position, fuel, and spark that is required to hit the torque-request target.

### *Ti-VCT System*

Adding a large level of sophistication is the Coyote's twin independent variable camshaft timing (Ti-VCT) system. The ability to change camshaft timing based upon driver needs enables the 5.0L engine to achieve power, economy, emissions, and drivability that was unobtainable with fixed camshafts. However, the Ti-VCT system also makes tuning more complex, as volumetric efficiency varies with camshaft position.

### *Wideband Oxygen Sensors*

A massive step forward for tuners is the Copperhead's wideband oxygen sensors. Previous systems used narrow-band sensors that only measured rich/lean from stoichiometric (closed loop) for part-throttle driving and relied on a preset (open loop) tune for wide-open throttle (WOT). The Coyote's wideband sensors measure exhaust oxygen over a much broader range, which allows full-time closed-loop feedback even during WOT. This makes tuning of the Coyote engine significantly easier.

### *MAF Sensor*

Coyote's digital mass airflow (MAF) sensor sends a digital signal to the Copperhead PCM. Higher digital frequencies (shorter wave periods) correspond to more air mass. There is no manifold air pressure (MAP) sensor. Load is inferred from MAF sensor readings and calculations based upon volumetric efficiency for various camshaft mapped points. Unlike previous generations, the inlet air

## Copperhead Engine Management Strategy Overview

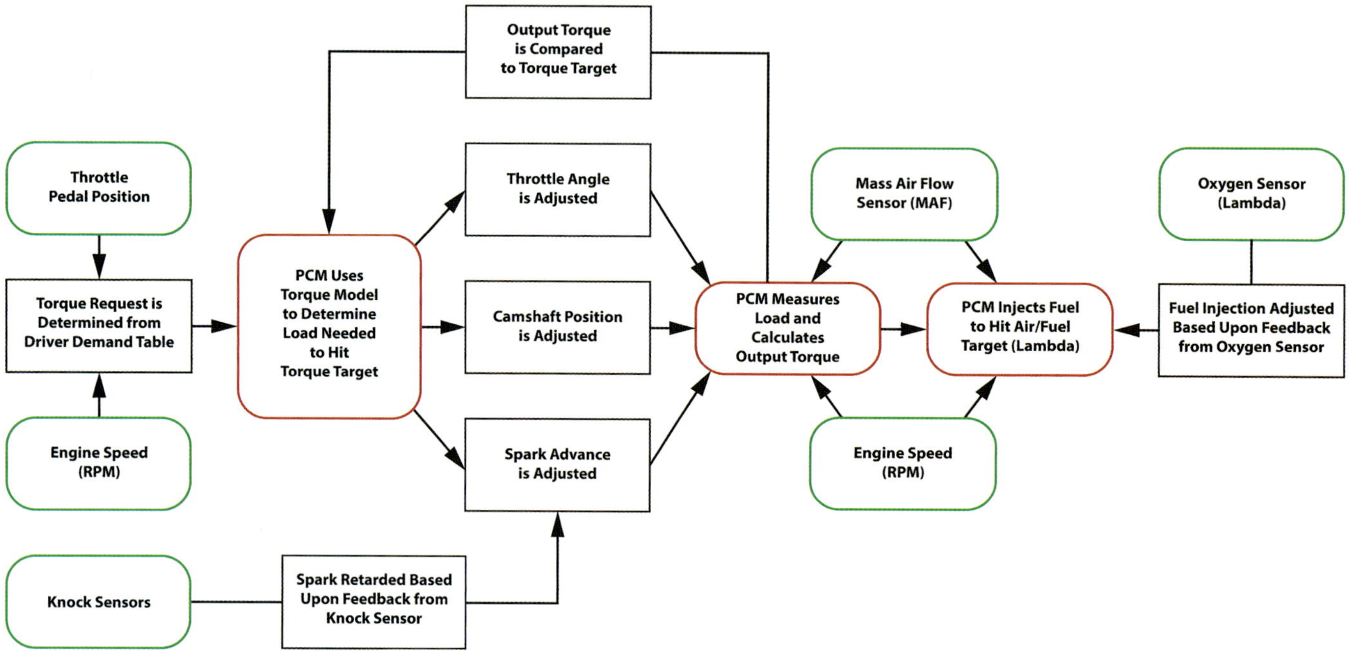


***At the risk of overcomplication, this flow chart may help visualize the the Copperhead's thought process. Rather than simply reacting to throttle position and load like previous strategies, the PCM adjusts the throttle based upon driver input, torque estimates, and torque output. Drivability problems result if the torque calculations are inaccurate (such as when aftermarket parts are installed and the torque model is not adjusted accordingly). However, when the engine is at wide-open throttle, much of the torque feedback calculations are ignored. The challenge to tuning the Coyote engine is to make good power at wide-open throttle without affecting drivability.***

temperature (IAT) is incorporated into the MAF sensor. There is not a separate IAT sensor.

### *Mechanical Returnless Fuel System*

Another departure from Fords of old is a mechanical returnless fuel system that has a fixed pressure regulator inside the tank. The absolute fuel pressure inside the system isn't referenced to intake manifold vacuum. Instead, it is inferred by calculations based upon the fuel flow of the injectors.

### *Knock Sensors*

These are another huge helper for tuners. The knock sensors in the Coyote engine are very effective at "hearing" knock, and the Coyote PCM quickly corrects for it. As always, it's best not to rely on these sensors for constant spark adjustments, but they're a great fail-safe to keep the Coyote's hypereutectic pistons in one piece.

## Electronic Throttle Control and Aftermarket Throttle Bodies

The Copperhead PCM reads the throttle pedal position to determine how much torque the driver is requesting from the engine and then opens the throttle body to deliver the airflow needed to meet the torque request. To complete this task successfully, the PCM needs to know how much air will flow at each throttle-blade position. Flow through the throttle body is related to throttle-blade valve size, blade angle, and pressure drop (vacuum) behind the throttle body. These variables make up the throttle body model that the PCM uses to predict throttle airflow.

If a larger throttle body is installed without adjusting the throttle-body model, more air will flow through the throttle body than the PCM expects. The engine load and torque delivered will be outside what the PCM predicted, which initiates a cascade of drivability issues. So, simply slapping on a larger throttle body to a Coyote engine isn't an option.

While the Coyote's factory 80-mm throttle body is more than enough for most naturally aspirated applications, larger aftermarket throttle bodies are available from some manufacturers. Any aftermarket throttle body will require new parameters for the throttle body. If a throttle body manufacturer doesn't supply this information, it's very difficult to gather the data without a flow bench and specialized equipment. Luckily, throttle-body model data for popular throttle bodies is usually available through the tuning community.

| Condition | Target Lambda | Air/Fuel Ratios | | |
|---|---|---|---|---|
| | | 100-percent Gasoline | E10 | E85 |
| Lowest Emissions | 1.00 | 14.64 | 14.08 | 9.76 |
| Power, Naturally Aspirated | 0.83 | 12.15 | 11.69 | 8.10 |
| Power, Supercharged | 0.78 | 11.42 | 10.98 | 7.61 |

Most traditional hot-rodders are comfortable tuning in air/fuel ratio. However, that's unwise with today's varied fuels because the stoichiometric air/fuel ratio varies with fuel type. The Copperhead PCM speaks lambda, so it's important to think in terms of lambda. This chart shows target lambda for different conditions and different fuels.

## Ti-VCT and Aftermarket Camshafts

Installing aftermarket cams is a tried-and-true hot-rodding trick. However, on a Coyote engine with Ti-VCT, it uses its understanding of the factory camshafts' profiles to estimate the air entering the cylinders at each camshaft position. The challenge is that remapping the engine's volumetric efficiency and expected torque output for each camshaft position can be time-consuming. Fortunately, the factory Coyote camshafts are adequate for all but the most extreme power levels.

## Wideband Oxygen Sensors and Tuning

This is the Copperhead's saving grace. If you've ever tried to tune an engine with a stand-alone wideband sensor, you know the value of factory wideband oxygen sensors feeding data into the PCM. The Copperhead PCM reads and adjusts fueling continuously, even at full throttle. The wideband oxygen sensors output a lambda reading, which is stoichiometric for the fuel being used. Keep in mind that the stoichiometric air/fuel ratio varies with different fuels.

## MAF Sensor and Changing Intake Tubes

The digital mass airflow (MAF) sensor directly measures incoming airflow and allows the Copperhead PCM to determine load. An incorrect MAF sensor reading results in a cascade of issues, so it needs to be as accurate as possible. The MAF sensor doesn't measure all the incoming air; instead, it takes a sample from the air stream and calculates the amount of intake air. Consequently, changing the shape or diameter of the intake tube throws the calculation off as the engine ingests a different amount of air per MAF sample.

Fortunately, the wideband oxygen sensors continually measure lambda and feed this information back to the PCM so that adjustments are made and recorded. These adjustments are called trims. There are long-term and short-term fuel trims, the sum of which are factored into the fueling. We can use these trim values to adjust the MAF sensor calibration—all without additional sensors. We'll cover this procedure at the end of this chapter.

## Mechanical Returnless Fuel System and Increasing Fuel Supply

Along with wideband oxygen sensors, the mechanical returnless fuel system is another departure from previous generations of Mustangs. Rather than continually vary the fuel pump duty cycle to maintain a set fuel pressure at the fuel rail, a conventional mechanical fuel-pressure regulator is placed in the tank immediately downstream of the fuel pump, and anything above 57 psi is bled back in the tank. The fuel pump has two speeds: low and high. To keep the fuel pumps cool and minimize evaporative emissions, the Copperhead PCM drives the pump at a low speed and switches the pump to high speed at high engine load.

## Knock Sensors and Spark Tuning

The knock sensors on 2011–2014 Coyotes work very well. There's usually no reason to turn them off, as they provide a valuable safety measure against knock and subsequent engine damage.

## Tuning Tools and Methods

There are two methods to tune the Copperhead PCM: 1) a handheld tuning device or 2) laptop tuning software. Handheld devices offer convenience, simplicity, and don't require a separate laptop computer to use. However, their tuning capabilities are limited to the functions enabled in the device. We covered some handheld tuning options in Chapter 6.

Laptop tuning software unlocks advanced tuning capabilities, as all parameters relevant to tuning are at a user's fingertips. The HPtuners VCM Suite software is popular among serious Ford tuners and includes two applications: VCM Editor and VCM Scanner.

## How-To Project: MAF Sensor Calibration

One of the most common upgrades to a Mustang is the installation of a larger air-intake tube. They add horsepower by reducing the air inlet restriction ahead of the throttle body. However, adding a larger intake tube skews the MAF sensor readings, as more air is entering the engine than estimated. The PCM will compensate for this additional flow by reading the oxygen sensors and injecting more fuel—but only within limits. As such, it's best to recalibrate the MAF settings in the PCM to normalize the flow and leave the necessary adjustment room for other factors.

Using HPtuners VCM Scanner, we will record the fuel injection adjustments at various airflow readings and then use VCM Editor to adjust the MAF calibration accordingly.

We're going to use HPtuners VCM Scanner and VCM Editor to recalibrate the MAF sensor readings after installing a Ford Performance Parts Cobra Jet cold-air intake tube.

To calibrate a MAF, we'll need the following:

- Microsoft Windows PC Laptop (or Mac running Boot Camp or Parallels Desktop)
- HPtuners MPVI2 interface device
- HPtuners VCM Editor software
- HPtuners VCM Scanner software

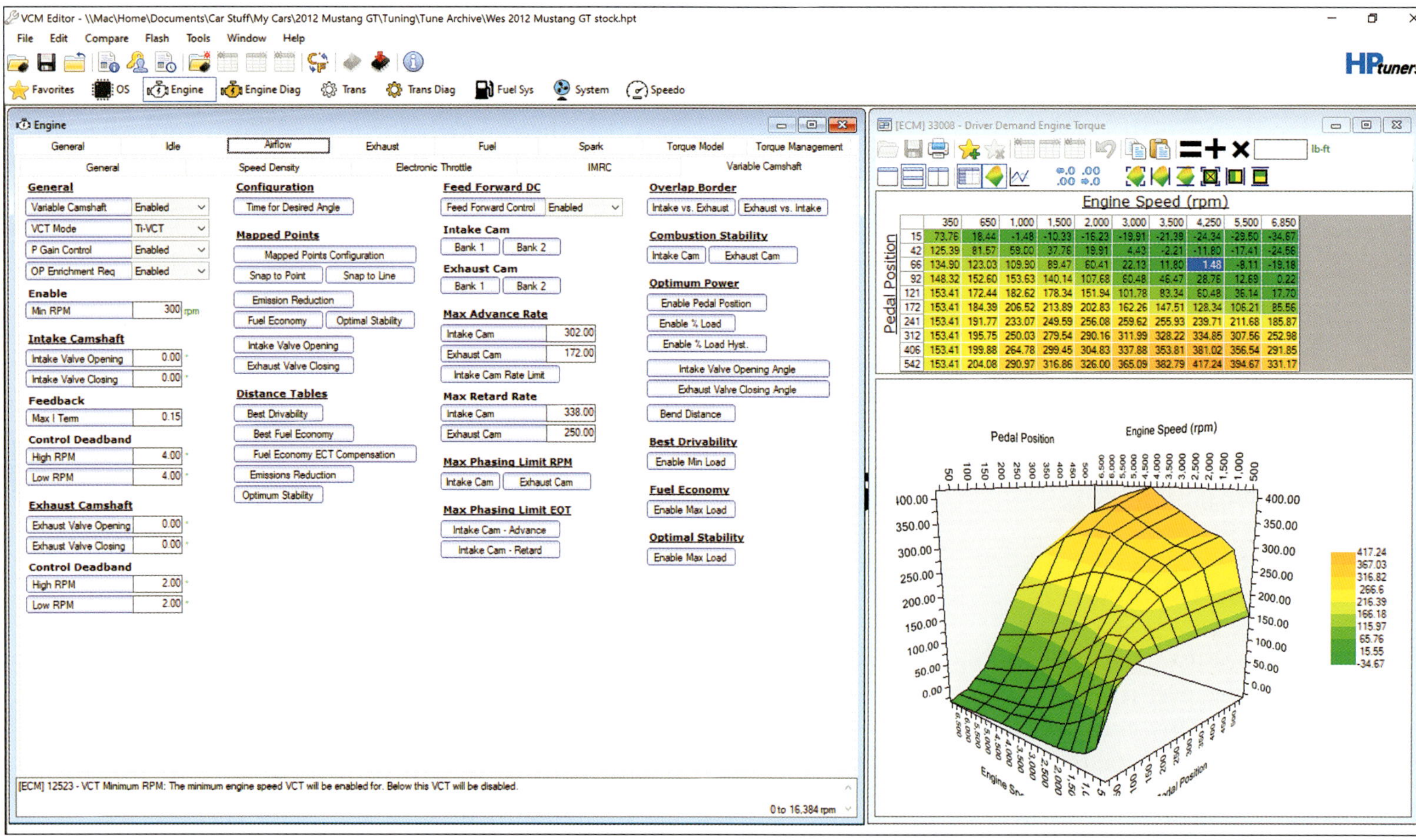


*The HPtuners VCM Editor is used to read, edit, and write calibrations that are loaded back in to the PCM. The calibration must be read, edited, and reloaded into the PCM before any changes take effect.*

*The HPtuners VCM Scanner gathers, displays, and records data from the stream of Parameter IDs into and out of the PCM. Both are invaluable tools used for tuning the Copperhead PCM. Recordings (logs) of data can be saved for later analyzation and used to diagnose problems or make tuning adjustments.*

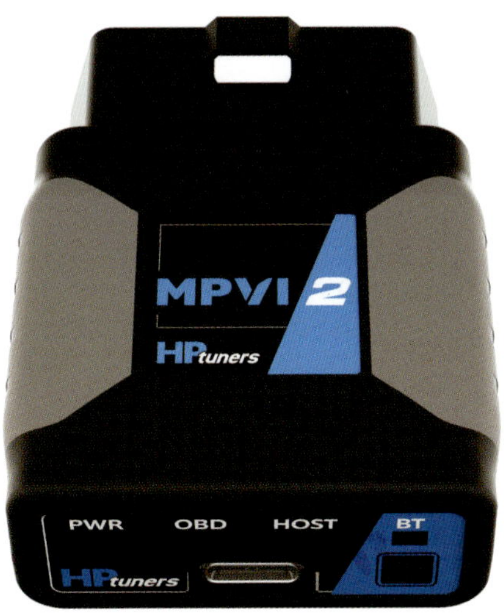


*The HPtuners MPVI2 is used to connect a laptop to a Mustang via the vehicle's OBD-II port so that the HPtuners software can communicate with the Copperhead PCM. (Photo Courtesy HPtuners)*

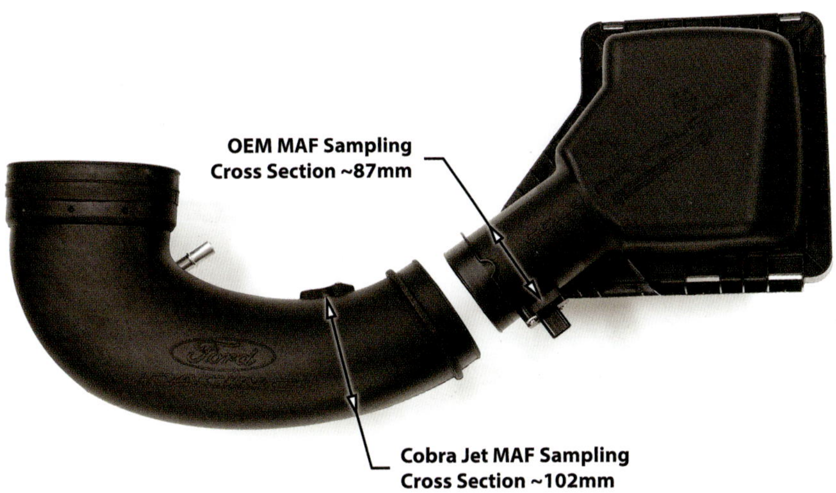


*The Ford Performance Parts Cobra Jet cold-air intake (left) is necessary when installing a Cobra Jet intake manifold, as a twin 65-mm throttle body requires an entirely different intake tube. The MAF sampling section of the Cobra Jet cold-air intake is significantly larger, which will require recalibrating our MAF sensor readings so that the amount of air entering the engine isn't grossly underestimated. The cross section of the OEM intake tube's MAF sampling section (right) is approximately 87 mm, and the Cobra Jet (left) is about 102 mm. We'll use the ratio of these figures as a rough starting point.*

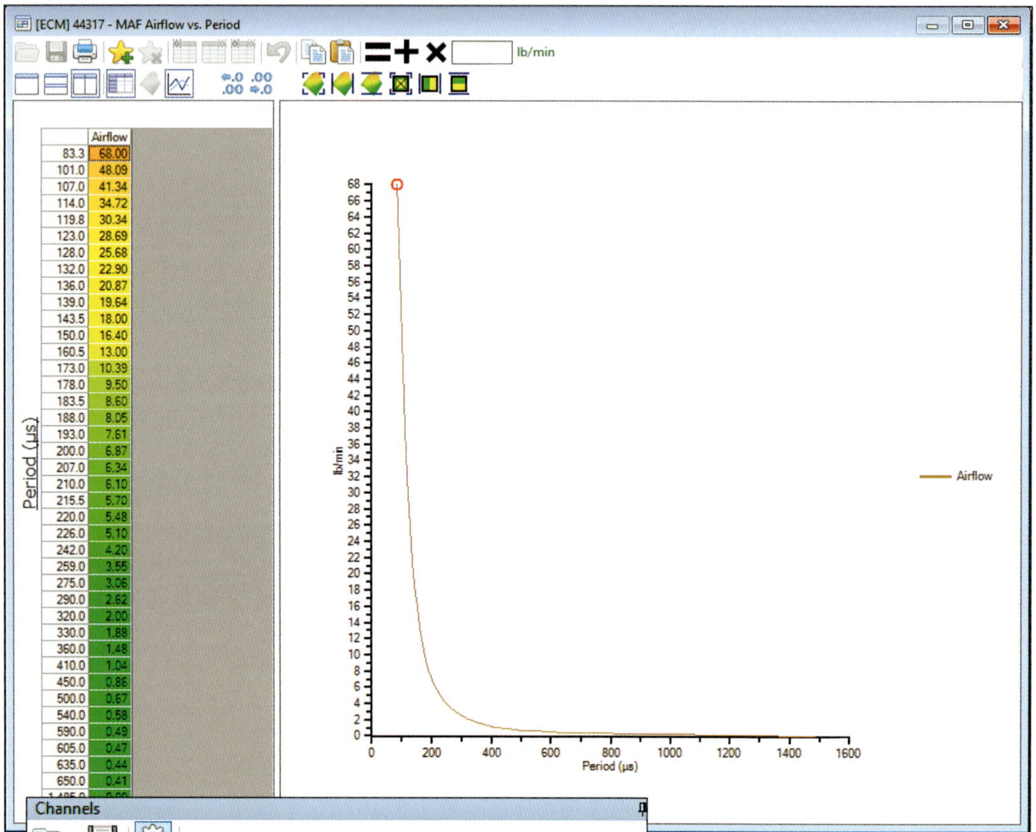


After saving our factory PCM file for later reference, we located the MAF calibration under Engine > Airflow > General > MAF Airflow vs. Period.

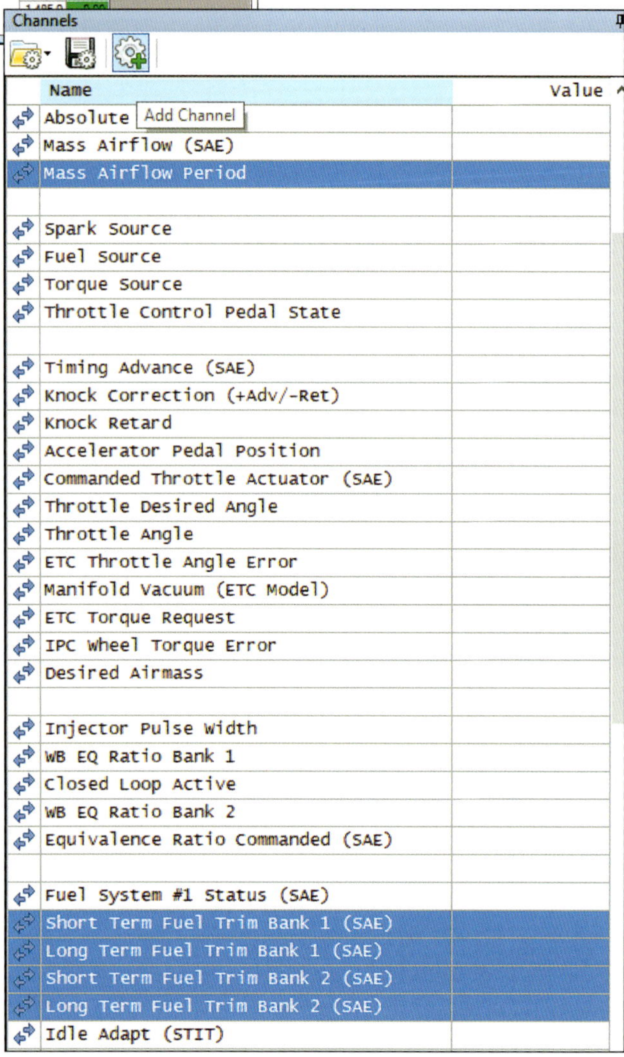


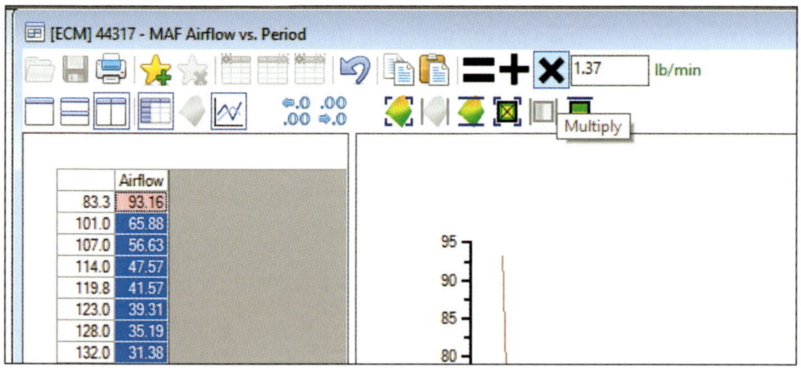


We found that the area of the Cobra Jet intake tube is 37-percent larger than the OEM tube by squaring the ratio of their diameters = $(102\ mm/87\ mm)^2$. We used that factor to multiply the factory values by 1.37, which got us in the ballpark.

After saving the file and loading the file into the PCM using the "Write Vehicle" button, we opened the HPtuners VCM Scanner software. To calibrate our MAF, we needed to be sure to gather the right data. We added "Mass Airflow Period" and the short and long fuel trims for both banks (all highlighted in blue) to our channel list using the "Add Channel" button.

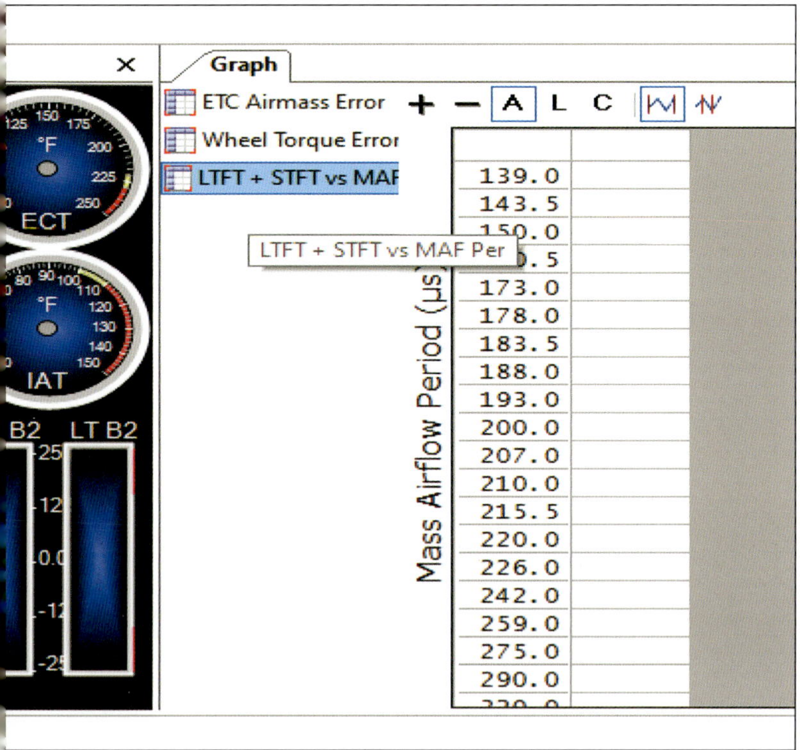


We set up the VCM Scanner to match the short-term and long-term fuel trims to the corresponding airflow period using the graphs feature (note that the Average "A" option is checked, as this will display the average of the data gathered). Results are recorded as a percentage.

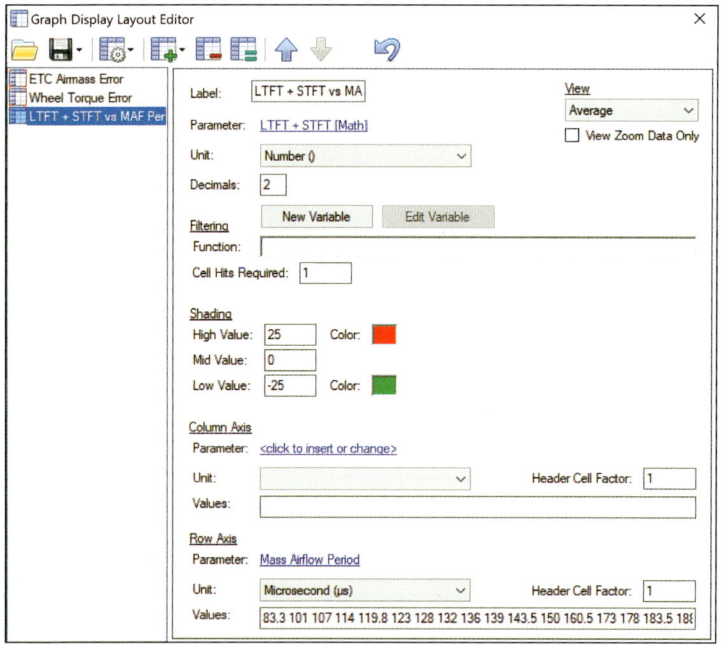


Here's how we set it up. The parameter "LTFT + STFT" is a math function that VCM Scanner performs. This graph displays the average of the sum of the short-term and long-term fuel trims that correspond to each MAF period, as noted in the "Row Axis" section at the bottom. Note that row axis values were copied from the "MAF Airflow vs. Period" graph in VCM Editor.

Here's the log file we created. Note how the graph of the "LTFT + STFT vs MAF" has a good range of data with no holes.

*We started the engine and had a datalogging helper hold the computer while we did some driving. It's best to do this on a dyno, as we needed to gather data from idle to wide-open throttle over a wide range of engine speeds. We saw the graph start to "fill in" the values as the engine ran over varying loads and speeds.*

SUM | fx =B2*(1+E2)

| | A | B | C | D | E | F |
|---|---|---|---|---|---|---|
| 1 | lb/min | Airflow | | Logged Trims | Smoothed | Cobra Jet tuned |
| 2 | 83.3000031 | 93.1600037 | 83.3 | | -0.100 | =B2*(1+E2) |
| 3 | 101 | 65.8833008 | 101 | | -0.100 | 59.29 |
| 4 | 107 | 56.631691 | 107 | | -0.100 | 50.97 |
| 5 | 114 | 47.5664024 | 114 | -0.09 | -0.100 | 42.81 |
| 6 | 119.800003 | 41.5657997 | 119.8 | -0.09 | -0.100 | 37.41 |
| 7 | 123 | 39.3112755 | 123 | -0.1 | -0.100 | 35.38 |
| 8 | 128 | 35.1876831 | 128 | -0.12 | -0.100 | 31.67 |
| 9 | 132 | 31.3775749 | 132 | -0.1 | -0.100 | 28.24 |
| 10 | 136 | 28.596571 | 136 | -0.11 | -0.100 | 25.74 |
| 11 | 139 | 26.9004707 | 139 | -0.1 | -0.100 | 24.21 |
| 12 | 143.5 | 24.6599998 | 143.5 | -0.11 | -0.100 | 22.19 |
| 13 | 150 | 22.4680004 | 150 | -0.11 | -0.100 | 20.22 |
| 14 | 160.5 | 17.8099995 | 160.5 | -0.09 | -0.100 | 16.03 |
| 15 | 173 | 14.2343006 | 173 | -0.07 | -0.088 | 12.98 |
| 16 | 178 | 13.0185785 | 178 | -0.04 | -0.076 | 12.03 |
| 17 | 183.5 | 11.7798824 | 183.5 | -0.04 | -0.064 | 11.03 |
| 18 | 188 | 11.0235224 | 188 | -0.03 | -0.052 | 10.45 |
| 19 | 193 | 10.419529 | 193 | -0.04 | -0.040 | 10.00 |
| 20 | 200 | 9.41819572 | 200 | -0.04 | -0.040 | 9.04 |
| 21 | 207 | 8.68265724 | 207 | -0.05 | -0.040 | 8.34 |
| 22 | 210 | 8.35754776 | 210 | -0.09 | -0.040 | 8.02 |
| 23 | 215.5 | 7.81224728 | 215.5 | -0.01 | -0.040 | 7.50 |
| 24 | 220 | 7.50099659 | 220 | -0.03 | -0.040 | 7.20 |
| 25 | 226 | 6.9807663 | 226 | -0.04 | -0.040 | 6.70 |
| 26 | 242 | 5.75399971 | 242 | -0.03 | -0.040 | 5.52 |
| 27 | 259 | 4.86350012 | 259 | -0.04 | -0.040 | 4.67 |
| 28 | 275 | 4.19219971 | 275 | -0.04 | -0.040 | 4.02 |
| 29 | 290 | 3.58939981 | 290 | -0.06 | -0.047 | 3.42 |
| 30 | 320 | 2.74000001 | 320 | -0.07 | -0.053 | 2.59 |
| 31 | 330 | 2.57559991 | 330 | -0.05 | -0.060 | 2.42 |
| 32 | 360 | 2.02760005 | 360 | -0.07 | -0.061 | 1.90 |

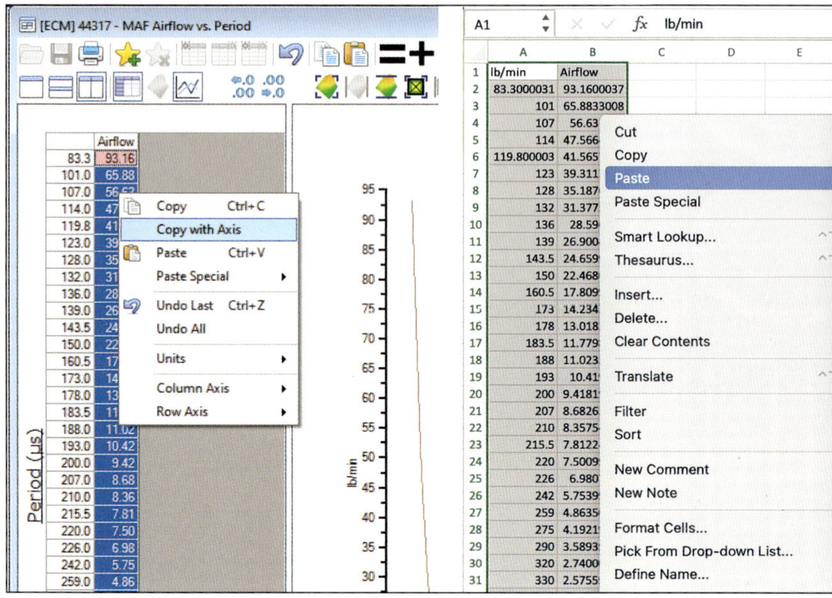


*In VCM Editor, we copied our MAF calibration (along with the axis) and pasted it into a spreadsheet.*

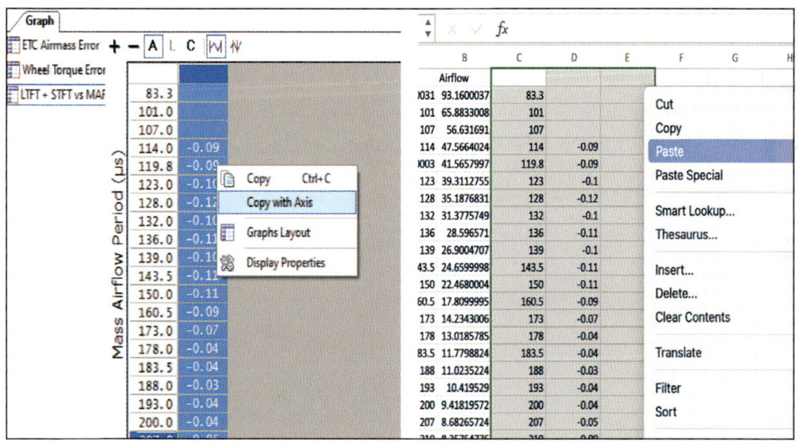


*Then, we copied our logged trim values from VCM Scanner over to the spreadsheet. (Note that we also copied the axis to make sure that the logged data matched up to the MAF calibration.)*

*We used the logged data as a guide to correct the MAF calibration. Note how we added a column "Smoothed" to the right of the raw trim values. We did this for two reasons: 1) it helped us fill in areas where we didn't have data (such as the upper reaches of the MAF flow), and 2) the calibration must step up or down incrementally from one value to the next in a smooth fashion. Using a smoothed correction factor ensured that our airflow values decreased as period increased. We then applied our correction to the MAF calibration by the formula shown.*

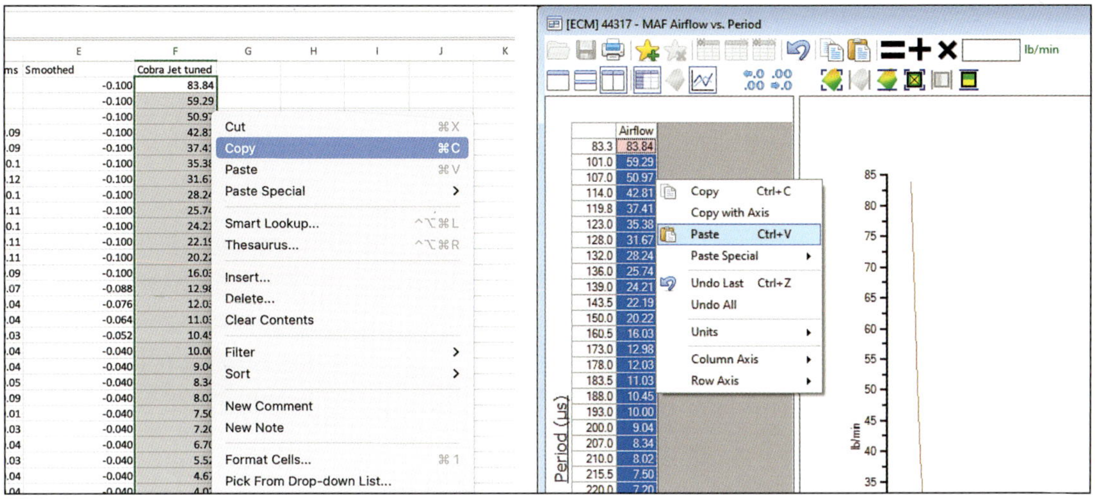


*Next, we copied the new calibration from the spreadsheet and pasted it into VCM Editor.*

*To verify our new MAF calibration, we did another data logging run. You can see on this logging run that the "LTFT + STFT vs MAF" graph shows significantly less trimming of fuel than before. Our trims were mostly under 3 percent, which was low enough for us.*

# EPILOGUE

The 2005 S197-chassis Mustang was leaps and bounds better than any previous Mustang, and in 2011, it received the Coyote engine that it needed to become legendary. Rather than spending resources addressing shortcomings, enthusiasts can concentrate on making their 2011–2014 Mustang corner faster, get down the drag strip quicker, or simply make it more enjoyable to drive. That's what this book is all about.

If you started this book with a mostly stock 2011–2014 Mustang and have come to the end, you have a car that will keep pace with sports cars costing 10 times the price as well as the satisfaction from doing the work yourself. The aftermarket is continually finding ways to unlock more performance from Mustangs, and the 2011–2014 Mustang will enjoy strong support for many years to come. When modifying your Mustang, choose your path, get wrenching, and enjoy the ride!

AP Racing
Wheler Rd.
Seven Stars Industrial Estate
Coventry
West Midlands CV34LB
United Kingdom
+44 (0) 24 7663 9595
apracing.com

BBK Performance
27427 Bostik Ct.
Temecula, CA 92590
386-624-0025
bbkperformance.com

Boundary Lubrication Systems
9573 County Rd. 2470
Royse City, TX 75189
833-786-7645
boundarypumps.com

Canton Racing Products
232 Branford Rd.
North Branford, CT 06471
203-481-9460
cantonracingproducts.com

Centerforce Clutches
2266 Crosswind Dr.
Prescott, AZ 86301
800-932-5882
centerforce.com

Circle D Specialties
14105 Packard St.
Houston, TX 77040
713-895-8834
circledspecialties.com

CorteX Racing
1280 State Route 28
Loveland, OH 45140
415-489-0866
cortexracing.com

DiabloSport
1790 E. Airport Blvd.
Sanford, FL 32773
866-404-6141
diablosport.com

Drexler Motorsport
Postgasse 12d
D-94121 Salzweg
Germany
+49 (0) 851 / 851 63 63 32
shop.drexler-motorsport.com

Eaton
eaton.com

Edelbrock
2700 California St.
Torrance, CA 90503
310-781-2222
edelbrock.com

Essex Parts Services
125 Hampton Ct.
Cramerton, NC 28032
704-824-6030
essexparts.com

Exedy Globalparts Corp.
8601 Haggerty Rd. S.
Van Buren Township, MI 48111
800-346-6091
exedyusa.com

Ford Performance Parts
performanceparts.ford.com

Garrett Motion
garrettmotion.com

H&R Special Springs
4108 Bakerview Spur
Bellingham, WA 98226
888-827-8881
hrsprings.com

Hellion Power Systems
2735 Della Rd. SW
Albuquerque, NM 87105
505-873-4670
hellionpowersystems.com

Holley Performance Parts
(Hays, Hooker, Hurst, Nitrous Oxide Systems, STS Turbo)
1801 Russellville Rd.
Bowling Green, KY 42101
866-464-6553
holley.com

HPtuners
hptuners.com

Jenvey Dynamics Limited
Building 2
Stanmore Business Park
Bridgnorth, Shropshire WV15 5HP
United Kingdom
+44 (0)1746 768810
jenvey.co.uk

Kenny Brown Performance
1416 Sadlier Circle E. Dr.
Indianapolis, IN 46239
317-396-2768
kennybrown.com

KohR Motorsports
5727 Executive Dr. E.
Westland, MI 48185
734-895-1543
kohrmotorsports.com

Koni North America
1961 International Way
Hebron, KY 41048
859-586-4100
koni-na.com

Kooks Headers
141 Advantage Pl.
Statesville, NC 28677
866-586-5665
kooksheaders.com

Late Model Restoration
7911 Panther Way
Waco, TX 76712
866-507-3786
lmr.com

Maximum Motorsports
3430 Sacramento Dr. Unit D
San Luis Obispo, CA 93401
888-378-8830

MGW Ltd.
4159 Mike Padgett Hwy.
Augusta, GA 30906
706-793-1770
mgwshifters.com

Michelin North America
michelinman.com

Moser Engineering
102 Performance Dr.
Portland, IN 47371
260-726-6689
moserengineering.com

Motive Gear
1001 W. Exchange Ave.
Chicago, IL 60609
800-934-2727
motivegear.com

ProCharger
14801 W. 114th Terrace
Lenexa, KS 66215
913-338-2886
procharger.com

Steeda
2281 Hammondville Rd.
Pompano Beach, FL 33069
800-950-0774
steeda.com

Stifflers
1511 Hancel Pkwy.
Mooresville, IN 46158
317-837-2444
buystifflers.com

Strange Engineering
8300 N. Austin Ave.
Morton Grove, IL 60053
800-646-7618
strangeengineering.net

Tilton Engineering
25 Easy St.
Buellton, CA 93427
805-688-2353
tiltonracing.com

TNT Wheel
643 N. Main St.
Goodlettsville, TN 37072
615-977-9072
tntwheel.com

Tremec
46643 Ryan Ct.
Novi, MI 48377
248-859-6500

Vortech Engineering
1650 Pacific Ave.
Oxnard, CA 93033
805-247 0226
vortechsuperchargers.com

Wilwood Engineering
4700 Calle Bolero
Camarillo, CA 93012
805-388-1188
wildwood.com